STUDIES IN THE ECONOMIC HISTORY OF SOUTHERN AFRICA

VOLUME I
THE FRONT-LINE STATES

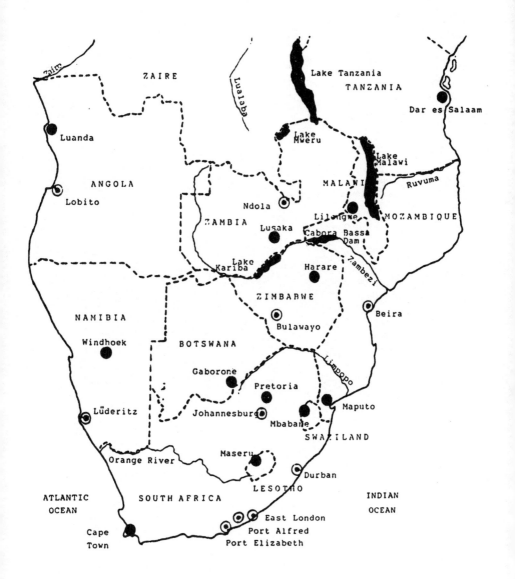

ZAIRE

Luanda

ANGOLA

Lobito

Lualaba

Lake Tanzania

TANZANIA

Dar es Salaam

Lake Mweru

Lake Malawi

MALAWI

Ruvuma

Ndola

ZAMBIA

Lusaka

Lilongwe

MOZAMBIQUE

Cabora Bassa Dam

Zambezi

Lake Kariba

Harare

ZIMBABWE

Bulawayo

Beira

NAMIBIA

Windhoek

BOTSWANA

Gaborone

Limpopo

Lüderitz

Johannesburg

Pretoria

Mbabane

Maputo

SWAZILAND

Maseru

Orange River

LESOTHO

Durban

ATLANTIC
OCEAN

SOUTH AFRICA

INDIAN
OCEAN

Cape
Town

East London

Port Alfred

Port Elizabeth

SOUTHERN AFRICA

STUDIES IN THE ECONOMIC HISTORY OF SOUTHERN AFRICA

VOLUME I

THE FRONT-LINE STATES

Edited by
Zbigniew A. Konczacki, Jane L. Parpart and
Timothy M. Shaw

Routledge
Taylor & Francis Group

LONDON AND NEW YORK

First published 1990 in
FRANK CASS & CO. LTD.

This edition published 2016 by Routledge
2 Park Square, Milton Park, Abingdon, Oxon OX14 4RN
711 Third Avenue, New York, NY 10017, USA

Routledge is an imprint of the Taylor & Francis Group, an informa business

Copyright © 1990 Frank Cass & Co. Ltd.

British Library Cataloguing in Publication Data

Studies in the economic history of southern
Africa.
Vol. 1: The front-line states.
1. Africa. Southern Africa, Economic
conditions, to 1988
I. Konczacki, Zbigniew A. II. Parpart, Jane
L. III. Shaw, Timothy M.
330.968

ISBN 0–7146–3379–8(cased)
ISBN 0–7146–4071–9(pbk)

Library of Congress Cataloguing-in-Publication Data

Studies in the economic history of southern Africa / edited by
Zbigniew A. Konczacki, Jane L. Parpart, and Timothy M. Shaw.
p.   cm.
Includes index.
Contents: v. 1. The front-line states.
ISBN 0–7146–3379–8(cased)(v.1)
ISBN 0–7146–4071–9(pbk)
1. Africa, Southern—Economic conditions.   I. Konczacki, Zbigniew
A. II. Parpart, Jane L.   III. Shaw, Timothy M.
HC900.S78 1990
330.968—dc 19   89–31405
                                                       CIP

ISBN 13: 978-0-71464-071-6 (pbk)

Typeset by Selectmove Ltd, London

Contents

Editors' Introduction

The unfolding history and historiography of Southern Africa pose profound challenges for both analysis and praxis in the last decade of the twentieth century. These challenges are reflected in the range of investigations and contradictions, some of which are treated here, which together constitute an intellectual and political conjuncture. The apparently snail-like pace of change in post-Second World War Southern Africa was only occasionally and briefly accelerated before repression and regression occurred – Sharpeville in 1960, the Portuguese coup in 1974 and Soweto in 1976 – until Zimbabwe's independence at the start of the 1980s and Namibia's freedom anticipated for the end of the decade. Yet underneath the appearances of continuity and hegemony, myriad forms of resistance have in fact developed, both theoretical and practical. The emergence of new studies and strategies for liberation in Southern Africa over the last decade confront not only orthodox approaches to the region but also traditional perspectives on Africa as a whole. The contemporary history and historiography of Southern Africa pose challenges, then, to African studies and states in general. Hence the preparation of our two-volume series of original essays on the past, present and prospective economic history of this most absorbing and exciting region.

It could be rightly claimed that a comprehensive economic history of each of the countries of Southern Africa deserves a book-size monograph. While fully realising this the editors of the present work undertook a less ambitious, if perhaps a no less demanding, task. By limiting this book to specialised studies they strove, instead, to cover the region as a whole and to bring out similarities, differences, conflicts and interrelationships between its various parts. In a follow-up collection of studies, the scope is extended to South Africa, Lesotho and Swaziland.

It is hardly necessary to justify the need for such a work at the present time, or its usefulness for future reference. It would be trite to say that the present cannot be understood without the knowledge of the past. An important reason for the timeliness of this work can also be found in the intensity and rapidity of changes which we are witnessing now and which are likely to be viewed in future as a watershed in the history of our century in general, and of economic history in particular.

In Southern Africa[1] the last three decades have abounded in conflicts of profound proportions. Here, the process of decolonisation, more peaceful in many other parts of Africa, went through the turbulence of the Angolan and Mozambican uprisings, the Unilateral Declaration of Independence (UDI) in (Southern) Rhodesia by the white regime, followed by guerilla warfare in that country, post-independence civil wars in the former Portuguese territories, strife for freedom in Namibia, and the overwhelming drama of the anti-apartheid struggle in the Republic of South Africa. The Southern African region inherited a particularly intense legacy of colonial and settler rule, including exceptional susceptibility to inter-ethnic conflicts related to boundary problems, the relative importance of white settlement with all its unacceptable trappings, lopsided economic structures, and various forms of neocolonialism which could be listed *ad libitum.*

The dramatic changes which we are witnessing presently show a snowballing effect and, as such, are unlikely ever to be reversed. Their outward appearance is political. However, beneath the surface, economic factors are of paramount importance. On the Southern African scene at the end of the 1980s a new development is the apparent willingness of the South African government to grant independence to Namibia, coupled with the prospects of the withdrawal of the Cuban troops from Angola. On the one hand, hard economic reality points to the effects of sanctions on South Africa, including the embargo on international credit and technology, the burdens of foreign debt and overstretched military expenditure. On the other hand, there are immense implications of *perestroika* in the Soviet Union which, among other things, put the material support for class struggles in the non-communist world on the back-burner. This decision affects, in no uncertain terms, the position of several Front Line States vis-à-vis South Africa. To many observers this is a radical change with far-reaching economic and political consequences; to those more open-minded among them, the possibility of unexpected important events in the Soviet Union, in the context of attempted reforms, cannot be excluded. To conclude, the Southern African scene of tomorrow is likely to be very different from what it was yesterday, or even today, albeit with some fundamental continuities.

Of special relevance, from our viewpoint, is also the evolution, if not always radical, yet often vital of the methods and approaches to the economic history of the region. Speculations regarding the direction of this process of change have intensified since the beginning of the present decade.[2] With some important exceptions, the 'old' economic history was the domain of historians; while its 'new' versions passed into the hands of social scientists, especially economists. Whereas this rather oversimplified view of the status of the latter discipline may fit most of the Western world, Africa is an important exception. The economic content of African history has always been considerable from its very beginnings, even though historians have played a far more prominent role than economists in African historiography. In Africa, economic history continued to be the domain of historians and historically minded anthropologists.

The new economic history (the cliometric school) never took root in the methodology of African history and continues to be of marginal significance.[3] The reason for this are complex. If one tries to identify the most obvious of them, one can find it in the preoccupation with the pre-colonial history, which does not lend itself readily to quantitative treatment and is bound to attract the attention of social scientists other than economists. Moreover, most of the colonial history did not provide a fertile ground for quantitative analysis of the 'cliometric' type. This also explains, at least partly, why African economic history extended its interest to the burgeoning fields of social and cultural history.

An even earlier development was the application of Marxian analysis which tended to imbue the discipline with the spirit of dialectical materialism.[4] It views history, in part, in terms of a dominant mode of production. Here, while the institutional aspects are not ignored and the material forces of production are emphasised, the appropriation of the surplus is viewed as a result of a conflict between classes. Useful as the concept of a mode of production may be, a recent discussion among Africanists has revealed a lack of willingness to accept it unconditionally as a methodological credo.[5] To narrow down the theoretical basis to the concept of class struggle, which for dialectical materialists is the driving force of history, can imply the neglect of many other vital factors – such as e.g. gender, ideology, demography, environment, etc.

In an attempt to find a more comprehensive approach, and to extend the basis for an explanatory effort, one may turn to the contribution made by the Annales group, whose interest has been in 'total history'.[6] Historians in the Annales school devote their attention to a number of disciplines with perhaps a stronger bias towards social history than economics. They are also reluctant to commit themselves to any rigorously defined method. Their open-mindedness permits them to be pragmatic and eclectic – a characteristic which deserves the attention of progressive economic historians, who ought to be aware of the fading boundary between social and cultural history and their own discipline. The protagonists of the Annales school do not reject the pre-statistical periods of history as unworthy of study. In this they show an affinity to most Africanists. Their open-mindedness permits them to recognise the methodological contribution of dialectical materialists to the extent that they find it useful.[7]

Editors' Introduction

As a holistic approach to Southern African or any other history represents an unattainable ideal, one can only attempt to approximate it. Economic historians following this path should proceed with caution so as not to lose their disciplinary identity. However, Douglass North's dictum about the Annales scholars that 'they provide no leadership to aid us in acquiring a more systematic and scientific understanding of the economic past'[8] should not discourage us from drawing a lesson from their extremely valuable contributions.

These aspects are taken into consideration when dealing with the pre-colonial past of Southern Africa. The first chapter attempts to outline the history from the Early Iron Age to the occupation of the region by the Europeans, over a period of four centuries, starting with the Portuguese intrusion and ending with the late nineteenth-century 'scramble' for Africa.

The geographically extended area of the Bantu migrations and the related wide range of economic, social, and cultural interactions between population groups, necessitated the coverage of the whole territory of Southern Africa. Plainly, this approach is intended to satisfy the requirements of the sequel volume on South Africa, the Lesotho and Swaziland. It serves to situate and indicate the extended tradition of regional relations. They thus constitute useful additions to the on-going development of Southern Africana. Regional studies of an interdisciplinary kind have multiplied during the decade of the 1980s. A few appeared before then, but these usually concentrated on either a subset of states (eg. BLS or the then 'unholy alliance' of settler regimes) or a subset of issues – strategic or economic or labour or infrastructure. Until the welcome appearance of contemporary collections by Joseph Hanlon, and by Phyllis Johnson and David Martin, in the mid-1980s[9] there were all too few comprehensive analyses of the political economy of Southern Africa. The independence of Zimbabwe in 1980 transformed the regional context, compelling scholars as well as statespersons to treat Southern African contradictions, both cooperative and conflictual, in a comprehensive manner.[10] The contemporary chapters in this collection identify and analyse the most salient of these.

Thus the essays on the colonial and the post-colonial period, presented in the five case-study chapters, concentrate on particular countries and on particular aspects of their economic history. In so doing, they point to similarities and contrasts, cooperation and conflict over time. They also reflect distinctive aspects of each political economy, notably degrees of authoritarianism and industrialisation, and debates over land and labour, food crops and export commodities. Southern Africa has witnessed considerable variation at the level of politics and rhetoric in recent

x

decades but its underlying cohesion and comparability remain. New regional institutions seek to advance such cooperation for development into the 1990s which may yet experience the liberation of South Africa as well as of Namibia.

One sector in which there has been considerable change and debate in the region over the last decade is that of food: food security has become a growth industry for consultants and scholars given the incidence of destabilisation and drought, with major disagreements about how to define and secure regional production, storage and distribution.[11]

Lastly, there is the problem of analytic emphasis on the various elements of human lives – Basic Human Needs over time – including the influence of natural environment. When these elements act as the variables which determine the course of historical events, the force of their impact varies with the length of time under consideration. Thus, throughout the millennia of the African Iron Age, demography, environmental, cultural and health factors played a prominent role. In a relatively short run, encompassing just a few decades, the number of factors and their strength changes, leaving more room for the all-important impact of politics on economic and social life; i.e. raw ecological vulnerability was moderated, at least for some societies. This is visible in the influence of internal political forces on economic life, as well as in the degree and mechanics of dependence between the Southern African 'periphery' and the highly industrialised Western 'centre', on the one hand, and the narrower 'periphery' of the Front Line States vis-à-vis the South African 'centre', on the other.

This theme of politics, with its roots deeply embedded in the rich soil of the controversial socio-economic issues, will appear in a widened perspective in the companion collection of studies on the remaining countries of Southern Africa.

NOTES

1. For the purpose of this study Southern Africa is taken roughly as the territories south of the line running between the estuaries of the rivers Zaire, in the west, and Ruvuma, in the east.
2. See a series of articles in the *Journal of Interdisciplinary History*, Vol. XII, No. 2 (1981).
3. For a useful survey and the discussion of the problems encountered by the school see: Donald N. McCloskey, 'The Achievements of the Cliometric School', *Journal of Economic History*, Vol. 38, No. 1 (1978), 13–28.
4. For a discussion of the role played in economic history by the Marxist School see: Jon S. Cohen, 'The Achievements of Economic History: The Marxist School', *Journal of Economic History*, Vol. 38, No. 1 (1978), 29–57.
5. See a series of articles in the *Canadian Journal of African Studies*, Vol. 19, No. 1 (1985), 1–174. An informative discussion of some of the problems faced by the Marxist methodologists can also be found in Mike Morris, 'Social History and the Transition to

Capitalism in the South African Countryside', *Review of African Political Economy*, Vol. 41 (Sept 1988), 60–72.

6. For a discussion of the role played in economic history by the Annales School see: Robert Forster, 'The Achievements of the Annales School', *Journal of Economic History*, Vol. 38, No. 1 58–80.

7. These important characteristics are well epitomized by the example of a collection of studies by Shula Marks and Anthony Atmore, eds., *Economy and Society in Pre-Industrial South Africa* (London, 1980), to mention one of the more recent works of this kind.

8. Cited by Robert Forster, *loc. cit.*, p. 80.

9. See Joseph Hanlon, *Apartheid's Second Front* (Harmondsworth: Penguin, 1986) and *Beggar Your Neighbours* (London: James Currey & CIIR, 1986) and Phyllis Johnson & David Martin (eds), *Destruction Engagement: Southern Africa at War* (Harare: Zimbabwe Publishing House, 1986).

10. For an overview of this literature see Timothy M. Shaw, *Southern Africa in Crisis: an analysis and bibliography* (Halifax: Centre for Foreign Policy Studies, 1986). See also David R. Black *et al, Foreign Policy in Small States: Botswana, Lesotho, Swaziland & Southern Africa* (Halifax: Centre for Foreign Policy Studies, 1988).

11. For insights into these issues see series of reports and annual collections from the University of Zimbabwe/Michigan State University Food Security in Southern Africa Project and Coralie Bryant (ed), *Poverty, Policy, and Food Security in Southern Africa* (Boulder: Lynne Rienner, 1988).

Contributors and Editors

Marcia M. Burdette has done research in Zambia and Zimbabwe as well as teach at Fordham, Columbia and St. Lawrence universities. Her most recent publication is *Zambia: Between Two Worlds* (Westview Press, Boulder, Colorado, 1988). Dr. Burdette's current focus is on possible linkages between mining and manufacturing in the developing world. She is exploring the possibilities for greater self-sufficiency in the agrosupport industry of Zimbabwe as well as its potential to supply the SADCC region.

Kenneth Good was Associate Professor of Political Studies at the University of Zambia 1982–88. He has taught and carried out research in a number of other African countries and in Papua, New Guinea. He is co-author of *Articulated Agricultural Development* which was published by Gower in 1988.

Zbigniew A. Konczacki is Professor Emeritus, Dalhousie University, Nova Scotia. He taught at the universities of Natal, Alberta and Dalhousie and specialises in economic development and economic history of Africa and Europe. His most important publications relating to southern Africa are *Public Finance and Economic Development of Natal 1893–1910* (Duke University Press, 1967), *The Economics of Pastoralism: A Case Study of Sub-Saharan Africa* (Cass, 1978) and a contribution to *From Shantytown to Township* edited by Gavin Maasdorp and A.S.B. Humphreys (Juta, 1975).

Philip Longmire studied African Foreign Policy and International Relations at Dalhousie University in Canada. He has worked extensively in Central Africa, Asia and the South Pacific as co-ordinator of educational programs and curriculum development. Currently he is a consultant in international programming based in Halifax, Nova Scotia.

Andrew C. Murray, formerly of the Department of History, University of Botswana, is now Assistant Representative, The British Council, Malawi. Author (with R.F. Morton and J. Ramsay) of *A New Historical Dictionary of Botswana*. Presently engaged in writing a History of Ngamiland, 1906–66.

Jane L. Parpart, Associate Professor of History, Dalhousie University, has done extensive research on women and labour in Africa. Her most important publications include a book on *Labour and Capital on the African Copperbelt* and *Patriarchy and Class: African Women in the Home and the Workplace* (co-edited with Sharon Stichter).

Neil Parsons received a doctorate in history from Edinburgh University. He has spent many years in southern Africa where he taught history at universities in Zambia, Swaziland and Botswana. He also worked as a research associate of Queen Elizabeth House at Oxford University. His publications include *The Roots of Rural Poverty in Central and Southern Africa* (London, Berkeley and Los Angeles, 1977), and *A New History of Southern Africa* (New York, 1983).

Yonah N. Seleti is lecturer in history at the University of Zambia. Has done extensive research in Portugal and Angola on the Angolan coffee industry. Received a doctorate in history from Dalhousie University.

Timothy M. Shaw is Professor of Political Science and Director of International Development Studies at Dalhousie University in Nova Scotia, where he has also served as Director of the Centre for African Studies. He has written extensively on African political economy and is the editor or author of *Economic Crisis in Africa, Southern Africa in the 1980s, Towards a Political Economy for Africa, Coping with Africa's Food Crisis,* and *Corporatism in Africa.*

Socio-Economic Formations of the Southern African Iron Age: An Overview

ZBIGNIEW A. KONCZACKI

INTRODUCTION

The antiquity of the *Homo sapiens* in Southern Africa[1] goes back at least 80–100,000 years as indicated by the discoveries of human remains which include the archaeological finding made in 1974 at Border Cave (kwaZulu) (21, pp.212–15). No evidence has been found for the presence of the Neanderthals or "Neanderthaloids" in the southern sub-continent or, for that matter, in Africa south of the Sahara. Instead the population is typified by an early *Homo sapiens* variant with some Khoisan-Negro affinities. It developed a relatively advanced Stone Age technology and economy indicated by the presence of specialised tools and the intense exploitation of marine resources (4, p.416).

A pertinent question arises – what were the conditions of life and the related distribution of the early populations of Southern Africa during the last glacial period? The important fact is that unlike during some previous periods of glaciation the sub-continent was not covered with ice, but climatic changes which took place on a large scale strongly influenced vegetation, human, and animal life. The last glacial maximum, with its cold and dry climate, occurred about 18,000 years ago. At that time, there were no significant changes in seasonal distribution of rainfall as compared with that of the present, but changes in total annual rainfall were considerable. The relevant archeological evidence has produced few traces of the population of hunter-gatherers, the ancestors of the San of Southern Africa, who depended for their subsistence on the natural environment. A visible change took place with the coming of the present interglacial epoch, some 12,000 years ago. Between 10,000 and 8,000 years ago, the largest increase in human population took place, when the climatic optimum led to greater productivity of environments. Subsequently, there was some deterioration in the conditions of life. An instance of extremely unfavourable conditions is found in the Transvaal highveld, where hunter-gatherer population was absent between 8,000 and 2,000 years ago, i.e. until the arrival of the Iron Age agriculturalists (16, pp.325–7).

Iron Age farmers, who practised shifting cultivation, contributed to the destruction of the original dry forest and shrub. Grazing herds also played a role in modifying plant cover. Of particular significance was the impact of grass fires both man-induced and natural. The age-old practice of grass-burning had been noticed by Vasco da Gama who, in 1497, because of the dense smoke seen along the coast of the south-western Cape, called it *Terra de Fume*. Grass burning had been used already in prehistoric times against wild animals, for hunting purposes, and later on by pastoralists to induce the growth of grass. Subsequently European immigrants adopted the methods of the local inhabitants in order to increase the utilisation of natural pasture. Seasonal burning has undoubtedly been an ecological factor of considerable importance for a very long time. Its effects were manifold: the most important was an adjustment in plant species, as only fire resistant trees and shrubs could survive; second, a reduction in the formation of humus, the lowering of the soil pH; and third, an increase in soil erosion caused by the seasonal disappearance of plant cover (45, pp.166–8).

The results of recent studies have radically altered our views on the pace and the nature of the long-term ecological change. The older 'wilderness model', relying on the reconstruction of the Southern African flora in AD 1400 by J.P.H. Ackocks, assumed that, at that time, the environmental impact of the Iron Age farmers and pastoralists was insignificant in comparison with the role played by commercial cultivation and livestock-rearing of the colonial period (1, passim). A number of subsequent archeo-botanical investigations carried out in various parts of the region point to far-reaching modifications in the plant cover during the last two thousand years. The presently existing forests are only a remnant of the earlier Holocene biome. While the higher lying areas were probably covered with grasslands, the valleys and coastal plains, on the other hand, were overgrown with woodlands which were removed prior to the arrival of the whites. In eastern Botswana floral characteristics of certain locations allowed them to be identified with the Iron Age middens dating back to the ninth and the thirteenth centuries. Similar detective work has been done by archeologists in the Transvaal lowveld where the presence of *Acacia* indicated early village sties. In Zululand, as well, woodlands dominated by *Euclea divinorum* had replaced the original forests

2

felled in the pre-colonial period as the result of extensive iron-smelting activities (35, p.12). The appearance of secondary savanna and the shrub encroachment following the cessation of cultivation are, as a rule, tangible evidence of Iron Age occupation (29, pp.150–1).

Vegetation is also affected by significant changes in humidity, whether represented by alternating long periods of wet and dry climate (pluvials and interpluvials) extending over centuries or even millenia, or the shorter term year-to-year variations in weather conditions.

It goes without saying that vegetational patterns have been formed over thousands of years as a result of slow changes. They have also been modified by man's interference. Thus the present plant cover cannot be considered as entirely 'natural' and the landscape which is seen today may be mainly anthropogenic.

EARLY IRON AGE (EIA): BANTU MIGRATIONS AND ECONOMIC CHANGE

Prior to the great movement of the Bantu-speaking agriculturalists from the north, Southern Africa was inhabited solely by the San and Khoi peoples.[2] In contrast to the immigrant black-skinned Bantu-speakers, the San and the Khoi were yellow-skinned and their languages were related. The San came from East Africa in the distant past. The penetration of the Bantu, who arrived long before the coming of the first European settlers in the seventeenth century, initiated the Southern African Iron Age. The spread and growth of Bantu-speaking groups among the local Khoisan peoples[3] was gradual and largely peaceful, unlike the rapid movement of the Europeans in the eighteenth and nineteenth centuries, which was often accompanied by armed conflict. Whereas the Bantu-speaking people brought with them the benefits of the African Iron Age to the Late Stone Age population, the impact of European technology had a traumatic and disruptive effect on the indigenous peoples.

The beginnings of the dynamic process of migrations of the proto-Bantu speakers throughout sub-Saharan Africa can be traced to the original settlements in Cameroun and neighbouring Nigeria around 1,000 BC or even earlier. It was a movement of neolithic population which had left traces of pottery, ground stone artifacts and grindstones, made use of oil palm and consumed fruit of *Canarium schweinfurthii*. It is important to note that the Western Bantu did not cultivate cereals (82, p.132). Subsequently, as these migrants moved further to the south they began to grow yams on the forest fringes and clearings. Their food supply, which was complemented by hunting and gathering, allowed for population growth.

3

In recent years views on the Bantu expansion have changed reflecting the rapidly growing archeological evidence, the re-evaluation of older archeological material, the accumulation of linguistic evidence, and the positive results of linguistic and archeological correlations.[4]

According to D.W. Phillipson (66, pp.210–20), the expansion of Bantu-speakers was channelled into two streams: the Western and the Eastern. Between 1000 and 400 bc[5] some Bantu-speakers moved eastwards, along the fringes of the tropical forest into the Great Lakes region of East Africa where they established an Early Iron Age culture. This occurred when they came into contact with mixed-farmers who were probably the speakers of ancestral Central Sudanic languages. Apart from adopting the herding of domestic cattle and sheep and certain cereal crops (including sorghum), the Bantu-speakers acquired metal-working techniques (66, p.227).

The Western Stream of Bantu-speakers moved into northern Angola and between 300 and 100 bc was joined by a splinter group which left the Eastern Stream and proceeded around the southern margin of the equatorial forest, bringing with them Iron Age technology. These two groups coalesced into the Western Stream, which by 100bc entered northern Namibia, and between ad 400 and 500 reached Shaba and western Zambia, spreading out from there, after ad 1000, to the eastern part of Southern Africa. Meanwhile, about ad 100 to 400 the Eastern Stream reached the coast of southern Kenya. From there through the highlands, west of Lake Malawi, they moved into the Transvaal. Another branch of that stream moving east of Lake Malawi reached southern Mozambique, Natal and the eastern Transvaal.

Some of the assumptions of Phillipson's two-stream hypothesis, and the facts on which it is based, have been the subject of a lively debate in archeological literature (43, p.135; 38, p.447; 42, pp.223–7; 20, p.11). The controversy is likely to continue until discovery of some new facts and the publication of new radiocarbon dates make further revisions of the present views on this matter possible. It is already known that some of the population movements took place earlier than was originally thought. For instance, it has been discovered that Bantu settlements were in existence on the Mozambican coast by AD 200, if not earlier.[6] It also appears that the Western Stream sites in Zimbabwe (Rhodesia)[7] were at least as early as the Eastern Stream sites in Natal, which have recently been dated to the fourth century AD (43, p.136), while widespread presence of EIA communities in north-western and north-eastern Botswana goes back to the middle of the first millennium AD (20, p.14).

With this framework in mind we can now pass on to the agricultural history of the Bantu-speaking settlers. The typical EIA villages consisted of small huts. These were made of mud (*daga*) which was applied over a pole and wattle frame and covered with a thatched roof. Storage bins raised above ground, and structured in a similar manner, as well as storage pits, were common. The preferred sites of these settlements were close to water-courses because of the growing dependence on cereals. Occupation was of relatively limited duration in keeping with the practice of shifting cultivation. In the areas of high soil fertility the occupation of land was more prolonged. Estimating population densities is difficult due to frequent changes of the place of residence. A small community on the move could easily create an impression of being numerically far larger. Nonetheless, it has been suggested that in many areas the EIA populations were too small to displace the autochthons. Low population densities permitted a peaceful coexistence between the newcomers and the indigenous population.

The acquisition of new crops by the former probably intensified their movements in search of suitable environments but, because of the largely different modes of procuring food supplies, the preferred environments of the two population groups did not overlap to any significant extent. Thus the open, dry country and densely forested areas remained the domain of hunters and gatherers (83, pp.138–9). Demographic pressures began to appear only many centuries later on.

Archeological evidence indicates the presence of domestic animals several hundred years before the advent of the Iron Age. The Late Stone Age herders were present in Western Zimbabwe (Rhodesia) by 200 BC, and in Namibia and the Cape at the beginning of the first millennium AD. Bones of domestic sheep, goats and cattle radiocarbon-dated to the fifth century ad have also been found at Broederstroom in the Brits District, west of Pretoria. In northern Botswana good grazing lands, in the area around the Okavango Delta and the Makgadikgadi Pans, may have been of crucial importance in the southward spread of livestock (66, p.120; 20 pp.4–6).

C. Ehret's study, based on linguistic evidence, dates the introduction of domestic animals into northern or northeastern Botswana to the second half of the first millennium BC. James Denbow indicates the early pastoral neolithic communities in East Africa of 3000–2000 B.C as a likely source of livestock for the Late Stone Age peoples of the Southern African region, and he finds the obstacle of a large geographical distance as 'not necessarily serious' (20, pp.6, 9).

The Khoi acquired their small stock from East Africa when their range extended much further north. Tsetse fly presented no barrier, hence one possible route to the south was via Mozambique. An alternative route led westward from the Makarikari Lake (northern Botswana) southwards through Namibia to the Cape of Good Hope. It permitted the Khoi sheep-herders to avoid the crossing of the Mopani scrub veld which was deficient in grass.

According to C.K. Cooke the first sheep to reach the southern Cape were of the fat-tailed variety. When the Khoi came into contact with Bantu-speakers, the possessors of hairy thin-tailed sheep, the Khoi animals were cross-bred with the latter (84, p.437; 12, pp.268–9, 271–3). The acquisition by the Khoi of the fat-tailed sheep was, most likely, due to the advantages derived from their coarse wool and the fat deposit on the tail.

The goat, on the other hand, was not raised by the southern Khoi tribes at the time of the first European settlement at the Cape. Its acquisition was due to the Bantu-speakers who, in turn, obtained goats from their neighbours in the north (26, vol.2, pp.255, 258).[8]

The archaeological evidence of domestic cattle in Southern Africa is derived from a fairly widespread occurrence of bone remains. According to Phillipson none of the Eastern Stream cattle occurrences predate the meeting with the Western Stream cattle, which probably took place in the vicinity of the Victoria Falls region between ad 400 and 500. Passage through tsetse-infested lands of southern Tanzania must have deprived the Eastern Stream migrants of their cattle. This loss was only remedied after contact with the Western Stream Bantu was established. The latter's cattle escaped a similar fate and entered the area of the Gokomere Tunnel Site in Zimbabwe (Rhodesia) sometime after AD 600. Cattle remains (*Bos taurus*)[9] recovered from that site and from Mabveni have been radiocarbon dated to ad 530 ± 120 (SR-26), 570 ± 110 (SR-79) respectively (66, pp.146–7, 230; 79, p.461)

Phillipson's hypothesis regarding the re-acquisition of cattle by the Eastern Stream after the two streams had met, has been recently questioned, as new evidence from Malawi points to the presence of the cattle already in the third century (60, p.436).

In so far as cultivation is concerned the archeological findings are sufficient to give us a broad idea of the crops adopted by the EIA farmers. Their distribution was, however, far from being widespread and general. The settlement depended largely on the ecology. Adequate rainfall and deep alkaline soils were sought for the cultigens like grains, legumes and cucurbits which were the main crops. Sweet grazing was preferred as well as places where a good supply of timber was available for domestic fires, construction of huts and iron smelting. The areas which satisfied these requirements were limited and as the EIA way of life extended to the south it followed the narrow belt between the sea coast and the interior grasslands. The latter suffered from such disadvantages as acid soils, drier climate, less palatable grazing and a shortage of timber. In fact, Tim Maggs used the Natal pattern as a predictive model for other parts of Southern Africa and suggested that a major environmental boundary is reached where the mean annual rainfall is less than 200 mm and the precipitation during the three summer months (December to February) becomes less than is required for the growth of the cultigens which were grown by the EIA farmers (55, pp.7–9). This explains the absence of cultivation to the south-west of the straight line drawn between Port St. Johns and Mafeking, with the exception of the coastal sites elsewhere and the deeply incised river valleys which provided a favourable environment for mixed farming of the Bantu migrants.

The earliest evidence indicates the presence of the EIA farmers on the east coast of Mozambique and in Natal at about AD 200 and in Malawi, Zimbabwe (Rhodesia), Zambia and the Transvaal a century and a half later[10] (43, p.135; 54, p.176; 28, p.160; 60, pp.436, 449, 452; 65, p.7; 75, pp.184, 185). The Natal site, at the rock shelter of Shongweni, gives direct evidence for the early cultivation of *Eleusine coracana* (finger millet), *Pennisetum americanum* (bulrush millet) and *Lagenaria sineraria* (bottle gourd) (55, p.5). In Malawi, the Munga Hill site cattle remains have been dated to the third or fourth centuries. Archeological data from Zimbabwe (Rhodesia) and from Makwe in Zambia's Eastern Province suggest that the beginnings of the EIA in that region were roughly contemporary with similar developments in Malawi. In the Transvaal traces of bulrush millet at the third-century Silver Leaves site are another confirmation of the appearance of EIA cultivators to the south of the Limpopo River (66, pp.113–20; 55, p.6; 60, p.449).

As regards the technology of the EIA industrial complex, the most common product encountered by archeologists is pottery, and ceramic traditions have been used by them for the purpose of identifying other finds. According to Phillipson, in contrast to the later practice among Bantu-speakers, women were the EIA potters, although there is some probability that men may have also participated in pottery-making. By contrast, T.N. Huffman's careful analysis points to the absence of any convincing evidence that would indicate that men were the potters during the early Iron Age. Their participation in this craft was probably an exception rather than the rule (66, pp.147, 150; 42, p.237).

Whether or not pottery vessels were the object of trade, other than local, is an unresolved question. The likelihood that it may have been transported over long distances is small. Nonetheless, the existence of the trade in salt, a rather bulky commodity, raises the possibility that pottery may have been transported, as well, over long distances. Alternatively, pottery whose style ran counter to the local tradition may have been the

7

work of migrant potters, who, prompted by the desire to acquire some foreign goods, such as copper, visited distant localities. Numerous finds of copper ingots in places far removed from the mines indicate extensive trade in this metal.

Whereas ceramic industry is traced back to the Stone Age, the smelting and working of iron initiated a distinctive new period in Southern African prehistory. Nevertheless, owing to the scarcity of iron, only small objects, such as arrowheads, knives and hoes were manufactured. Larger tools continued to be made of stone and the coexistence of the two industries practised by the Bantu-speakers lasted for many centuries.

The absence of both the Copper Age and the Bronze Age in Black Africa can be explained in terms of the relative scarcity of copper and tin, prior to the discovery of copper in Zaïre and Zambia, as compared to iron. This does not mean that other metals were unknown to the Iron Age metal workers of Southern Africa. In order of importance iron was followed by copper and gold.

In Angola, the earliest Iron Age radiocarbon date goes back to the second half of the first century ad, and is related to a location (Furi, Lunda) in the north-east. There are still vast areas in the centre and the south of that country where no systematic excavation has taken place (17, pp.491, 504).

The regions extending to the South – Namibia, Botswana and the northern parts of the Cape Province – because of their climatic characteristics, were not likely to attract settlers who were primarily interested in good farming land and adequate supply of wood. All these regions could offer were pastures of highly varying quality, and in comparison to the contemporary settled farmers, nomadic pastoralists, who used them, left very few traces of their existence. Little evidence is available and not much weight should be attached to isolated radiocarbon dates. At their best they can indicate the location and the earliest appearance of a given phenomenon but not its magnitude and its full territorial coverage.

Iron ore, which exists in many parts of Southern Africa, was obtained from surface exposures or from shallow pits. Archeological evidence indicates that it was smelted in tall, cylindrical furnaces fired by natural draught, capable of attaining temperatures in excess of 1110°C. It also appears that the later taboo forbidding contact between smelters and women may not have existed at that time, as not infrequently smelting took place in villages.

The occurrence of copper is far more restricted than that of iron ore deposits, and apart from the Shaba–Zambia Copperbelt it is limited to only a few areas. Prehistoric copper mining sites had been largely damaged by modern mining operations; however, many objects made of

8

this metal, discovered by archeologists, are traceable to the EIA. These are mostly small items of personal ornament, or bars and cross-shaped ingots, which were used for exchange purposes. On the whole, the surviving objects from the EIA industrial complex suggest a relative scarcity of copper. Its working took place on a far smaller scale than that during subsequent centuries. The same is true of gold mining, which developed towards the end of the first millennium in Zimbabwe (Rhodesia) and in the neighbouring territories. Out of the numerous gold mines traced there, only four are known to have been worked during the EIA. They were located in the eastern part of the country in the valleys of the Mazoe and the Sabi rivers linking the interior with the coast.

Archeological data pertaining to trade patterns has been corroborated by written Arabic sources, which also indicate that gold was exported. Significantly, the beginnings of the mining of this metal coincided with the appearance of imported glass beads in the areas. The EIA trading activities between the interior and the coastal regions were on a very small scale. Written sources did not record any exports of gold and copper from the interior prior to the tenth century, whereas such other items of the Indian Ocean trade mentioned by them, as rhinoceros horn, ivory and turtle shells, may have originated in the coastal belt (66, pp.144–52).

To sum up – our knowledge of the EIA industrial complex relies mainly on the evidence provided by archeology. The Bantu-speaking immigrants brought with them rudimentary agriculture, herding, pottery manufacture, metallurgy and a settlement pattern based on semi-permanent villages consisting of pole-and-daga huts. An outstanding and hardly unexpected characteristic of the EIA settlements was their location in areas which environmentally suited the requirements of the contemporary methods of farming. Local, as well as long distance trade remained very limited in scope.

These new forms of economic life continued to co-exist in many localities with the indigenous stone-tool-using societies. The continuation of the microlithic industry by the latter suggests that cultural contacts were limited. The demise of the stone-tool-using hunter-gatherers was the result of their inability to withstand the competition for the territory as the Bantu-speaking population grew. It appears, for instance, that in parts of central Zambia, where the EIA immigrants of the Western Stream had settled, and in much of Zimbabwe (Rhodesia), the local population was displaced or assimilated before the end of the first millennium ad. By contrast, to the south of the Limpopo, the sparseness of EIA occupation resulted in relatively little contact between the two population groups. Where that contact was closer, it is likely that some form of temporary client relationship developed, whereby the original inhabitants rendered hunting and herding services to the Bantu-speakers in exchange for food and other products, such as pottery, prior to the adoption by them of the pot-making technology (66, pp.248–67).

LATER IRON AGE (LIA): SOCIAL-ECONOMIC CHANGES

The LIA in Southern Africa goes back to the early centuries of the present millennium. Compared to the EIA our knowledge of the LIA suffers from a relative paucity of data due to less comprehensive research. As one progresses in time, archeological studies tend to concentrate primarily on the more spectacular sites, such as the Great Zimbabwe, and a few other comparable ruins.

Among the regions that have been investigated more thoroughly one should mention southern Zambia, where the Kalomo and Kangila cultures have been identified on the basis of distinct ceramic traditions. The beginnings of the Kalomo industry overlapped with that of the final phase of EIA, and within a few centuries it gave way to the Kangila culture which spread from the north and had reached the Victoria Falls area around the late twelfth century ad. The richest archeological evidence of that culture comes from three sites: Sebanzi Hill north-west of Monze, Ingombe Ilede close to the Lusitu/Zambezi confluence, and Kangila approximately mid-way between the two latter sites. The Sebanzi occupation ended around the eighteenth century, while that at Ingombe Ilede was intermittent – it first appeared early in the present millennium and again about the fourteenth century or later. Kangila village was occupied in the fifteenth century for a relatively short time of a few decades.

The economies of these two cultures were largely comparable and it seems that no major technological progress was made as compared with the level achieved in the EIA. The only improvement of any significance was the use of iron-smelting furnaces fired by artificial draught which can be inferred from the presence of tuyère pipes and bellows' nozzles. In contrast to the EIA practice, the smelting took place away from the village as no traces of furnaces were ever discovered on the village sites. Ironworking was performed by means of the simple hammering of bars, rods or strips of the metal. The technique of welding was unknown. Iron hammers were not in use; instead stones with battered surfaces are commonly found. The manufacture of iron tools had been practised on a small scale. Copper continued to be imported and its use was limited to the manufacture of bangles.

On the other hand, there were major differences in the scale of activity in herding and in trade. Faunal material discloses a higher proportion of cattle and small stock vis-à-vis wild animals as a source of protein. An outstanding example of such a change was the dramatic increase in the size of herds in the central district of Botswana as early as the late part of the EIA (after about AD 700). This may have been the result of the occupation of an area particularly suited for grazing. The increased dependence on pastoralism in many parts of Southern Africa can be correlated with the rise in the number of liquid-holding pots, suggestive of a greater reliance on milk in the diet.[11] The location of many settlements on the borders of grasslands favoured livestock-raising, and grassland pasture provided a better protection from predators than the woodlands. The examination of the mandibles points to the slaughtering of young as well as old and infirm beasts by the villagers. This may indicate that there was an adequate supply of animals over and above herd maintenance requirements. The cattle were approximately of the same size as nineteenth century Tonga animals. The latter were of Sanga shorthorn breed with cervico-thoracic humps.

The mixed-farmers of the Kalomo and Kangila cultures, practising shifting agriculture, were limited in the choice of land by their primitive methods of cultivation based on the simplest implements consisting mainly of digging sticks. Iron hoes were rare, due to the scarcity of iron, and so were iron axes, which precluded any extensive clearance of woodlands. Edaphic grasslands, savanna woodlands and sites situated on the edge of *dambos* (the waterlogged depressions) provided the most favourable environment. Sorghum (*Sorghum caffrorum*) was the main cereal crop. Other crops included bulrush millet (*Pennisetum*), cowpeas (*Vigna unguiculata*), the Livingstone potato (*Coleus esculentus*), yams (*Dioscorea sp.*), Bambara groundnut (*Voandzeia subterranea*) and various cucurbits (66, pp.169–72; 27, pp.59–91; 20, p.15).

The patterns of production point clearly to the prevalence of a subsistence economy where trade played an insignificant role and very few commodities were exchanged. Small quantities of sea-shells of the 'trade' type as well as glass beads, probably of Indian or Persian origin, were the objects of the long-distance trade with the east coast. Imports of Central African origin included copper and graphite. The latter had been used for burnishing clay pots. It may be presumed that salt also formed an item of the regional exchange as its production was limited to only a few places.

As to exports, there were very few natural resources to attract traders from afar. One of them was ivory used both domestically and for trade. Hence, little could be offered in payment for imports. Nonetheless, archeological evidence points to the fact that the coastal trade routes had penetrated to the interior (27, pp.85–87, 216).

A similar type of economy existed in many areas scattered over Southern Africa. It extended to Zambia, in the west into Angola, in the east into Malawi, and in the south into Mashonaland (Harare and Musengezi industries), the Inyanga highlands – associated with terrace cultivation on mountain slopes north of Umtali, Matabeleland and the Limpopo valley, where numerous sites centring around Bulawayo have provided valuable archeological evidence.

Of particular importance in that area is the industrial succession named after the Leopard's Kopje site (Nthabazingwe). The Leopard's Kopje tradition began with the Mambo phase in the eleventh century ad, which has been identified by its distinctive pottery. The economy of this culture was based on mixed farming. The second phase, known as Woolandale, made its appearance around the thirteenth century. It differed from the Mambo phase by a change in the typology of its pottery, presumed initiation of cotton cloth manufacture (indicated by the discovery of spindle whorls), construction of stone structures and gold-mining. Imported glass beads became more common. Both Mambo and Woolandale sites extended westwards to Botswana, whereas the southward extension of the Leopard's Kopje culture developed two phases: Bambandyanalo and Mapungubwe, named after the two, closely located, sites on the Transvaal side of the Limpopo river. In terms of their broad characteristics they corresponded to the Mambo and Woolandale succession.

The Mapungubwe phase distinguished itself by some new socio-economic phenomena such as the extensive use of organised labour and a degree of social stratification indicated by the differences in the quality of the houses (66, pp.169–85; 41, pp.247–8).

The most impressive of the numerous stone structures, in the region, are those of the Great Zimbabwe,[12] and so are the finds indicating the economic and socio-political significance of that centre of LIA activity. It is, to some extent, paralleled by the Manekweni site, on the coastal plain of southern Mozambique, and that of the Ruanga Ruin of northern Mashonaland (32, pp.25–47; 31, pp.107–43).

Of particular interest, in the Transvaal Lowveld, extending to the east of the Great Escarpment, is the Phalaborwa region where copper was mined on a substantial scale since the early centuries of the LIA, by sinking shafts and driving horizontal passages. The tools commonly used included iron chisels and stone hammers. Iron ore was mostly collected from the surface.

The practice of cultivation is indicated by the presence of iron hoes, grindstones and the terraced hill-sides. Faunal remains of domestic animals include cattle, goats and chicken. A number of sites provided salt which was obtained by the evaporation of brine in soapstone bowls, manufactured locally.

In the Orange Free State, to the south of the Vaal, the evidence of LIA settlements goes back to the fourteenth or fifteenth centuries ad. The inhabitants of the drier areas of this region depended more on livestock-raising than on cultivation.

In Natal the spread of the LIA population to the south dates from the eleventh century and five centuries later the Kei River, in the Cape Province, was reached. More research is needed in order to improve the knowledge of the expansion of Bantu-speaking people in this important area during the pre-colonial times. The data on the western parts of Southern Africa is also fragmentary but all available evidence points to the settlement of long duration of the Bantu-speakers. In Angola the site at Feti la Choya, some 300 kilometres north of Kunene, had been occupied for many centuries of the present millennium.

Iron Age pottery of a distinctly Bantu style, from the north-western corner of Botswana (Tsodilo Hills), is comparable to that made in Zambia in the twelfth century ad. Moreover, seventeenth-century radiocarbon dates from the Depression Cave in the Tsodilo Hills indicate contacts between the Late Stone Age and the Iron Age people. Regional differences were largely related to ecological conditions, which is indicated by the sandveld (Kalahari) and hardveld sequences. Late Stone Age sites of the pastoral Khoi peoples occurred mainly in the sandveld whereas the intrusive Iron Age settlements concentrated in the hardveld. The two areas were linked by exchange based on rudimentary specialisation.

In Namibia pottery associated with the Khoi people, found at Conception Bay, has been dated back to the fourteenth century, while in the northern part of that country a seventeenth-century LIA site has been discovered at Vungu Vungu (Okavango) (66, pp.199–205; 44, p.230; 18, p.474; 19, pp.404–7).

Compared to the geographical distribution of the ethnic groups during the EIA, the seventeenth-century dividing line between the settlement areas of the Khoisan and the Bantu-speakers receded far to the west and ran between the present localities of Windhoek in Namibia and Port Alfred on the south-east coast of the Cape Province (66, p.198).

The study of the economies of the Southern African Iron Age, thus far undertaken in this chapter, has been based mainly on archeological data. However, if a broader view is to be taken, including the vital aspects of socio-economic and political organisation, archeology offers limited assistance. The methodology of reconstruction of these aspects of a culture from archeological data has not been adequately developed as yet, and the inferences one can make from this type of evidence are usually of a rather general nature. In most cases they indicate a combination of quantitative and qualitative changes. For instance, increases or decreases in human population can be inferred from the variations in the number and size of sites and the duration of their occupation. Differences in the quality of individual houses point to social and economic stratification (see above, the Mapungubwe phase). Furthermore, the existence of higher-order political systems is indicated by the regional distribution of sites as well as the differences in their size and in the nature of ecology. As settlements move away from the capital such as Great Zimbabwe or Mapungubwe socio-political cohesion undergoes a weakening process. Ecological factors in combination with political considerations played an important role in the location of sites either on hilltops or in the lowlands. The former were further away from productive resources but provided protection from cattle raiders and enjoyed a position of dominance. The latter, while benefitting from the proximity of good soils and water, were less secure and exercised less social and political power.

A process which is quite well documented by archeological evidence is the development of pastoral economies, often linked to a rapid growth of herds, as exemplified by a change which took place in the eastern part of the Kalahari between the seventh and thirteenth centuries AD, when herding became more important than cultivation. The most vital long-term consequences of this type of dynamic quantitative change tended to be largely of a qualitative nature. One of them was a transition from a matrilateral to a patrilateral type of society. Both these forms of kinship system were present in the prehistoric Bantu societies, but the growth of herding meant a shift in emphasis which was related largely to the division of labour in pastoral societies, along gender-lines. By taking charge of the large herds of cattle men strengthened their economic dominance over women.

The consequences of the increased significance of pastoralism also became visible in the greater differentiation of the factors of production. In contrast to cultivation, which relied primarily on scarce labour inputs, herding depended on capital represented by cattle. This opened the way to the accumulation of that asset by individuals, giving rise to economic and social stratification with concomitant political consequences resulting from inequalities in wealth and power. It was a rudimentary form of early family capitalism in a basically pre-capitalist society. In contrast to cattle-herding, cultivation ensured a fair degree of equality, and one is inclined to agree with James Denbow when he views this difference as a possible clue 'to one of the most interesting problems in southern African prehistory: the formation of hierarchical social systems and thus states' (20, pp.15–17, 21–3; 72, p.152; 50, p.41).

SOME METHODOLOGICAL ISSUES

An analysis of the process of state formation goes far beyond the confines of archeological evidence in that it takes advantage of protohistory and touches upon a variety of data recorded by various other disciplines. One has to start with that form of society in which the state organisation was still absent and the forces contributing to its formation were relatively weak. Whether one thinks of it as 'primitive communism' – the first of Marx's four stages of development – or as the 'original affluent society' as suggested by modern anthropologists, like Marshall Sahlins (71, chapter 1), in each case stereotyping is unavoidable.[13]

Unlike Marx, who concentrated on the Asiatic mode of production which, in his time, provided the best available case study, modern Africanists of neo-Marxist orientation diverted their attention to the socio-economic formations found in pre-colonial Africa. Thus, attempts were made to replace the characteristics peculiar to the static hydraulic agriculture of Asia with traits of a more generalised nature, capable of explaining change in a variety of early manifestations of social organisation. A stage theory of socio-economic evolution was eschewed, with the emphasis placed on the concept of a mode of production.[14] This was supposed to free the analyst from the constraints imposed by the unconvincing idea of a predetermined and irreversible sequence of stages.

As an analytical device a mode of production relies on two components: (1) the forces of production such as technology, labour and raw materials, and (2) the relations of production which are concerned with the manner of the extraction and distribution of the surplus (49, p.9). The latter component is a reflection of class structure. In the writings of contemporary Africanists the concept of the mode of production has assumed a variety of formulations. Thus, for example, Samir Amin proposed five modes: (1) the primitive-communal mode; (2) the tribute-paying mode; (3) the slave-owning mode; (4) the simple petty-commodity mode; and (5) the capitalist mode (3, pp.13–15). Amin abandoned the Marxian stage sequence but one can still detect its original structure in his classification. Catherine Coquery-Vidrovitch formulated an African mode of production which relies upon the combination of a patriarchal-communal economy and the control of the long distance trade by a privileged group (13, pp.33–51).

Claude Meillassoux and Pierre P. Rey developed a concept of a lineage mode of production with an emphasis on the control over the means

15

of reproduction which they regarded as of decisive importance to the distribution of wealth (59, pp.38–67; 69, pp.27–79).

More recently, the preoccupation with these new conceptualisations has led to an attempt to assess their theoretical soundness and practical value as a tool of analysis. An exchange of views took place between anthropologists and historians of Marxist and non-Marxist orientation.[15] A full summary and an assessment of the results of this debate is beyond the scope of the present chapter. Briefly, a wide spectrum of opinions were expressed ranging from those which recognised the usefulness of the concept of the mode of production, with the proviso that further improvements be made (47, pp.64–72), to those which suggested that a 'massive conceptual overkill' took place when the desired theoretical and political aims could well have been achieved by other means. Gavin Kitching insists that 'there are altogether humbler, more disaggregated concepts which can do these jobs, and which are, in addition, a lot more historically and empirically flexible than the modes of production' (48, p.118).[16] Still others, while insisting on the usefulness of alternative approaches and methods, admit that the rejection of the mode of production concept would deprive us of an important heuristic device and thus impoverish our understanding of the African past (2, p.18; 14, p.63; 11, p.19).

With the exception of the simplest and earliest form of society, dominated by the primitive-communal mode of production, the pre-history of Southern Africa displayed a variety of formations characterised by a considerable degree of analytical complexity. As one progresses in time the modes of production cease to appear in their pure form implied by their original definitions. In real life, social formations are the result of a combination of several (at least two) modes of production of which one is dominant (79, p.345). The subordinate modes are usually inherited from the preceding period, while the new mode germinates to reach full florescence in the succeeding period when it, in its turn, assumes the role of the dominant mode. In this process of change the modes lose the original sharpness and become blurred by mutual interactions and frequently by the impact of exogenous forces. This analysis may be taken a step further by identifying the key economic institution pertaining to the dominant mode of production. Such a key institution has been defined by Judy Kimble as one 'through which the domination (formal or real) of those productive processes pertinent to the appropriation of surplus labour is exercised.' The main characteristic of this institution is that it ensures the effective possession of the means of production (47, pp.65–6).

The empirical approach of social scientists who attempt to reconstruct and analyse the life of the societies of the more distant past encounters

16

the obvious data problem. In addition to the fragmentary results of archeological research there are descriptions by travellers and explorers who encountered indigenous societies in pre-colonial and early colonial times.[17] What they saw, however, differed in many respects from the state these societies were in many centuries ago. Intensification of contacts with the outside world, man-made and natural changes in the environment, demographic movements, interactions between ethnic groups (Bantu-speakers and Khoisan) and, in more recent times, resistance to the European intrusion – all had an impact on the life of these peoples which, in many respects, made their socio-economic organisation unlike that of their more distant ancestors. Survival of age-old forms, suspected in these cases where conditions did not alter too drastically, permits us a glimpse into the economic pre-history. Nonetheless, this procedure cannot claim to be anything more than informed guesswork.

A confrontation of the theoretical framework, relying on the concept of the mode of production, with the empirical evidence, imperfect as it is, confirms the reservations about the ability of a single mode to account adequately for the phenomena of real life. A number of important examples, taken from the pre-colonial economic history of Southern Africa, can be used to substantiate this point.

According to Samir Amin the primitive-communal code is characterised by (a) the collective ownership of land by the clan and its use by nuclear families (individual use) and partly by extended families (collective use); (b) absence of exchange; and (c) distribution of the product based on kinship. In fact, in the case of the San people, who were hunters and gatherers, and that of the Khoi people, who were also pastoralists, there were significant exceptions to the collective ownership of land, particularly when rights were created, through one's personal effort, to the use of a natural resource. Thus, e.g. an individual who dug a waterhole had the exclusive right to it. Furthermore, there were important exceptions to the principle of distribution based on kinship. Hunting was often done by groups of hunters, who were not necessarily linked by the bond of kinship and the meat of the hunted animal was divided between the members of the party on the basis of mutual agreement and not along the rules inherent in the kinship system (74, pp.47, 49, 50; 73, pp.290–1).

A vital characteristic of the primitive-communal mode is the absence of exchange. More advanced forms of trade were absent from the San society, but the flow of goods between families took on the form of gift-exchange, which was equivalent to informal barter. Exchange transactions of the Khoi people were incidental to the production for subsistence. Exchange was limited to barter carried on not only between

17

families but also with other groups, such as the Bantu-speakers, the San, and later on with the Europeans (73, pp.317–19).

The evident conclusion to be drawn from the above discussion is that empirical studies provide little evidence for the existence of a mode of production in its 'pure' form. History suggests that as socio-economic change progressed, in addition to the original dominant 'primitive-communal' mode of production there began to appear the subordinate modes *in statu nascendi*, such as the 'tribute-paying' and the 'African mode', which subsequently replaced the original one and, in turn, assumed the position of dominance.

LATER IRON AGE: THE RISE AND FALL OF THE KINGDOMS

The Southern African population groupings of the LIA displayed a rich mosaic of social, economic and political forms ranging from stateless, diffuse and miniscule groups, often of a village size, through chieftaincies of more substantial territorial extent, to kingdoms possessing a hierarchical organization involving tributary chiefs and headmen subordinated to them.[18]

In Angola the two most important were the Kongo and the Lunda kingdoms; in the central parts of the region the dominant role was played by the kingdom of Great Zimbabwe, and the related Rozwi kingdom of Mashonaland, while in the east there were the Chewa kingdoms of Malawi, the kingdom of Swaziland and the Zulu kingdom of Shaka and his successors. Also, several Southern African chiefdoms, including those of Botswana, Lesotho, Ciskei and Pondoland, came into prominence.[19]

With the exception of the Great Zimbabwe, which between the twelfth and eighteenth centuries went through several phases in its history of foreign trade – gold-mining, farming and cattle-herding – the origins of most of the other kingdoms go back to the second half of the present millennium.

The nature of the support systems for the population of the Southern African kingdoms, the superstructural activities related to the payment of tribute and the carrying on of the various crafts and forms of trade, reflected the wide environmental and demographic diversity of the region and, last but not least, the availability of minerals. The sub-regional patterns of food production, which have already been presented in their bare outlines, were affected by the rise of kingdoms and the accompanying increase in the size of settlements.

At Zimbabwe a system of economic and political power, based on tribute and on the control over long-distance trade, was established quite clearly, with the integration of the various branches of production by the ruling Shona dynasty (20, pp.22–3; 33, pp.490–3). The Portuguese sources mention a tax amounting to the produce of one field in every village and one day of labour in 30 on the part of the king's subjects. The ivory, exported by the ruler, came from the tribute of one tusk of every pair. More lucrative than ivory was the trade in gold. Mining was a community task, performed by the population of villages, who sold the output of gold to the king.[20] In one recorded instance the payment was made with cattle; however, the method of fixing the price is unknown. The king's power over trade was enhanced by the fact that foreign traders from the East Coast, originally the Arabs and later on the Portuguese, were subject to his control and could not travel freely over his territories (30, pp.176–7).

The decline of Zimbabwe was probably due to an ecological imbalance related to heavy reliance on pastoralism, as the main source of food for the highly concentrated population. In the opinion of T.N. Huffman, 'The constant demand for firewood . . . and the gradual exhaustion of the soil must have made it increasingly difficult to live there without a more efficient agricultural system . . .' (40, pp.365–6). A changeover from meat to the products of cultivation, brought from distant areas, was not practicable in the absence of adequate transport. The wheel never reached pre-colonial sub-Saharan Africa and animal power was not used for any form of traction.[21] By contrast, cattle could be driven to Zimbabwe on the hoof from pastures situated at a considerable distance. Also, in the absence of the plough, there were no means of substantially increasing agricultural productivity in a society where, at best, cultivation meant hoe farming (34, passim). Huffman's hypothesis also explains the subsequent fragmentation of Zimbabwe. By the middle of the fifteenth century food shortages and a disruption of trade occurred and were followed by the dispersion of the population. As a result, the centre of political and economic control moved to the north, to an area bordering on the middle Zambezi River, but the Great Zimbabwe managed to survive as a state under a ruler bearing the title of Mwene Mutapa.

In other states, located in what is now Zimbabwe (Rhodesia), the development of foreign trade reached its peak during the second half of the present millennium. This occurred in the sixteenth and seventeenth centuries on the northern Mashonaland plateau, and in the seventeenth and eighteenth centuries in Matabeleland. While both these states were linked to the Great Zimbabwe, the southern Mashonaland became the Rozwi kingdom of Guruhuswa ruled by the Changamire (Mambo) dynasty. The rulers of that kingdom exercised strict control over foreign trade. They relied on a monopoly of the export of gold and on the prohibition of non-African merchants from entering their lands.

19

Instead, the services of the African *mussambazes* (professional agents) were used. Here again, the system of exchange was based on the tribute network which benefitted a small oligarchy (66, pp.192–3; 78, pp.258–9). The Rozwi state came to an end when it was attacked by the Matabele in the early 1800s (66, pp.195–6; 10, pp.47–8).

In Angola both the Kongo and the Lunda kingdoms collected tribute, which in the case of the former consisted of payments in raphia cloth, ivory, hides, slaves and labour services (82, pp.41, 44, 246–8). The export of slaves developed as a result of demand on the part of the Portuguese; they acquired both goods and slaves from the king, who accumulated these by way of tributary payments. The wars of conquest, dating from the second half of the sixteenth century, enabled the Portuguese to exact tribute directly from the chiefs, who were subjugated by them (82, pp.184–5; 7, pp.171–2; 6, pp.37, 41, 78). The weakened state of the Kongo survived until the second half of the sixteenth century, when it fell prey to the invading Jaga people (36, pp.20–1; 6, ch.6).

The kingdom of Lunda achieved the peak of its expansion in the eighteenth century, which enabled it to extract tribute from a number of satellite states. At that time, Lunda became the major slave exporting area (6, pp.148–9, 152–4, 161). Cessation of the slave trade in the nineteenth century spelled an end to the prosperity of Lunda's ruling class, who did not succeed in competing in ivory exports with the Cokwe, the neighbouring people, who proved to be more dynamic and versatile traders. In time, however, the system of integrating large numbers of alien women into their society created overpopulation in the Cokwe country.[22] Their inability to feed the increasing population forced them to emigrate from Quiboco, where they originally lived. In the course of their migrations the Cokwe overran the Lunda kingdom, thus putting an end to its existence (61, pp.194–201).

In the eastern part of the region the most important were the Chewa kingdoms of Malawi and in particular those of Kalonga, Undi and Lundu, which controlled many tributary chiefs. It is likely that the development of these states was partly due to the ability of the kings to distribute foreign imports to subordinate rulers and administrators, who had little opportunity to participate in foreign trade. The king's power depended on the monopoly of the collection of tribute in ivory, which was also the most important export commodity. Exports of slaves were of little significance prior to the nineteenth century. The breaking of the king's monopoly in ivory and the decentralisation of his control over tribute and trade, in general, led to the decline of the Malawi kingdoms. This, in turn, was due to the development of direct trade relations between some of the minor kings and chiefs and the Portuguese in the peripheral areas, where the central power was unable to enforce its authority. By the middle of the nineteenth century economic and administrative decentralisation, combined with external political pressures, led to the fragmentation of Malawi's kingdoms.[23]

The rise, in the early nineteenth century, of Shaka, the king of the Zulus, and his way of establishing control over environmental exploitation in the face of the breakdown of physical resources, form a unique episode in the economic history of Southern Africa. The Zulus, who were stock-keeping cultivators, practised concentrated grazing over long periods, thus steadily reducing the carrying capacity of the pastures. This long-term trend was drastically accentuated during the catastrophic famine, known as the *Madlathule*, which occurred in the first decade of the nineteenth century (37, p.111). Shaka speeded up the centralisation process, initiated by his predecessors, reorganised the army and, during the early 1820s, used his military strength to conquer land, which permitted the distribution of cattle over a much greater area. The series of raids and wars (*Difaqane*) displaced whole Bantu communities (53, p.107). Shaka's other measures led to the adaptation of population size to food supply. This was achieved by the king's right to withdraw permission to marry to his warriors and to the women, who formed age-sets. As a result, their average age at first marriage was quite late, with a consequent decline in population. The king's control over men was very extensive as all of them, from the age of puberty, were required to serve in the army for some 15–20 years (37, pp.103, 111–18).

In the remaining years of the nineteenth century, Zulu kings gradually lost their powers and territory to the whites, and the conflict between the two ethnic groups reached its climax in the wars of 1879 and 1883–4. Zululand lost its independence in 1897, when it became part of Natal.

The Swazi kingdom – a close neighbour of the Zulus, and a survivor of *Difaqane* – underwent a profound transformation in the last decades of the eighteenth and during most of the nineteenth century. Its lineage-based structure, relying on the monopoly of trade, exercised by the elders, which facilitated access to cattle and other assets exchangeable for wives, was transformed under the impact of the *Madlathule* famine. By drastically intensifying the competition for resources it led to territorial conquests, oppression and levies of tribute exacted from the subjugated people. The newly-introduced age-regiments (*amabutho*) provided a coercive intervention in lineage reproduction and the appropriation of tributary labour services. Also a change from an exogamous to a cross-cousin form of marriage allowed for the concentration of wealth, consisting mostly of ivory, cattle, and captives, within the ruling group. During the course of the nineteenth century the Swazi society, based on lineage and tribute,

21

began to experience struggles within its embryonic class system and the weakening of the central authority (5, pp.33–5, 88, 209–14; 8, pp.85, 87, 92–7). The arrival of European settlers, following the discovery of gold and tin, and the pressures exerted by both the British and the South African Republic, introduced an element of economic and political dependence, which was formalised in 1902 with the establishment of British administration.

To conclude, the decline and fall of the African kingdoms was due to a number of causes ranging from the inability to deal with ecological imbalances to the destructive impact of foreign intrusion. On the whole, Africans could cope better with the former than with the latter problems. One may presume, as Jan Vansina did, that 'the development of the African states would have gone on had there been no influence from outside' (82, p.248). This brief survey of the attempts to cope with the imbalance between population and resources has identified several courses of action which, regardless of the original intentions of the decision-takers, tended to relieve the pressures. They included efforts to adapt population size to food supply by emigration, birth control and conquests of new lands. Such measures were largely undertaken in those states where decision-taking was concentrated within a centralised system of government.

Emigration to another area was a solution typical of the Bantu-speakers practising shifting cultivation. They abandoned exhausted lands and took advantage of the open and sparsely populated spaces elsewhere. It should be borne in mind, however, that there were other societies with different systems of decision-taking, where the diffuse system of power precluded drastic actions, and where the methods of dealing with environmental imbalance were more spontaneous and wide open to external influence active over long periods of time. The most successful were the efforts to increase food supply by the introduction of new crops, which required a modification of the dietary habits. This involved a changeover from less productive crops to maize and other plants which could offer higher food-value yields per unit of land (9, p.385). Between 1548 and 1583 maize entered Central Africa, probably through the kingdom of Kongo, and in the seventeenth century cassava came under cultivation, supplementing the diet based on millet, bananas and yams. Despite its poorer nutritional value this plant became popular because of its resistance to attack by locust and as a hedge against famine (46, pp.66; 62, p.94; 82, p.21).

Maize was brought to South Africa by the Dutch in 1658, and in the nineteenth century it became an important staple food of the African population. Approximately at the same time it gained a predominant position in Malawi, whereas in Mozambique, Zambia, Zimbabwe (Rhodesia)

22

and Botswana the twentieth-century evidence indicates its paramount importance as the foodstuff consumed by the local populations (62, pp.144–7, 155–69). It thus appears that in most of Southern Africa, maize has replaced the traditional and more nutritious foods, such as millets and sorghums, largely because of its role in increasing the productivity of agriculture.[24] The substitution of maize for other cereals has also been influenced by the dispossession of Africans of their land under colonial rule, and more recently by the accelerated population growth.

EPILOGUE

It took approximately 300 hundred years for the Southern African Iron Age to come to an end. The beginning of the end came in the sixteenth century with the Portuguese designs on Angola and Mozambique. Originally, the small settlements of colonists and traders were limited to the coastal areas and the conquest of the interior was slow. Control over most of what was later known as 'Portuguese Africa' was achieved by the end of the nineteenth century. Resistance, however, continued as late as 1917 in the case of Angola's Moxico region and in Mozambique's Barué region (22, pp.226–34).

In South Africa the earliest victims of the European intrusion were the Khoisan people in the Cape and subsequently the Bantu-speaking carriers of the Iron Age culture. As a result of the growing pressure exerted by white colonists, who founded their first settlement in the Cape of Good Hope in 1652, the Khoi people were dispossessed of both their land and cattle. This did not come about without their active resistance. White colonisation was linked to the 'frontier policy' of prolonged strife with the local tribes.[25]

European occupation of the remaining parts of Southern Africa followed the Berlin Conference of 1884–85, a portentous episode in modern history, which led to the indiscriminate dismemberment of African tribal units and ethnic groups.

In 1884 Germany declared a protectorate over Namibia and a year later Bechuanaland (Botswana) came under British control. With the establishment of the British South Africa Company in 1889, a framework was created for the occupation, administration and exploitation of the territories north of Bechuanaland, the Transvaal, and west of Mozambique, which became known as Northern Rhodesia (Zambia), Southern Rhodesia (Zimbabwe), and Nyasaland (Malawi).

Events pertaining to the subsequent economic history of these countries are the subject matter of this volume. At this stage, attention will only be focused on the early impact of European intrusion which, in many parts of Southern Africa, took place within a few decades of effective colonial occupation. This impact assumed three basic forms. The first was the redistribution of agricultural and pastoral land in favour of the white colonists. In most cases this was achieved through the establishment of the so called 'native reserves' in which frequently the local population was resettled. As a rule the poorest lands were allocated to Africans.

Secondly, the colonists brought with them the demand for African labour. The initial inadequacy of the labour supply led to the application of ruthless methods of eliciting it, thereby disrupting the customary way of life. These methods ranged from slavery, in the early history of South Africa, to resort to various forms of direct and indirect force. The former relied on communal labour for public works and the use of convict labour. Direct labour drafts for private employers were rather unpopular in the territories under British control but prevalent in Portuguese Africa.

Indirect force relied on the imposition of poll taxes, hut taxes, curtailment of African land rights and the system of formal or informal recruiting which often implied the use of veiled force, to round up African manpower. The most subtle method of procuring labour services was to entice a villager into buying goods and thereby entangling him in monetary obligations which he could not pay off except by seeking wage employment. This was the essence of the 'advances system' widely practised by traders who, at the same time, acted as labour recruiters (5, pp.403–11; 23, pp.184–7).

Thirdly, European colonialism spelled the end to the centuries old industrial complex of the African Iron Age. Local crafts and mining industries of a pre-capitalist economy were destroyed with the coming of Western capitalists and the appearance of imports of mass-produced manufacturers from the metropolitan countries. The age-old traditions of craftsmanship were irretrievably lost to a population which a few decades later strove to assimilate the skills required by the new industrial age.

All in all, the colonial brand of capitalism, while destroying the pre-colonial socio-economic systems, substituted for them a form of dualism, which quite efficiently performed a function assigned to it by the newcomers. The purpose of it was to exploit the artificially created class and wealth distinctions and to guard against the 'dangers' of educational, economic and political progress in the African sector of colonial society. All this was done under the guise of introducing civilisation. Ironically, African poverty was its most conspicuous result, which should not surprise those who tend to agree with Marshall Sahlins' dictum that 'Poverty is a social status. As such it is the invention of civilisation' (71, p.37).

NOTES

1. The geographical area with which this study is concerned can be roughly defined as that part of the African Continent which extends to the south of the line drawn between the points where the northern borders of Angola and Mozambique reach the Atlantic and the Indian Ocean respectively.
2. The San and the Khoi were also called Bushmen and Hottentots by the European settlers. At present the latter names are no longer in usage as they are regarded as derogatory terms.
3. According to I. Schapera the term 'Khoisan' was coined in 1928 by L. Schultze who combined the names 'Khoi-Khoin' by which the 'Hottentots' called themselves and 'San' as they called the 'Bushmen' (73, p.5).
4. For a fair idea of this evolution see: *References*, items 39, 43, 63, 66 (ch.8–10), 82.
5. The lower-case bc and ad denote radiocarbon years, whereas the capital letters BC and AD denote calendar years. For the explanation of the difference between the radiocarbon age and the calendar age see: R.C. Soper, 'New Radiocarbon Dates for Eastern and Southern Africa', *Journal of African History*, Vol.15, No.2, 1974, p.175.
6. The earliest radiocarbon date for Matola IV (Delagoa Bay) is R-1327: ad 70–50. Its acceptance would necessitate a revision of the chronology of settlement along this part of African coast (38, pp.440, 455).
7. This designation is used throughout this chapter to distinguish the modern state of Zimbabwe from the ruins known under that name.
8. Linguistic evidence points to a hypothesis that Bantu took over livestock-keeping from people who spoke Central Sudanic languages (25, passim).
9. There are differences of opinion about the origins and the domestication of *Bos taurus* which made its appearance in Africa in the Sahara during the humid period. The later shorthorn variety was preceded by the longhorn type depicted in the earliest rock paintings in West Africa (26, Vol.1, pp.292, 293).
10. This account relies on published information relating to radiocarbon dates available prior to 1986.
11. Linguistic evidence suggests that the milking of cattle was practised by the Bantu-speakers of Southern Africa but its diffusion took place after their advance into that region was well under way (24, pp.11–17).
12. *Zimbabwe* in the Shona language means 'stone houses' or 'venerated houses'. This term, or its plural 'madzimbabwe', has been applied to many structures in that area, which were built by the Shona ruling groups (33, p.479).
13. Today, people living in the Galbraithean version of the 'affluent society' view the hunters, gatherers and pastoralists of old as suffering from poverty. They tend to forget, however, that the adequacy of the means of livelihood is a relative concept and it ought to be measured in relation to one's needs.
14. For the most succinct statement of Marx's stage theory of development see his *Capital*, Vol.1 (57, p.316). Marx distinguished four stages viz: 1. primitive communism; 2. ancient slave state; 3. feudalism; and 4. capitalism. Later on Lenin considered modern imperialism as the last and highest sub-stage of capitalism, where Western colonialism intruded upon the mostly pre-capitalist societies.
15. See: *The Canadian Journal of African Studies*, Vol.19, No.1, 1985, pp.1–174.
16. The author of this remark stops short of making any explicit suggestions as to what those other concepts might be. From among many contributions, in this field, that by Karl Polanyi comes to mind as one of particular relevance. More than 30 years ago Polanyi directed his interest to the vital distinction between market and non-market economies. Concentrating mainly on the case study of the slave trade of Dahomey, he viewed it as a non-market, administered form of exchange, based on a state monopoly (67, 68 passim). Most of the critics questioned the validity of empirical evidence used by Polanyi. The debate appears to be far from over and among the most recent critics of Polanyi's substantivist position

25

are: Philip D. Curtin, Bruce G. Trigger, Werner Peukert, and Robin Law (15, 80, 64, 52 passim), and among his supporters Abraham Rotstein (70 passim). The discussion would have undoubtedly been enriched by a more generous inclusion of case studies which could provide better empirical evidence, and by taking into account criticism put forward by the supporters of methodology based on the mode of production concept, who pointed out that, in formulating his 'substantivist' thesis, Polanyi paid attention primarily to the nature of exchange, while underestimating the importance of production and the tribute on the supply side of the equation (78, pp.340–1). This example may suggest a way out of the controversy between the supporters of the mode of production method and its critics, which may be found in an eclectic and more empirical approach to methodology.

17. For an indication of the sources of this kind see: Monica Wilson (84, I, ch.2); Izaak Schapera (73, pp.439–45); George W. Stow (76, passim).
18. Some of the kingdoms, e.g. the Manyika kingdom paid tribute to the Mwene Mutapa and later on to the Rozvi Changamire, hence some of the authors, in recognition of this hierarchical relationship, are inclined to speak of Mwene Mutapa and Rozvi empires. See H.H.K. Bhila, *Trade and Politics in a Shona Kingdom* (Burnt Mill, Harlow, Essex, 1982).
19. A useful survey of the relevant literature can be found in Patrick Harries, 'Modes of Production and Modes of Analysis: The South African Case', *Canadian Journal of African Studies*, Vol.19, No.1, 1985, pp.30–7. See also Judy Kimble, 'A case for Defence' (ibid., pp.64–72), for a discussion of the tributary mode in Lesotho.
20. Archeological research has identified two different gold mining techniques used in that part of Africa: open stopes and shafts. The former consisted of trenches which followed ore bodies, until the ore gave out, or some obstacle, such as water, prevented further digging. Shafts were applied to horizontal ore bodies which outcropped on the slope of a hill. The absence of timbering techniques to support the overhanging rocks made mining very dangerous and archeologists found evidence of many mining accidents. The skeletons of victims were frequently those of young females, which indicates that women were employed in underground work. Gold was obtained by crushing in stone mortars rock extracted from the mines. An alternative source was the alluvium of rivers (77, pp.464–6).
21. Some years ago the author saw, in one of the villages in South Africa, a sort of a sledge drawn by a team of six oxen and used for the transport of farm produce for short distances. It was not possible, however, to ascertain the antiquity of this method of transport.
22. Instrumental in this process of integration of alien women was the pawnship system, the essence of which was 'the transfer of rights over an individual from one lineage to another'. Its widespread application was prompted by the tensions inherent in the matrilineal social system of the Cokwe (61, p.181).
23. See Harry W. Langworthy, 'Chewa or Malawi Political Organization in the Precolonial Era' in Bridglal Pachai (ed.), *The Early History of Malawi* (Evanston, Illinois, 1972), pp.104, 113, 117–20.
24. Today, in many parts of Africa local populations are malnourished because of the almost exclusive reliance on such staples as maize, cassava, or plantains, which contain very little protein. In pre-colonial times their diet was more diversified and richer in protein.
25. For details of the Khoisan resistance see *References* No.56.

REFERENCES

1. Ackocks, J.P.H., *Veld Types of South Africa*. Pretoria, 1953
2. Alpers, Edward A., 'Saving Baby From the Bath Water', *Canadian Journal of African Studies*, Vol.19, No.1, 1985
3. Amin, Samir, *Unequal Development. An Essay on the Social Formations of Peripheral Capitalism*. New York and London, 1976
4. Beaumont, P.B., De Villiers, H., Vogel, J.C., 'Modern Man in Sub-Saharan Africa Prior to 49,000 Years B.C.: A Review and Evaluation with Particular Reference to Border Cave', *South African Journal of Science*, Vol.74, Nov. 1978

Socio-Economic Formations of the Southern African Iron Age

5. Berg, Elliot J., 'The Development of a Labour Force in Sub-Saharan Africa', *Economic Development and Cultural Change*, Vol.13, No.4, Part I, 1965
6. Birmingham, David, *Trade and Conflict in Angola*. Oxford, 1966
7. Birmingham, David, 'Early African Trade in Angola and its Hinterland' in Birmingham, D. and Gray, R., *Pre-Colonial African Trade*. London, 1970
8. Bonner, Philip, 'Classes, the Mode of Production and the State in Pre-Colonial Swaziland', in S. Marks and A. Atmore (eds.), *Economy and Society in Pre-Industrial South Africa*. London, 1980
9. Boserup, Ester, 'The Impact of Scarcity and Plenty on Development', *Journal of Interdisciplinary History*, Vol.14, No.2, 1983
10. Chanaiwa, David, *The Zimbabwe Controversy: A Case of Colonial Historiography*, Syracuse University, Eastern African Studies, VIII, 1973
11. Clarence-Smith, Gervase, 'Thou Shalt Not Articulate Modes of Production', *Canadian Journal of African Studies*, Vol.19, No.1, 1985
12. Cooke, C.K., 'Evidence of Human Migrations from the Rock Art of Southern Rhodesia', *Africa*, Vol.25, No.3, 1965
13. Coquery-Vidrovitch, Catherine, 'Research on an African Mode of Production', in Martin A. Klein and G. Wesley Johnson (eds.), *Perspectives on the African Past*, Boston, 1972
14. Cordell, Dennis D., 'The Pursuit of the Real: Modes of Production and History', *Canadian Journal of African Studies*, Vol.19, No.1, 1985
15. Curtin, Philip D., *Cross-Cultural Trade in World History*, Cambridge, 1984
16. Deacon, H.J., 'Another Look at the Pleistocene Climates of South Africa', *South African Journal of Science*, Vol.79, Aug. 1983
17. De Maret, P., Van Noten, F., Cahen, D., 'Radiocarbon dates from West Central Africa: A Synthesis', *Journal of African History*, Vol. 18, No.4, 1977
18. Denbow, J.R., 'Early Iron Age Remains from Tsodilo Hills, North-Western Botswana', *South African Journal of Science*, vol.76, 1980
19. Denbow, J.R. and Wilmsden, E.N., 'Iron Age Pastoralist Settlements in Botswana', *South African Journal of Science*, Vol.79, 1983
20. Denbow, James, 'A New Look at the Later Prehistory of the Kalahari', *Journal of African History*, Vol.27, 1986
21. De Villiores, Hertha, 'A Second Adult Human Mandible from Border Cave, Ingwavuma District, KwaZulu, South Africa', *South African Journal of Science*, Vol.72, July 1976
22. Duffy, James, *Portuguese Africa*. Cambridge, Massachusetts, 1959
23. Duffy, James, *Portugal in Africa*. Harmondsworth, Middlesex, 1962
24. Ehret, C., 'Cattle-Keeping and Milking in Eastern and Southern African History: The Linguistic Evidence', *Journal of African History*, Vol.8, No.1, 1967
25. Ehret C., 'Sheep and Central Sudanic Peoples in Southern Africa', *Journal of African History*, Vol.9, No.2, 1968
26. Epstein, H., *The Origin of the Domestic Animals of Africa*, 2 vols. New York, London, Munich, 1971
27. Fagan, B.M., *Iron Age Cultures in Zambia*. London, 1967
28. Fagan, B.M., 'Radiocarbon Dates for Sub-Saharan Africa: VI', *Journal of African History*, Vol.10, No.1, 1969
29. Freely, J.M., 'Did Iron Age Man Have a Role in the History of Zululand's Wilderness Landscapes?' *South African Journal of Science*, Vol.76, April, 1980
30. Garlake, P.S., *Great Zimbabwe*. London, 1973
31. Garlake, P.S., 'Excavations at the Mhunguza and Ruanga Ruins in Northern Mashonaland', *South African Archeological Bulletin*, Vol.27, 1973
32. Garlake, P.S, 'An Investigation of Manekweni, Mozambique', *Azania*, Vol.11, 1976
33. Garlake, P.S., 'Pastoralism and Zimbabwe', *Journal of African History*, Vol.19, No.4, 1978
34. Goody, Jack, 'Land Tenure and Feudalism in Africa', *The Economic History Review*, Second Series, Vol.22, No.3, 1969
35. Granger, J.E., Hall, M., McKenzie, B., Freely, J.M., 'Archeological Research on Plant and Animal Husbandry in Transkei', *South African Journal of Science*, Vol.81, Jan. 1985

36. Gray, Richard and Birmingham, David, 'Some Economic and Political Consequences of Trade in Central and Eastern Africa in the Pre-Colonial Period', in Gray, R., and Birmingham, D. (eds.), *Pre-Colonial African Trade*. London, 1970
37. Guy, Jeff, 'Ecological Factors in the Rise of Shaka and the Zulu Kingdom' in Marks, Shula and Atmore, Anthony, *Economy and Society in Pre-Industrial South Africa*. London, 1980
38. Hall, M., and Vogel, J.C., 'Some Recent Radiocarbon Dates from Southern Africa', *Journal of African History*, Vol.21, No.4, 1980
39. Hiernaux, J., 'Bantu Expansion', *Journal of African History*, Vol.9, No.4, 1968
40. Huffman, T.N., 'The Rise and Fall of Zimbabwe', *Journal of African History*, Vol.13, No.3, 1972
41. Huffman, T.N., 'Radiocarbon Date from Zimbiti Ruin, Inyanga, Rhodesia', *South African Journal Of Science*, Vol.7, 1975
42. Huffman, T.N., 'African Origins', *South African Journal of Science*, Vol.75, May 1979
43. Huffman, T.N., 'Archeology and Ethnohistory of the African Iron Age', *Annual Review of Anthropology*, Vol.11, 1982
44. Jacobson, L. and Vogel, J.C., 'Radiocarbon Dates for Two Khoi Ceramic Vessels from Conception Bay, South West Africa/Namibia', *South African Journal of Science*, Vol.75, 1979
45. Joubert, D.M., 'Ecological Effects of Fire: An Overview', *South African Journal of Science*, Vol.73, June 1977
46. July, Robert W., *Precolonial Africa, An Economic and Social History*. New York, 1975
47. Kimble, Judy, 'A Case for Defence', *Canadian Journal of African Studies*, Vol.19, No.1, 1985
48. Kitching, Gavin, 'Suggestions for a Fresh Start on an Exhausted Debate', *Canadian Journal of African Studies*, Vol.19, No.1, 1985
49. Klein, Martin A., 'The Use of Mode of Production in Historical Analysis', *Canadian Journal of African Studies*, Vol.19, No.1, 1985
50. Konczacki, Zbigniew A., *The Economics of Pastoralism. A Case Study of Sub-Saharan Africa*. London, Cass, 1978
51. Kraut, H. and Cremer, H.D. (eds.) *Investigations into Health and Nutrition in East Africa*. München, 1969
52. Law, Robin, 'Royal Monopoly and Private Enterprise in the Atlantic Trade: the Case of Dahomey', *Journal of African History*, Vol.18, No.4, 1977
53. Lye, William F., 'The Difaqane: the Mfecane in the Southern Sotho Area 1822–24', *Journal of African History*, Vol.8, No.1, 1967
54. Maggs, T., 'Some Recent Radiocarbon Dates From Eastern and Southern Africa', *Journal of African History*, Vol.18, No.2, 1977
55. Maggs, T., 'The Iron Age Sequence South of the Vaal and Pongola Rivers: Some Historical Implications', *Journal of African History*, Vol.21, 1980
56. Marks, Shula, 'Khoisan Resistance to the Dutch in the Seventeenth and Eighteenth Centuries', *Journal of African History*, Vol.13, No.1, 1972
57. Marx, Karl, *Capital*, Vol.1, London, 1887
58. McIlroy, R.J., *An Introduction to Tropical Cash Crops*, Ibadan, 1963
59. Meillassoux, Claude, 'Essai d'Interprétation du phénomène économique dans les Sociétés Traditionelles d'Auto-Subsistance', *Cahiers d'Études Africaines*, Vol.4, No.1, 1960
60. Mgomezulu, G.G.Y., 'Recent Archeological Research and Radiocarbon Dates from Eastern Africa', *Journal of African History*, Vol.22, 1981
61. Miller, Joseph C., 'Cokwe Trade and Conquest in the Nineteenth Century', in Gray, R. and Birmingham, D. (eds.), *Pre-Colonial African Trade*. London, 1970
62. Miracle, Marvin P., *Maize in Tropical Africa*. Madison, Milwaukee, and London, 1966
63. Oliver, R., 'The Problem of the Bantu Expansion', *Journal of African History*, Vol.7, No.3, 1966
64. Peukert, Werner, *Der Atlantische Sklavenhandel von Dahomey, 1750–1797*. Wiesbaden, 1978
65. Phillipson, D.W., 'Notes on the Later Prehistoric Radiocarbon Chronology of Eastern and Southern Africa', *Journal of African History*, Vol.11, No.1, 1970

28

66. Phillipson, D.W., *The Later Prehistory of Eastern and Southern Africa*, London, 1977
67. Polanyi, Karl and Others (eds.), *Trade and Markets in the Early Empires*. Glencoe, 1957
68. Polanyi, Karl, *Dahomey and the Slave Trade: An Analysis of an Archaic Economy*. Seattle, 1966
69. Rey, Pierre P., 'The Lineage Mode of Production', *Critique of Anthropology*, Vol.3, 1966
70. Rotstein, Abraham, 'Innis: The Alchemy of Fur and Wheat', *Journal of Canadian Studies*, Vol.12, No.5, 1977
71. Sahlins, Marshall, *Stone Age Economics*. Chicago and New York, 1972
72. Sansom, B., 'Traditional Economic Systems', in Hammond-Tooke, W. (ed.) *The Bantu-Speaking Peoples of Southern Africa*. London, 1974
73. Schapera, I., *The Khoisan Peoples of South Africa*. London, 1965
74. Silberbauer, George B., *Report to the Government of Bechuanaland on the Bushman Survey*. Gaberones, 1965
75. Soper, R.C., 'New Radiocarbon Dates for Eastern and Southern Africa', *Journal of African Studies*, Vol.15, No.2, 1974
76. Stow, George W., *The Native Races of South Africa*. London, 1905
77. Summers, Roger, 'The Iron Age of Southern Rhodesia', *Current Anthropology*, Vol.7, No.4, Oct. 1966
78. Sutherland-Harris, Nicola, 'Trade and Rozwi Mambo' in R. Gray and D. Birmingham (eds.), *Pre-Colonial African Trade*. London, 1970
79. Taylor, John, 'Marxism and Anthropology', *Economy of Society*, Vol.1, 1972
80. Thorp, C., 'Cattle from the Early Iron Age of Zimbabwe–Rhodesia', *South African Journal of Science*, Vol.75, Oct. 1979
81. Trigger, Bruce G., *Natives and Newcomers: Canada's 'Heroic Age' Reconsidered*. Kingston and Montreal, 1985
82. Vansina, Jan, *Kingdoms of the Savanna*. Madison and London, 1966
83. Vansina, Jan, 'Western Bantu Expansion', *Journal of African History*, Vol.25, 1984
84. Willcox, A.R., 'Sheep and Sheep-Herders in South Africa', *Africa*, Vol.36, No.4, 1966
85. Wilson, Monica and Thompson, Leonard (eds.), *The Oxford History of South Africa*, 2 vols. Oxford 1969

2

The Development of Dependent Capitalism in Portuguese Africa

YONAH N. SELETI

INTRODUCTION

A systematic account of Portuguese colonialism in Africa in the nineteenth and twentieth centuries requires consideration of the dynamics of Portuguese expansion prior to this period. Yet in a chapter of this scope the necessity for brevity entails the sacrificing of the details. However, without the consideration of particular, concrete situations, the general picture cannot emerge. Considering that the collection and analysis of data are on-going activities, I attempt here to delineate the evolution of Portuguese colonialism from the materials available so far, with an emphasis on the tension between political change and economic stagnation, external dependence and internal ideology.

Portuguese ambitions to begin with were limited but, having met with early successes in the fifteenth century, they became enmeshed in economic and strategic structures of world dimensions and complexity (36, pp.40–1). Boxer's reference to the system as the 'Portuguese Sea-Borne Empire' is quite appropriate (14, p.2). Until this century, the form of capital which had dominated Portuguese operations had been merchant capital. The tendency of such capital to depend on the extraction of profits through the exploitation of the existing interconnections between productive and social systems resulted in Angola and Mozambique playing different roles in the Portuguese sea-borne empire prior to the twentieth century. While merchant capital was dominant, the Portuguese presence in Africa did not necessitate significant changes in socio-economic systems.

The dominance of the slave trade in Portuguese Africa stifled all other forms of commerce and industry. The abolition of this trade, the harbinger of economic constriction, was a significant episode in the history of Angola and Mozambique. The timing and implementation of its abolition has been correlated to broader trends in the ideological and economic transformation of Portugal, notwithstanding the local factors which determined the different responses of the two African territories under consideration.

The inadequacy of the Portuguese economy to generate capital for colonial investment was a critical factor in the development of dependent capitalism. As Portugal allowed other colonial powers to participate in spoilation, Angola and Mozambique were subjected to contradictory patterns of transformation, destruction and preservation of their internal structures which resulted in a variety of systems of colonial occupation and exploitation (7, p.166). The resulting variations which emerged in Angola and Mozambique were a product of particular forms of external capitalist penetration, heterogeneous structures and distinctive responses of the indigenous people. The local ecologies and natural endowments were very important factors as well.

The *Estado Novo's* economic nationalism, with its acclaimed aim, of 'Portugalisation' of foreign capital, had limitations placed upon it by the centrality of foreign capital in the colonial economies. The success of the *Estado Novo's* attempt to nationalise foreign capital in the colonies has been overestimated (66, p.4). In fact the participation of foreign capital in the extractive sectors in the colonial economies increased greatly in the post-Second World War period.

The launching of the peoples' liberation struggles in the 1960s served to accelerate Portugal's dependency on foreign capital and military support for perpetuating its colonial presence in Angola and Mozambique. At the collapse of this nexus in 1974, Portugal bequeathed colonial economies which had been dominated by foreign rather than Portuguese capital. Western capitalists and the white supremacists of South Africa who stood to lose most from the liberation of Angola and Mozambique have continued to undermine the People's Republics of Angola and Mozambique.

ANGOLA AND MOZAMBIQUE TO 1800:
A HISTORICAL BACKGROUND

The historical development of Angola and Mozambique since coming in contact with the Portuguese from the fifteenth century has been quite complex. In the early centuries the two territories played different roles in the Portuguese sea-borne empire. Their different roles were determined by local circumstances and by shifting Portuguese commercial interests and fortunes. At the time the Portuguese came to Angola, the region had no sea-borne trading networks within the Atlantic zone which they could have exploited. The existence of the strong African kingdoms of Kongo and Ngola, which could not be easily swept away, determined the extent of Portuguese influence (10, passim).

The Portuguese who had come to Angola in search of land and precious minerals for the Iberian monarchs soon discovered that the real wealth of the region lay in its human population. The colonisation of Brazil and the evolution of sugar cane plantations and mining of minerals produced the need for labour to work them. The native Indian population of Brazil having proved to be reluctant and 'unreliable workers' left the Portuguese no alternative but to look to Africa for the supply of this much needed labour (68, pp.66–7).

The existence of an incipient slave trade between the islands of São Tomé and the continent provided a foundation for the Trans-Atlantic trade. Initially in Portuguese commercial strategy Angola was only important in so far as it serviced the more lucrative colony of Brazil through the supply of slaves.

By contrast, Mozambique like the rest of Eastern Africa had been involved in international trade for centuries before the advent of the Portuguese in the Indian Ocean. The constellation of Indian Ocean trading networks centring on the circulation of great quantities of high quality merchandise gave the Portuguese a great challenge (67, p.221). The Muslim traders who had established themselves along the Eastern African coast had penetrated the inland regions to the source of gold and ivory and thus created trading networks and exchange relations with the African peoples. Through the use of force the Portuguese intimidated, bombarded and pillaged the cities of the African coast with the aim of establishing a monopoly over the gold trade from the Zambezi plateau (67, p.221). They also aimed at controlling the shipping lanes of the Indian Ocean. Thus, while Angola was drawn into the Trans-Atlantic slave trade network, Mozambique continued to function as a part of the Indian Ocean system supplying ivory, gold and later slaves.

In the period before the scramble for Africa, Portuguese weakness and African resilience helped to forestall the complete subjugation of the Angolan and Mozambican people and their incorporation into dependent peripheries of the world economy. For centuries, Portugal's presence in the interiors of Angola and Mozambique was through the agency of adventurous backwoods traders and *moradores*.[1]

The Portuguese authorities only managed to impose a marginal military and administrative presence in both territories and concentrated their efforts on the coasts. When the itinerant merchants – African, Muslim and Portuguese – who dealt with interior production centres began to bypass these coastal authorities the Portuguese embarked on the policy of conquering the production centres of gold, ivory, copper and slaves. They hoped that the conquest would enable them to enforce a much needed monopoly (9, p.34). But efforts to conquer the interior of Africa were not successful as the African kingdoms held their ground. The result was that until the 1880s the Portuguese controlled only stretches of land along the Zambezi and the Kwanza river valleys in Mozambique and Angola, respectively.

The earliest Portuguese institutions of any economic value for Mozambique were the *prazos*. The *prazo* system was a device for the establishment of Portuguese rule by legitimising the claims of *degradados* (convict colonists) to the tracts of land they had seized for themselves, mainly by conquest but also by marriage alliance with African chiefs along the Zambezi and in Manica (74, p.8). In Angola the *moradores* were granted *sesmarias* (land grants) by authorities for similar purposes. The present state of knowledge tends to suggest that this system of occupation was more elaborate in Mozambique than in Angola, where the preoccupation with the slave trade only allowed activities supporting it. In Mozambique the *prazeiros* eked out a living from the rights to levy annual tributes from the indigenous population and the exercising of a trade monopoly within the *prazos*.

In Angola the authorities through the *chefes de postos* collected the tax and tribute from the Africans directly (24, Vol.1, pp.166–8). These patterns were to be maintained in the twentieth century through the concessionary companies, which in Mozambique exercised governmental authority while in Angola the privileges were served for the state in the majority of cases. The policy of creating substantial settler populations of direct Portuguese descent in the colonies, was never achieved at all in the period before the Second World War.

In Angola the *moradores* who were in command of the inland slave trade and supplied the foodstuffs for Luanda and the slave ships were in constant conflict with the metropolitan merchants who strove to bring the entire enterprise under their control (48, pp.146–8).

In Mozambique the beginning of the nineteenth century witnessed conflicts of interest between the authorities wishing to promote agricultural production on the basis of the economy and the *prazeiros* who wanted to maintain their traditional *modus vivendi* (54, p.148). In the first decades of the nineteenth century, *prazo*-based agricultural production and trade in ivory and gold was ravaged by the slave trade. The avaricious and rapacious agent of mercantile capitalism – the slave trade – was now ravaging both Angola and Mozambique and thus eliminating possibilities of the colonies' regeneration without any external help.

33

Portuguese relations with their African possessions were transformed by a series of events triggered by the Napoleonic invasion of Portugal in 1807 which forced the Portuguese royal family to flee to Brazil under the protection of the British (17, pp.61–2). Through British pressure Portugal enacted a policy of free trade, opening up Portuguese ports to trade with its allies (64, p.127). This step contravened the mercantilist principles on which the Portuguese empire was founded: the reservation of colonial trade for Portuguese ships and merchants.

This was followed in 1822 by the independence of Brazil, the most lucrative colony. The loss of Brazil led to the shrinkage of opportunities for commercial operations open to the Portuguese commercial class. The political struggles within Portugal between the absolutists constituted by the landed aristocracy, on the one hand, and the commercial and urban bourgeoisie otherwise called 'liberals', on the other, was another significant undercurrent in changing relations. The 1834 liberals' victory signalled the beginning of attempts at the destruction of the last vestiges of feudalism in Portugal (17, p.71). The liberal politicians such as Sá da Bandeira devoted their energies to the strategy of using colonial revenues to develop the metropolis (22, p.12).

THE ABOLITION OF THE SLAVE TRADE IN PORTUGUESE TERRITORIES

Beginning with the liberal victory in 1834 the Portuguese colonial authorities developed a general strategy for their African possessions of increasing the colonial revenues by legitimate means. In both colonies this led to the abolition of the slave trade in 1836, with the purpose of freeing labour for other activities.[2] The abolition of the slave trade in Portuguese vessels was followed by the setting up of customs posts, increased taxation of Africans and stimulation of a plantation economy (19, p.50; 57, p.439). However, the reluctance of the Portuguese traders and *moradores* to give up the most lucrative business and the resurgence of the Atlantic slave trade thwarted these efforts to regenerate the colonial economies. Although this trade subsided in Angola after the closure of Brazilian ports to slaving vessels after 1850, the situation was different in Mozambique, where it continued well into the 1880s (3, pp.216–19). It continued to flourish in Mozambique under the *engagé* system sparked off by the emerging plantation economies of the Indian Ocean islands and the clandestine slave trade with Brazil and Cuba (74, pp.30–7).

As the authorities considered how best they could exploit these colonies, the metropolitan bourgeoisie attempted to form colonial companies with the aim of developing closer commercial relations with them than hitherto.

In Angola a settler economy, based on agricultural production, emerged from the 1840s onwards. The cultivation of cotton in Southern Angola started when the state transported 300 Portuguese nationals who were fleeing from xenophobic persecution in Brazil in 1849 (22, p.15). In Northern Angola, sugar cane cultivation and the foraging and planting of coffee provided new avenues of economic activity and growth (68, p.623; 11, passim; 29, passim; 63, chapters 1 and 2). While an agriculturally based economy was evolving in Angola, Mozambique continued to be a domain of the *prazo*-based economy. Although the principles for agricultural development had continued to be reiterated from the time of Sá da Bandeira, their implementation was rendered unattainable by a number of factors. The Portuguese hoped to fulfil agricultural development in a country which was largely outside their control. Because of their inability to bring the African people and the *prazo* holders under direct Portuguese authority they adopted a strategy of working through the latter, whose interests were diametrically opposed to official policy. Thus by 1870 Mozambique was still dominated by the *prazo*-based system, while Angola was increasingly falling within the metropole's sphere of influence.

After the liberal victory of 1834, the Portuguese attempted to regenerate the colonial economies through the promulgation of liberal legislation which banned the slave trade and slavery and introduced new land and customs laws. They were unsuccessful largely because they lacked both the will and the means. They often capitulated to the pressure from the *prazo* holders, slave traders and others who wished the colonial economy to remain unchanged. While the reconstruction of the metropolitan economy was in progress, there was little capital available for investment in the colonies. The battles raging between different contenders for power in Portugal allowed little attention to be paid to the overseas territories (17, p.71). Thus it may be argued that all these factors forced the Portuguese to let the colonies evolve on their own, while they contented themselves with the extraction of revenue.

FORMULATION OF A STRATEGY FOR COLONIAL ECONOMIC GROWTH AND THE WEAKNESS OF THE PORTUGUESE ECONOMY

From the 1870s there was a definite change in Portuguese colonial policy as new attempts were made to formulate a strategy for colonial economic growth. The emergence of this strategy was a result of changes in the dominant political forces in Portugal, the growth in industrial productive capacity, the effects of the world economic depression, which started in 1873, and the subsequent scramble for Africa. Clarence-Smith has noted that between 1870 and 1910 a more complex and diversified urban bourgeoisie moved to the centre of the political arena with much more direct interest in the colonies (23, p.172). The conflicting designs of the urban bourgeoisie, the industrialists and the commercial and financial interest groups, for the African colonies, greatly influenced the course of events. Portuguese industrialists turned to Africa for protected markets for their surplus goods provided by the growth in industrial capacity, especially in the textile industry (17, passim). They sought opportunities for expanding sales in the colonies rather than engage in the extraction of raw materials for their industries. The commercial and financial interests sought monopolies in the fields of transport and credit and favoured an induced re-routing of all colonial trade through the metropolis (23, p.172). As is well-known, the development of Portugal from the 1850s had fallen into the hands of a comprador bourgeoisie (17, passim; 56, Vol.2, pp.7–9). This group also sought to expand its field of mediating for foreign capital in the colonies. Clarence-Smith, who has clearly demonstrated that the Portuguese bourgeoisie was the most economically motivated of all European bourgeoisies during the 'scramble', has dismissed Hammond's uneconomic imperialism as a myth (23, p.174).

As the public sector of the Portuguese economy was chronically bankrupt and could not generate sufficient capital to invest in the colonies, the government aimed at inducing Portuguese private investment to fill the gap. In Mozambique it hoped to attract investors through the judicious granting of concessions which would be used as proof of 'effective occupation', a condition arising from the Berlin Conference. In 1874 the state granted the first concession of 20,000 hectares of land to Paiva Rapose for the plantation of opium. This concession was taken up in 1877 although it came to nothing owing to many factors, one of which was the resistance put up by Africans to labour demands (74, p.59).

In Angola, where an embryonic plantation economy, based on coffee and cotton, was already in existence, favourable high prices for these two commodities in the international markets stimulated their expanded production.

The Portuguese comprador bourgeoisie believed that economic development could only come upon the improvement of communications and the building of infrastructure. In fact, in Mozambique the port facilities at Quelimane were improved in 1874. A year later the authorities granted a concession to a Portuguese company – the Empresa Miniera e de Navigação a Vapor de Zambeze – to improve shipping on the Zambezi (74, p.63). This concession was later revoked due to the protests of the British, who were in the Lake Malawi area and wanted the Zambezi to be opened to foreign trade.

In Angola, where the need for improved transportation was being recognised, the state took drastic steps in revoking a shipping monopoly on the Kwanza, granted to an American citizen A.A. de Silva in 1865 (13, passim). The Banco Nacional Ultramarino, which was already involved in the agricultural sector of Angola, through the provisions of credit facilities, was granted a concession to organise a navigation company on the Kwanza to supersede de Silva (59, p.405). On the whole, however, the development of the colonies was thwarted by the weakness of the Portuguese economy. With increased European activity in Africa, as the scramble intensified, Portugal was petrified about the German and British designs over its African possessions. The British ultimatum of 1890 aimed to put an end to Portuguese claims over what today is Malawi. This event led to the convergence of the interests of the bourgeoisie and popular opinion over colonial affairs. When the partitioning of Africa ended by the turn of the century, Portugal held on to its colonies.

In analysing the relationship between Portugal and its colonies some historians, such as e.g. Alan Smith, have maintained that its most outstanding feature, before the rise of Antonio Salazar to power, was the indifference of the mother country (66, p.654). To sustain this argument, Smith considered the absence of public interest in the colonies, the lack of emigration to Africa, refusal of the Portuguese capitalists to become involved, the high turnover of administrations and the government's willingness to transfer its functions and privileges to foreign chartered companies as manifestations of indifference. He further argued that in granting concessions to foreign companies the Portuguese gave up the idea of maintaining sovereignty over colonies (66, pp.654–7). Yet to make the pathetic state of affairs in the colonies between 1890 and 1926, and the drastic drop in public interest in the colonies, synonymous with indifference in the mother country is to fail to identify the historical forces shaping this relationship. To evaluate the situation properly, a comprehensive analysis of the relationship between Portugal and its colonies should be cognizant of the range of historical forces at play in metropolitan and colonial societies. The economic and political crises of metropolitan Portugal, since the 1870s, and the commercial crisis at the turn of the century, were important determinants of the context of the relationship between Portugal and its empire. The period from 1870 to 1910 was characterised by the liberals' concern for economy at home and abroad. The growth of state expenditure on colonies depended upon the economic and financial situation in Portugal. The concern of the liberals for the economy, resulting from the financial condition of the country, was compounded by their struggles with the remnants of the high nobility over the destruction of the constitutional monarchy (56, Vol.2, pp.173–5).

While political battles raged for the control of the state machinery by the emergent bourgeoisie, Portugal's economy was continuing to face hardships. The financial position of the country in the last quarter of the nineteenth century revealed the existence of deficits in the public accounts averaging more than 5,000 cantos per year. The financial crisis was also reflected in the declining value of the escudo – the exchange rate with the pound sterling fell from 53 to 33 escudos (56, Vol.2, p.75). Owing to these financial difficulties the Portuguese abandoned the gold standard (28, p.40). Portugal's budgetary problems were magnified by the fact that the colonial possessions did not pay off. By the turn of the century, the Portuguese monarchy attempted unsuccessfully to salvage the country through external borrowing (32, p.95).

Due to the deteriorating economic conditions, marked by the decrease in real wages, the workers responded by forming trade unions. The number of these associations increased from 24 in 1876 to 135 in 1903. By 1910 there had been 91 strikes, most of which were successful.[4]

While the people of Portugal struggled, the nation drifted more and more into the control of an oligarchy of rich men. When in 1906 King Carlos challenged this oligarchy by claiming a limited dictatorship to deal with the chaotic situation, his action resulted in upheavals which led to his and his eldest son's assassination in 1908. The intensifying political crisis culminated in the republican revolution of 5th October 1910.

As far as the Portuguese economy was concerned, the period of the Republic from 1910 to 1926 did not change the course of events. The republican government's intentions were liberal and democratic, promising a new era of social reform, but all they equipped themselves with was goodwill which proved inadequate for the task before them. An analysis of the Portuguese economy during that period reveals the continued devaluation of the escudo, deterioration of the balance of payments, bank failures, reduction in real earnings of the middle classes and a succession of worker's strikes.

The political scene during the Republic was disastrous. In 16 years there were seven general parliamentary elections, eight presidential elections and 44 governments (56, Vol.2; 15, p.25; 76, p.46). The history of the first Portuguese Republic includes futile efforts to erect a liberal parliamentary system, general governmental weakness and a record of bribery, corruption, assassinations, bombings, mudslinging and filibustering on the part of the minorities. Explanation of the failure of this democratic experience is not difficult. Ranking high on the scale was the inexperience of the politicians, mismanagement and incompetence. During this period the emergent social forces were still inchoate and too disorganised to contend for power. With the increasing weariness among the people it became apparent that there was no further line of political evolution in Portugal and that the Republic had to be replaced with something different. The military coup d'etat of 17 June 1926, which was greeted with popular support, opened the door wide to the implementation of a policy which gave priority to Portuguese national interests.[5] It can be seen, then, that the attempts at colonial development at that time reflected inadequacies in the growth of the social and economic forces far more than a presumed fundamental indifference of Portugal to its colonies.

CONSOLIDATION OF PORTUGUESE COLONIALISM 1890 TO 1926

The Portuguese had always viewed the colonies as sources of revenue to be used for the development of the metropole. As far as Africa was concerned, Portuguese colonial policy stressed imperial consolidation through the integration of the scattered territories and the exploitation of African labour (21, passim). The public interest in colonial affairs in Portugal occasioned by colonial rivalries, conflicting interests of the bourgeoisie, and insufficient capital to invest in the colonies were responsible for the type of colonialism that emerged in Angola and Mozambique. For the Portuguese to achieve integration of and impose their authority over the vast scattered territories which fell under their sphere of influence, they needed effective occupation and the subjugation of the African peoples. Efforts to promote Portuguese emigration through the judicious granting of land had failed lamentably for Mozambique. Clarence-Smith has argued that the Portuguese policy of parcelling out large areas of the colonies to foreign companies with very wide powers was a product of internal struggles within Portugal. He maintains that members of the comprador bourgeoisie who pushed for this policy obtained highly-paid positions on the boards of directors of those foreign companies (22, p.173). With the scarcity of capital prevalent in the metropole, the Portuguese were prepared to allow foreign capital to participate as long as they were able to uphold the overall sovereign rights of Portugal.

Whatever the role of the comprador bourgeoisie Portugal, in emulating other imperial powers, hoped that the chartered companies, with the capital it lacked, would stimulate economic growth. These chartered companies were expected to set up a network of administration, to establish a system of transportation, to facilitate communication and exploitation, and to revitalise *Prazos* in Mozambique. They also enjoyed wide powers as they had the right to raise customs duties, police the territory and levy taxes on the indigenous inhabitants. In this regard the chartered companies operating in Mozambique were not unique, as the British South African Company (BSACo) exercised the same responsibilities in the two Rhodesias.

In Mozambique, three principal companies came to dominate nearly two-thirds of the colony. The first was the Companhia de Mozambique (Mozambique Company), the creation of Paiva d'Andnade, chartered in 1891 (56, p.104). It took the form of a joint stock company with its headquarters in Lisbon. British capital, holdings 40 per cent of the shares, came to dominate the company (72, p.384). Soon after, Albert Ochs, a British national competing with Cecil Rhodes for the domination of Southern Africa, came to control the company. By a 25-year charter, extended to 50 years in 1897, Lisbon granted extensive powers and a tax holiday for 25 years in return for 10 per cent of the sold shares and 7.5 per cent of the profits (74, p.113). The lands of the company coincided with the districts of Manica and Sofala. Within this region the company exercised a monopoly in mining, fishing, public works, communications services and African taxation. Although it had few problems in raising money, it starved the local administration of funds while preferring to place its capital in European banks to earn interest instead of investing in Africa (72, p.395). The company was more interested in speculation than in developing the territory under its administration.

The Portuguese expectations of the Mozambique Company in stimulating economic development were only partially fulfilled. The Mozambique Company's main economic concern was in the transit trade to the interior through the railway to Southern Rhodesia. The BSACo had controlling shares in this railway. The Mozambique Company dealt in the export of locally produced goods. African males were neither allowed to work outside the territory nor to engage in cash crop production for their own benefit. They were 'reserved' for labour on local sugar plantations and for public works. Women were compelled to grow cotton and other crops and to sell them to the company's agents (72, p.396). The African population was further subjected to a high hut tax which compelled it to enlist for wage labour. Despite the extraction of wealth from its territories, however, the Mozambique Company failed to provide essential social amenities such as hospitals and schools. The British South Africa Company's interest in the labour of this Company's territory, port development and rails rates continued up to 1910 while leaving the territory in economic stagnation. British interests in the Mozambique Company continued to be strengthened to the detriment of the region as they did very little to develop the areas under their control.

The second charter in Mozambique was granted to the Companhia de Niassa (Niassa Company) in 1891 for 25 years. It enjoyed the same powers as the Mozambique Company and was also largely British financed (41, p.104). It was to administer the region bordered by the Lurio River to the South and the Rovuma river to the North. Most of the area designated for this company lay beyond any direct Portuguese influence at the time of granting the charter. The Makua, Yao and Makonde people of the region, contrary to Vail's designation of it as an economic backwater (72, p.397), had been engaged in market oriented production and exchange relations long before company rule. In fact the Niassa Company initially obtained its revenue from the custom duties on the pre-company trade and production (52, p.144).

The Niassa, unlike the Mozambique Company, had problems with raising capital, however. In fact, throughout the period of its existence it remained undercapitalised and Tomlinson in consonance with Vail attributes its failure to develop the concessions to this factor (52, p.126). The company, unable to conquer the African people, to establish control throughout the territory or to develop the infrastructure in the period following the granting of the charter, found itself pressed for time to undertake profitable short-term investments. Because the Niassa Company could not operate profitably, the people of the area were subjected to brutality and crude exploitation as it attempted to cut its losses and recoup part of its investment (52, p.125). Having abandoned all hopes of economic development, it opted to function as a supplier of labour to South Africa's mines whose interests in it were reflected by the shares they held through Niassa Consolidated. Realising that Portugal was not going to extend the Charter after its expiry in 1929, the company attempted to recoup part of its investments through heavy taxation on Africans. Although the Niassa Company failed miserably in its economy endeavours, it did manage to secure Northern Mozambique for the Portuguese.

The largest of the concession companies operating in Mozambique, the Companhia de Zambezia (Zambezi Company), was founded in 1892 upon the old concession granted to Paiva de Andrade in 1877. This concession had been transferred in 1879 to a French concern, Société des Fondateurs de la Compagnie Générale de Zambezi. The Zambezi Company, its predecessor, was a creation of Albert Ochs, the British speculator in competition with Cecil Rhodes (74, pp.112–14). Although the company's initial interests lay in mining, it acquired *Prazos* in Quelimane district. It raised its profits/revenue through the taxation of Africans and trade in African-produced goods in its *Prazos*. The Zambezi Company, besides exercising a *de facto* monopoly of trading in peasant produce in its *Prazos*, was also involved in plantation agriculture of coconuts, tea and sisal.

The Zambezi Company was in the practice of making money through subcontracting *Prazos* under its control. For example, the Companhia do Boron, a Portuguese company, obtained *Prazos* from it in 1895 (74, pp.112–14). As it made its money from the trade monopoly, with the collapse of trade in 1900, coupled with popular African resistance to taxation, the company moved into the exploitation of sugar, sisal and coconuts through plantation agriculture. The British-financed Sena Sugar Estates, which continued to crush sugarcane and distill alcohol into the 1970s, was an important subsidiary of the Zambezi Company (41, p.165). The demand for taxes to be paid in labour in the company's territories caused many Africans to flee into the neighbouring Mozambique Company's land where taxes were paid in goods or in money. Besides enjoying the most diversified investment, the Zambezi Company was the most successful of the charters.

In Angola, by contrast, the mechanism of using concession companies to preserve Portuguese sovereignty was not employed as extensively as in Mozambique, simply because in Metropolitan strategy Angola was reserved for Portuguese capital. As Portuguese interests in the south of Angola came to be threatened by the Germans, in 1894 they granted a vast concession to a French consortium – the Companhia de Moçâmedes – to check German advances (22, p.17). The Companhia de Moçâmedes was deprived of the fiscal rights of taxing Africans, collecting customs dues and circulating its own currency like the companies in Mozambique. Another contrast with the Mozambique companies was that the concession excluded coastal regions in accordance with the laws regulating such concessions in Angola. Without any existing revenue to live on, the company turned to mining and railway construction as avenues for profit-making. The original French consortium did not have the resources to work the rumoured gold deposits of Cassinga nor to construct a railway to serve Cassinga and the Otavi-Tsumeb copper mines in northern South-West Africa (Namibia). Cecil Rhodes wishing to outflank his rivals in the construction of the transcontinental railway took over the company with this goal among other motives. Efforts to mine the Cassinga gold and construct the railway were only partially accomplished. This move by Cecil Rhodes did not prevent his rivals from constructing their railway in Central Angola (Robert William's Benguela railway) and the German Otavi-Swakopmund railway in South-West Africa (22, p.18).

The Companhia de Moçâmedes was reduced to a small foreign concern by the early 1900s. Having failed to promote mining and railway construction under Cecil Rhodes, it fell back again to the hands of French owners. Before its privileged charter was ended in 1923, it had achieved a modest success in establishing cotton plantations and cattle ranches (23, passim). The company proved to be a failure and did not meet with the success of the Mozambique companies whose lands were fertile, unlike the semi-arid lands granted to the Companhia de Moçâmedes.

The success of the mechanism of using concession companies to preserve Portuguese territories and stimulate economic development in the colonies has received mixed evalution from historians. Leroy Vail has argued that in Mozambique the strategy failed to develop the economy and that foreign capital participation failed to block the imperial expansion of Portugal's rivals. And for Angola, Clarence-Smith concluded that the Companhia de Moçâmedes was a total failure (72, p.417). The most plausible evaluation, however, is that of Tomlinson who maintains that the charter company was essentially meant to preserve Portuguese sovereignty in the sense that the territory should be internationally recognised as Portuguese and that Portugal should take on the administration of the area once the charter expired (23, p.174). Yet Tomlinson's evaluation overlooked the fact that the chartered companies had a responsibility to develop their lands. In this regard, the chartered companies failed to invest in productive activities and resorted to plundering the labour resources of Africans and extracting revenue through heavy taxation. Although this system led to the perpetuation of quasi-feudal relations of production through semi-servile labour, low levels of productivity and a general retardation of the development of capitalist relations of production, it did manage to incorporate and subordinate large areas of Mozambique to the world capitalist system. The failure of the companies to invest capital for economic development had been realised in Portugal long before the 1920s (54, p.76). With no threats to Portuguese sovereignty then in existence, the metropole terminated the charters on their expiry dates as they had outlived their usefulness.

SPECIALISED CAPITAL ENTERPRISES

Another approach taken by the Portuguese in their attempts to make their colonies economically viable was through the granting of lucrative monopolies in the fields of banking and transportation. The Banco Nacional Ultramarino (BNU), founded in 1865 by the Lisbon and Oporto commercial bourgeoisie with the purpose of investing money in the colonies, became the leading financial institution in them. The bank worked very closely with the government. It had obtained the exclusive right to issue colonial currency in 1890 and lived on the manipulation of exchange rates (74, p.202). The general policy of the BNU of linking the currency to the pound sterling and making it convertible to gold led to the chaotic situation of shortages of its currency and the circulation of numerous other currencies in Mozambique. In Angola, BNU, which had been granting mortgages to settler planters since the 1870s, became the biggest land owner as more and more mortgaged plantations fell into its hands (60, passim). The fall in commodity prices especially of coffee at the end of the nineteenth century drove many settlers into bankruptcy, forcing the bank to take their plantations as payment for their debts. This practice of the bank led to the formation of the Companhia Agricola de Cazengo in 1900 in which the bank was the major shareholder. The BNU was thus forced to engage in the productive sector of the Angolan economy, where it became, in 1905, a shareholder in the following companies: Nova Companhia de Navegacao no Quanza; Companhia Congo Portuguese; Companhia Agricola de Dande and Companhia de Cabinda (61, p.19). While BNU continued to be dominant in Mozambique, it was liquidated in Angola in 1926 owing to its malpractices in the issue of currency (65, pp.9–10). However the bank continued to operate in Angola through the companies in which it held shares.

The Portuguese desire to improve communication between the colonies and the metropole led it to grant in 1880 a shipping monopoly to a Portuguese company, the Empresa Nacional de Navegação. The latter started a regular non-subsidised service between Lisbon and Angola via the islands of Cape Verde and São Tomé e Principé. A regular line between Lisbon and Mozambique proved difficult until 1903 when the Empresa Nacional, through a government subsidy, extended its navigation lines to Mozambique (56, Vol.2, p.100).

In the Portuguese colonies of Angola and Mozambique, railway building, which involved huge sums of money, was carried out almost entirely by foreign capital. Although entrepreneurs seeking specific railway building concessions were granted their request, they all had problems of undercapitalisation. The first railway from Lourenço Marques to the Transvaal provided for by 1877, had problems finding an entrepreneur with enough capital (1, p.84). An American colonel, Edward McMurdo, who had been granted the concession to build this railway, died insolvent having failed to raised capital for the railway. The Beira–Rhodesia railway was constructed by Rhodes because the Mozambique Company did not have the capital. In Angola the Luanda–Ambaka railway had difficulties in attracting investment.

The concession granted to Robert Williams of the Tanganyika Concessions Company in 1902 also had problems raising the necessary capital. Williams' problems of undercapitalisation are said to have arisen because of the opposition from the Angolan, Rhodesian and South African sources envious of his envisaged success (64, p.90). While the aim of the railway was to connect the copper mines to the coast through Portuguese territory, this was not achieved until 1930.

GROWTH IN THE ANGOLAN ECONOMY

Until colonies prove to hold promise for investors, very little capital is forthcoming. The economy of Angola continued to be depressed after the last decade of the nineteenth century. The plantation economy, based on cotton, coffee and sugar, was rendered unprofitable by the crisis in the world economy at the turn of the century. The prices of coffee reached their lowest in 1916 and coffee exports never exceeded the 1895 level of 11,066 tons until 1930 when 11,839 tons was exported (70, p.39; 71, p.42). Other commodities, such as rubber which had risen to the rank of number one foreign exchange earner for Angola, were also subjected to low prices after 1910. Rubber had helped the Angolan economy to service the economic slump, as rubber prices evolved in a very untypical manner (22, p.176).

In 1895, when coffee was the leading export commodity, rubber constituted 34 per cent of Angola's exports; by 1910 the latter's share had risen to 77 per cent, so indicating its prominence (50, pp.238–9; 24, p.80). But then the bubble burst and prices nose-dived. Sousa Lara, a Portuguese *Colono* in Angola, observed that the commercial crisis in Angola was a result of the Portuguese dependence on trading in commodities produced by Africans such as coffee and rubber (45, passim). The situation was the same in Mozambique where African produce constituted a large share of companies' business.

However, beginning with Governor-General Paiva Henrique de Conceiro (1907–09) the Portuguese began to take more positive measures throughout Angola in encouraging a plantation economy based on the exploitation of African labour rather than produce.[6] Although efforts were made towards diversifying the economy through plantation agriculture, fluctuating commodity prices, lack of credit facilities, and transportation problems served to deter new capital until the following decade.

The decade of the 1920s in Angola was characterised by the advent of metropolitan capital domination in the colonial economy. Foreign capital was also represented in the emerging plantation economy. Metropolitan

Studies in the Economic History of Southern Africa

came together with Angolan capital in the formation of joint stock companies for the exploitation of agriculture resources. The Companhia de Amboim illustrates the process of capital formation in Angola. The *Colonos* in Amboim, tired of their perpetual indebtedness to the commercial houses in the coastal towns, came together with metropolitan based credit firms to form companies. The Companhia de Amboim, formed in this way, became so successful as to construct its own railway from Porto Amboim to Gangela. Bernardinho Correria founded the Companhia Agricola de Angola (CADA) with the participation of Belgian capital from the Banque Belga Hallet. Although CADA became the biggest coffee enterprise in Angola up to the time of Angolan independence, it was just one of the many sub-companies operating in other sectors.

The Fomento Geral de Angola (FOGERANG, in existence since 1924) was another one of these companies which emerged in this period. The capital of the company was subscribed by commercial banks. Several colonial companies also had shares in FOGERANG (58, p.3). Among the subsidiary companies under its control were the Companhia de Pescarios de Angola (ANGOPEXE), which had been catching and drying fish since 1926, and the Companhia Agricola-Pecuaria de Angola (CAPA). A company which promoted cotton-growing in Angola was the Companhia Geral des Algodões de Angola. In the industrial sector the Companhia de Combustiveis do Lobito (CARBONANG) was formed in 1927.

The Companhia de Pesquisas Minerais de Angola (PEMA) formed in 1912 was the first such enterprise through which the direct interest in the international monopolies in Angola was revealed. This company was succeeded by the Companhia des Diamantes de Angola (DIAMANG) in 1917, with the exclusive prospecting rights over 81 per cent of Angola's territory (58, p.7).

Mining companies and minerals have played an important role in the transformation of the social and economic structures of Africa in the last one hundred years, including Angola. The DIAMANG was originally financed by Belgian capital but was later joined by Oppenheimer's Anglo-American Corporation based in South Africa. It found workable diamonds in the independent Luanda district in Eastern Angola. By 1925 DIAMANG was already producing and exporting diamonds worth £250,000, which constituted 11.8 per cent of Angolan exports (44, p.65). The colonial state, lacking resources, encouraged DIAMANG to take on administrative functions. As Clarence-Smith observed, 'DIAMANG quickly became a kind of state within the state, ensuring its power vis-à-vis the colonial government by lending large sums of money to it' (23, p.177). In return for its financial aid to the state, the company was assisted in the recruitment of labour. As correctly observed by Newitt, hitherto

46

the government had frowned on the practice of employing administrative pressure to supply private concerns with labour, but when it came to DIAMANG it made an exception. However, the monopoly control of diamond-mining in Angola, exercised by DIAMANG, should not be considered only in the benevolent terms of Newitt (55, pp.92–93). Such mining companies in Africa, as shown by G. Lanning and and M. Müller, have undermined Africa through their control of mineral resources. The mining of diamonds in Angola was inextricably linked to the development of advanced capitalist economies and any investment made in the infrastructure and other services was meant to entrench this domination of Angola by capital. In Eastern Angola, where DIAMANG mined, the Portuguese exercised virtually no authority, leaving the territory to the mercy of mining capital.

All these efforts by local, metropolitan and foreign capital to exploit the resources of Angola were dependent upon the employment of African labour. The question of labour has received the most attention to the point of overshadowing other issues of Portuguese colonial history (18, 27, 31, 53, 62 passim). In theory the Portuguese had abolished slave labour in 1878; however, in practice the system of contract labour did not lead to any changes in the working conditions of the Africans. The role of the chartered companies of Mozambique in the plunder of African labour has already been discussed. However, Mozambique became an integral part of the Southern African economic region through its supply of labour to the South African mines following the mineral revolution in the last quarter of the nineteenth century.

The mining industry of South Africa was built on the migrant labour system because this provided greater opportunities for cost minimisation. The cost of reproduction of labour under such a system was subsidised by the pre-capitalist economies left in the hands of women and children.

The pattern of 'economic development' and labour utilisation which emerged in Mozambique reflected its subordination to the foreign interests of the chartered and the South African mining companies. Portugal's eagerness to earn money from its exports of labour, the taxation of chartered companies and transit trade with British territories made them indifferent to forced labour and labour abuses of the chartered companies. One of the consequences of this state of affairs was the dislocation and distortion of African social formations through the forced extraction of labour and the fleeing of Africans. Portuguese labour practices in Mozambique as well as in Angola received attention and criticism from the League of Nations. White and Vail have documented the African reaction (74, passim). Owing to the preponderance of very strict labour control methods and brutality of Portuguese capital in the *prazos*, there was very little overt resistance.

The liberal reforms of the Republic did little to change the situation in practical terms. A few Governor-Generals of Angola, among them Colonel Manuel Maria Coelho (1910–12) and Norton de Matos (1913–15 and 1921–23) did attempt to reform the system (73, p.109). But they met with little success as the settlers and the commercial houses tenaciously resisted any reforms. The power and influence of the settler-trader alliance was shown by their successful lobbying for the dismissal of the Governor of Moçâmedes, Carvalho Henrique, who had acquired a reputation for opposition to forced labour (73, p.110). It is worth noting that despite the Republican rhetoric on reform, the extractive system based on the exploitation of forced labour under the guise of 'contraction-labour' was to be perpetuated by the Salazar regime.

The conflict over labour between the designs of the metropole and those of the local bourgeoisie in the colonies, especially in Angola, was just one of the struggles aimed at weakening settler influence. Another area of conflict was over the colonies' demand of autonomy or decentralisation. Leading colonial officials and settlers in both Angola and Mozambique who were dissatisfied with the concentration of power in the Colonial and Marine ministry advocated decentralisation. The official metropolitan position was that any decentralisation would lead to independence and the fragmentation of the empire (68, p.231). The colonial Governors-General noted for supporting decentralisation were Mousinho and Freire Andrade of Mozambique and Paiva Coureiro of Angola. The latter deplored the fact that as colonial officials they had no power to initiate projects, like the extension of the Ambaka railway to Malanje, without metropolitan approval. Such moves towards decentralisation were not attempts to break away from the metropole but rather to acquire more power in determining directions in the colonies.

Although measures had been taken since 1907 towards granting administrative autonomy to Mozambique, it was only in 1914 that the Republican parliament passed the laws concerning administrative and financial autonomy to the colonies. By 1920 only the making of war or peace, alteration of judicial systems or the contracting of loans requiring guarantees were reserved for the metropolitan government (30, p.10). It was argued by the opponents of decentralisation that the financial and economic problems of Angola were due to the effectiveness of decentralisation and so called for an end to it. However, the problems of Angola were already apparent before this date. Norton de Matos, writing about his term as Governor-General of Angola from June 1912, observed that the financial and economic state of crisis was deplorable (46, p.4). Although the Republicans believed strongly in a more rational exploitation of the colonies in the interest of Portugal (23, p.176), they were unable to implement anything owing to the instability already discussed. For about ten years local interests in Angola came to play an important part in determining the events of the colony. The demise of the Republic brought such autonomy to an end.

Governor-General Norton de Matos' second term from 1921 to 1924 could be characterised by his efforts to suppress settlers' inclination towards separation from Portugal (73, p.114). De Matos was so determined to reestablish imperial domination that he banned all the African and Mestizos associations which articulated Angolan interests. He was credited with the establishment of the first comprehensive and effective colonial administration in Angola. Through village regrouping and supervised communities, de Matos set about the systematic splitting up of ethnic collectives to small ones called *aldeias* directly under the appointed chiefs (27, p.139). This process made it easy for the administration to control the Africans and expose them to further exploitation by capital. The process of eliminating decentralisation had thus started before the end of the Republican period – 1926. The taxation of Africans was greatly enhanced under the administrations of Norton de Matos. However, his policy of increasing the numbers of civil servants led to strong criticism (26, passim). While it is true that the petty bourgeoisie in Portugal demanded colonial jobs as payment for their services in the revolution, it should be noted that the expanded colonial administration, following the integration of tributary societies, necessitated even more colonial functionaries.

FINANCIAL AND ECONOMIC INSTABILITY

Throughout the Republican period Angola had traversed a difficult path of financial and economic instability. In the pre-war period the treasury was drained by the payment of interests and amortisation on loans from the Banco Nacional Ultramarino, subsidies to the Empresa Nacional de Navegação, repayment of a loan from the Caminho de Ferro de Moçâmedes and the extension of the Ambaka railway. The banning of the sale of locally produced Angolan and Mozambique liquor resulted in the state paying huge amounts of money in compensation. The total debt when de Matos assumed the Governorship of Angola in 1912 was 6,000 contos (46, pp.4–5). The collapse of rubber prices in 1913 accentuated the fiscal crisis. The outbreak of the First World War did nothing but accelerate this financial disorder (47, p.7).

Throughout this period to 1926, the Banco Nacional Ultramarino played a very important role in attenuating the economy of Angola and Mozambique. It has been accused of malpractice and shortsightedness in its handling of the colonial banking and monetary systems. Mozambique, unlike Angola, enjoyed favourable balances of payments in the years before the war which were dissipated by the dubious practices of the bank (74, p.202). White and Vail observed: 'It had tremendous powers of disruption, yet little ability to contribute meaningfully to the country's economic development' (74, p.204). The Banco, having enjoyed vast privileges, soon became a law unto itself.

Although the banking and monetary systems in both colonies were subjected to the fraudulent practices of the Banco, long before the First World War, it was only in the inter-war period that the curious and suspect practices became apparent. The great monetary crisis of Angola started with the contract of 1922 between the Government and the Banco. This permitted the latter to introduce in Angola 50,000 contos of notes; prior to this issue only 12,000 contos had been in circulation. The money situation was further compounded by the government loan of 162,000 contos from the Banco. The oversupply of money caused the Angolan escudo to plummet against British sterling from 4$50 escudos to a pound to 300$00 escudos (34, p.21). As the exchange rate of the escudo to foreign currencies changed from day to day colonial commerce was transformed into a game of chance (*jogo de azar*). The prices of imported goods went up. This situation gave rise to spiralling inflation with too much money, too many buyers, but too few goods available. The colonial state was caught up in a dilemma of having to increase the salaries of functionaries to cushion them against the effects of inflation while at the same time it was unable to increase receipts proportionally. Faced with perennial deficits, the colonial state was forced to borrow from the metropole.

Unable to solve this problem through borrowing, it tried to tackle it by introducing into circulation more cedulas (30,000 contos) and nickel coins (7,081 contos). The Banco also committed yet another mistake by opening credits to all who cared, i.e., *bona fide* traders and adventurers picturesquely called *comerciantes miliciavos*. In this chaotic financial environment, the Banco embezzled 200,000 contos from Angola deposited in London and Paris without the equivalent being transferred back to Angola. It was out of this situation that the necessity for a colonial exchange system arose. Although measures to check the crisis were being worked out it became evident that the Banco, the force behind this malignancy, had to go. On 31 October 1926, the Banco ceded its rights to the Banco de Angola. The process of stabilising the monetary system initiated in 1924 through the suspension of transfers and credits continued into the Salazar period (34, p.23).

The effects of this monetary crisis on Angola were far-reaching. Leal Cunha, at one time Governor of the Banco de Angola, was outspoken about the disadvantages of the flight of capital from Angola (26, p.19). As the figures demonstrate, there was a decline in the commerce of the colony; between 1924 and 1926 this decline was 28.7 per cent. Oscillations in the balance of payments continued to affect the economy. In fact the rapid growth of the export economy during the short period was blunted by the financial and monetary crisis after 1922.

TABLE 1

ANGOLA: EXTERNAL TRADE IN MID-1920S

Year	Imports (Contos)	Exports (Contos)	Total (Contos)
1924	333,098	275,914	609,012
1925	253,146	235,638	486,784
1926	233,916	200,040	433,956

Sources: A.A. Lisboã de Lima, 'Reflexos na Colonia de Angola da Crise Mundia.' Bol. Agencia Geral Aug. 9, No.95, 1933, 67 and Vicente Ferreira, *O Sistema Monetario de Angola*, p.24.

Mozambique was not spared from the villainy of the Banco. Its monetary problems were sparked by the war-time measures of the government to stop selling gold to the Banco in exchange for its notes. These were taken because of the gold shortage originating from the South African government's prohibition of gold exports and gold payments to foreign workers for the duration of the war. These shortages meant that the Banco could not function normally as it was unable to convert bills of exchange to gold or convertible currencies.

In 1919, a seemingly workable formula of linking the Banco's currency to the metropolitan paper money and not to gold was included in the renegotiated charter. White and Vail considered this linking of the monetarily healthy economy of Mozambique to the unhealthy economy of Portugal as having placed this territory structurally in a truly colonial position *vis-à-vis* the metropole.

The Banco took several steps to counteract the deepening crisis. In 1920, it declared that all its notes were inconvertible into gold. It further affirmed that no foreign currencies could circulate legally in Mozambique. These measures created confusion in local commerce, leading to a shortage of money in circulation which consequently gave rise to the illegal circulation of other currencies. To resolve the shortage of notes the Banco was allowed to issue unbacked fiduciary notes in 1921,

51

inundating the colony in a wave of inflation. This measure was similar to the one taken in Angola with the issue of cedulas (74, pp.203-205). In examining the impact of the Banco on Mozambique White and Vail concluded:

> Linked by law to the plummeting Portuguese escudo and hence suffering great inflation and drained by the Banco of all the gold entering the country, Mozambique was placed in a position of structural underdevelopment at the very time when it was supposed to be enjoying unprecedented self-government (74, p.205).

Unlike in Angola where the contract with the Banco was revoked in 1926, in Mozambique it outlived the Republic. In Angola the Banco did not face competition from foreign banks as in Mozambique where Barclays and Standard Bank were very visible.

It became apparent that by the end of the Republic, both colonies were facing extremely difficult financial problems just like the mother country. Both colonies were experiencing negative balances of payments. Although autonomy or decentralisation had been granted, the metropolitan interests had entrenched themselves much more in Angola than in Mozambique. The economies of the two colonies came to be closely linked with the metropolitan through the financial and monetary system dominated by the Banco. In the inter-war period the African societies were integrated under the hegemony of the Portuguese. Although they had not managed to eliminate forced labour or stabilise the economies, their sovereignty was not questioned and the economies had somewhat grown. However, the chaotic financial *status quo* was soon used as justification for the interventionist, stern measures of the corporate state, which is the subject of the subsequent discussion.

PORTUGUESE CORPORATISM AND THE EMPIRE

The essence and ethics of the corporate state 'Estado Novo' which came into being through a military putsch on 26 May 1926, were historically determined and were significant in charting the course of history in the colonies. The view that Salazar, the new dictator of Portugal, devised corporatism because of his craving for power and that this scheme reflected his subtlety and cunning is a gross misrepresentation of the historical process (35, p.64). Salazar's coterie represented a group of people who had held on to the traditional Portuguese conception of the state and society as a unified organic corporate entity whose socio-economic and political relations were hierarchically ordered (75, p.122). The 1910 Republican Revolution, the apogee of the liberals' struggle to free Portugal from the shackles of the old regime, introduced democratic institutions for the first time.

As A. de Oliveira Marques, a Portuguese liberal, commented, the supporters of the old regime, fearing the loss or curtailment of their privileges, gathered together to oppose the Republic (56, Vol.2, pp.177–9). The revival of the corporatist ideology in this period is traced to the rise of a right-wing ideology of *'Integralismo Lusitano'* in 1914 which provided a rallying point for those opposed to the democratic Republic. Although *Integralismo Lusitano* appealed to the elites originally, the deepening of Portugal's financial and political crisis provided vast opportunities for winning more proselytes who were disillusioned with their Republican saviours (15, p.28). There were other right-wing groups which formed the core of opposition to the Republic, namely the Centro Academico de Democracia Crista and the Centro Catolico. Integratist ideology, which was authoritarian, nationalist and corporatist in character, found support among the military leaders who seized power in 1926.

Portuguese corporatism was officially defined by the Political Constitution of 1933 and later approved by a national plebiscite of 19 March 1933 (51, p.3). However, by 1929 Antonio Oliveira Salazar had begun expounding his philosophy for the New State in a series of public lectures. In a major speech on 30 July 1930, Salazar spelled out the principles of the new structure (51, p.23). The 1933 Decree-laws served to rationalise and legitimise a corporate system which was already coming into existence.

Portuguese corporatism was nationalistic, repudiating all foreign institutions such as the parliamentary system, which it considered not only as alien and detached from Portuguese society but, much worse, as divisive. In its nationalist vein, it rejected dependency, economic or otherwise. To help mobilise the people it created the mystique of a glorious past. The restoration of the prestige which Portugal had enjoyed in the international community was to be through the means of historical corporatism which was rooted in Portuguese society.

Portuguese corporatism included both 'state corporatism' and *corporatismo d'associacão* where society was viewed as organic and hierarchical.[7] The architects of modern corporatism in Portugal considered society as having functional specialisations which were hierarchically organised. Accordingly, the national interest was to reign supreme over and above all the needs of the individuals. Unlike liberalism, the pillar of capitalist society, which was built on individualism, seeking and protecting individual liberties, corporatism subjected individual liberties and interests to those of the nation. What was significant was that individuals or groups of interests participated economically, socially and politically through state-approved and carefully regulated associations and institutions (28, ch. 3; 76, ch. 3 & 4). The purpose of this was to ensure harmonious relations between all the sections of society and thus avoid the scourge of capitalist destructive competition and the plague of communist class conflict. However, the methods of implementing these ideals, chosen by the regime, transformed it into a fascist state. One of the first measures taken by Salazar, once in power, was to establish a secret police, the Policia International para Defiesa de Estado commonly known as PIDE. The influence of PIDE extended to the whole of Portugal and its colonies. PIDE was further supported by police forces, the Policia Judiciaria and the Policia de Sequarança Publica, and by a special military body well equipped for street battle known as the Guarda Nacional Republica. On the economic front the Guarda Fiscal, an armed force of customs officers, helped to enforce the military siege of Portugal and the colonies (37, p.165).

The *modus operandi* for the societal organisation was the so-called 'natural way'. At the grass-root level the primary units of the New State were to be based on the family, the municipalities (local councils), the syndicates (workers' organisations) and the 'gremios' (the professional associations). At the provincial and regional level, the unions and federations of the primary units constituted the broader units. All these organs would come together into 'corporations'. These would then be organised in accord with chief productive sectors such as fishing, agriculture, commerce, industry and transport. The corporations would then be represented in the Chamber of Corporations. The corporative agents were not to be mere agents of private interests but institutions of public interest integrated into the state. The above description of Salazar's corporate state shows that it was centralised, concentrated and monistic (76, pp.5–9). The problems and affairs of the Portuguese corporate state do not constitute the subject of this chapter apart from application of corporate theory to the colonies.

The principles to be followed in the administration of the Portuguese colonial empire were defined by the Colonial Act of 8 July 1930 drawn up by Salazar, who had assumed the Ministry of Colonies for that purpose (28, p.28). The 1933 Political Constitution adopted the Colonial Act of 1930 as one of its statues. The Colonial Act of 1930 was an attempt to apply corporate theory to the rest of the empire. In principle, as the nation was an organic whole so was the empire. The corporate principles as they applied to the colonies were defined further by the 1937 Decree-law No. 27552 and also in 1961 (51, p.6).

The Colonial Act of 1930, as Z.A. Konczacki has noted, became a dogma, unlike other previous laws, which were ignored (43, p.72). This act did not propose significant alterations in the direction of colonial policy. What it did achieve, though, was the consolidation and the codification of the legislation of the past. However, the concept of the colonies being part of the organic whole functioning in subordination to the 'national interest' was significant. There was a change of terminology; the colonies were to be provinces because the empire was one whole. In corporate theory extensive powers are reserved for corporate entities. The colonies were conceded the greatest possible measure of autonomy equivalent to that given to each corporation. Here decentralisation was allowed so far as it was consonant with the high sense of common destiny and responsibility.

Nonetheless, the high degree of centralisation of the Portuguese empire eroded the autonomy of the colony. The process started by Norton de Matos of curbing separatist tendencies of the settlers in Angola was completed in the period of the Estado Novo (73, passim). Although theoretically the colonial Governor-General had been delegated the responsibility of implementing corporatist organisation and of carrying out studies which would help with this task, in practical terms powers were limited in relation to the colonial office (51, p.7). The application of organic theory to Angola implied the coordination of the activities of all sectors of the colony for the first time. The system was so pervasive that the state could intervene in the affairs of the colony whenever it felt its interest threatened. (Basil Davidson refers to the new administrative structures as the extractive system (27, pp.107–120).)

The corporate system for the colonies was merely a vehicle for the implementation of the ultimate goal of integrating colonial economies with the metropole. The Portuguese constitution proclaimed the incorporation of the overseas territories into the 'economic organisation' of the Portuguese nation and gave the metropole full control over the economic and financial management of the colonies. The aim of the Estado Novo was

(a) the systematic utilisation of the territories' existing and potential natural resources;

(b) European settlement and the regulation of the migration of labour;

(c) the progressive nationalisation of activities which, by reason of their nature of capital structure, should be integrated into the national economy as a whole (4, p.11).

It was often stated by Salazar that the colonies were to provide solutions to the metropolitan problems of overpopulation and to supply raw materials for Portugal, while functioning at the same time as protected markets for industrial and consumer goods from Portugal and help in closing Portugal's foreign exchange gap. In short, the aims of the imperial colonial system of the Estado Novo were the exploitation of the colonial resources and the promotion of European or colonial settlement.

Portugal's parasitism was epitomised by its manipulation of prices for exports, which it bought at ridiculously low levels compared to the world market prices, and the foreign currency arrangements. Portugal received in foreign currency (dollars) credits stemming from the exports of the colonies, but it repaid the colonies in colonial escudos. This process involved double conversion: dollars to Portuguese escudos and Portuguese escudos to Colonial escudos. It is at this juncture that Portugal then re-exported to the colonies foreign manufactured goods which its industries could not produce. It over-charged the colonies for the products manufactured in Portugal as a method of transferring the wealth of the colonies to the metropole (4, p.11).

The corporate experiment of the Portuguese had rejected dependence on foreigners for the financing of development. In the colonies Salazar aimed at restoring internal financial discipline by establishing economic solvency and probity. But measures to enforce balanced budgets without external financing were opposed by colonial officials. In Angola the Governor of the Bank of Angola, Leal Cunha, and the Governor General Vicente Ferreira were outspoken critics. Salazar, bent on stability, could not stand any obstruction and he responded by dismissing the resistant officials (66, p.665).

The general assumption made concerning the balanced budgets in Angola, which had been achieved by 1931/32, was that it would lead to the stagnation of the economy. Commenting on the new Governor-General of Angola, Filomeno da Camara, whose task it was to balance the budgets, Alan Smith said: 'Subsequent events were to prove that da Camara was indeed the harbinger of constriction on colonial growth' (66, p.663). The situation in Angola in the first decade of the Estado Novo contradicts this view, however, as there was an upsurge in economic activities.

The positive balance of payments enjoyed by the colonies following the stringent measures passed by the Estado Novo played an important role in closing Portugal's foreign exchange gap outside the Escudo Novo. Mario de Andrade, who based his conclusions on a 1959 study, noted that the overseas provinces made the major contribution to the balance of payments of the Portuguese empire. Table 2 illustrates the role of the colonies in closing the foreign exchange gap (4, p.31).

Angola's balance of payments showed a slight deficit from 1957 to 1960 owing to the convergent trends of the deteriorating terms of trade

TABLE 2
1959 BALANCE OF PAYMENTS BETWEEN PORTUGAL'S ESCUDO ZONE
AND OTHER COUNTRIES CURRENT PAYMENTS (CONTOS)

Balance for the Metropole	*Balance for the Provinces*	*Overall Balance*	*Capital Transactions*	*Errors and Omissions*
−4,061,000	+2,807,000	−1,254,000	+1,389,000	−135,000

Source: Andrade, Mario de and Olliver, Marc, *The War in Angola: A Socio-economic Study*. Dar es Salaam, 1975, p.31.

and imports of capital goods to equip primary sectors. While Angola was experiencing negative balances of payments, Mozambique enjoyed a positive balance and thus played an increasing role in supplying foreign exchange for the Escudo Zone.

It is undeniable that the policies of the Estado Novo, coupled with better terms of trade, contained the financial and economic crisis of the 1920s. However, this was done at the expense of the colonies and at the cost of the increasing integration and subordination of the colonial financial systems to the metropole. Thus the colonies not only served as reservoirs of agricultural and industrial raw materials for Portugal, and as protected markets for Portuguese textiles and wines, but also as suppliers of the Escudo Zone's foreign exchange resources (4, p.31).

Throughout the period of the Estado Novo, the colonies functioned mainly as suppliers of raw materials to the metropole. The structure of the colonial economies remained heavily dominated by the primary sector, with agriculture as the cornerstone.[8] The Estado Novo, it must be emphasised, did not attempt to diversify the colonial economies. Thus by 1960, 96 per cent of Angola's total exports still consisted of raw materials, with coffee (35 per cent) and diamonds (14 per cent) continuing, as ever before, to occupy the same importance. The heavy concentration of exports (coffee, diamonds, sisal) remained unchanged up to 1960. The situation in Mozambique was the same. In the export sector, Castro pointed to the huge concentration of exports, as nine products corresponded to 95 per cent of the tonnage exported by 1958 (20, pp.130–4).

In both colonies also the structure of the agricultural sector remained the same, with African producers at the lowest level, followed by European settlers and, at the top, the monopolist companies. The only novel element introduced by the Estado Novo was the forced cultivation of crops in the concessionary zones. Settler agriculture continued to thrive on the exploitation of African labour supplied under the contract labour

57

system. As Castro puts it, 'Many of these farmers are also traders . . . and many of the traders are also farmers' (20, p.128). This applied more to Angola than to Mozambique. In Angola this sector was bigger than in Mozambique.

MONOPOLY CAPITAL IN ANGOLA AND MOZAMBIQUE

The success of the Estado Novo's attempts to nationalise foreign capital in the colonies has been overestimated by historians. In both colonies, the reliance of Portugal on the participation of foreign capital in the extractive sector remained central. Admittedly, the politico-administrative privileges of the *companhias majesticas*[9] were curtailed and passed on to the state. But the refusal to renew the contract of the Niassa company was not typical.

It should be noted here that when considering the question of the Portuguese section of foreign capital, different patterns of foreign capital participation in the two colonies should be recognised. In Angola, unlike in Mozambique, international capital participated largely through partnership in the social capital of the metropolitan and colonial enterprises. The incidences of direct investment as in the Benguela railway and DIAMANG remained unscathed by Salazarist strategies. Besides, international capital continued to participate in the colonies through the granting of loans to the metropolitan state and the supplying of technology.

An examination of the four major agricultural companies reveals the degree of international capital presence in Angola throughout the era of the Estado Novo. Until 1949, Belgian capital continued to play an important role in the Companhia Angolana de Agricultura (CADA) which was the biggest coffee company in Angola. CADA's history illustrated clearly the role of the state in assisting finance capital against local Portuguese capital. In 1949 the direct participation of the Belgians came to an end through their selling of CADA to Banco Espirito Santo de Commercial de Lisbõa (BESCL) and Eduardo Quedes. It is worth noting that the social capital of BESCL, notwithstanding its Portuguese base, was constituted as well by foreign capital, thus making the whole situation much more complex and not easily open to simplistic analysis (20, p.134).

The Sociedade Agricola de Cassequel, another big monopoly, was controlled by Portuguese finance capital through BESCL and international capital. It was founded with British capital in 1927 for the purpose of producing sugar. The Cassequel Company and the Angolan Sugar

Company (Companhia de Açucar de Angola) were among the privileged companies who were granted monopolies in the production of sugar. After the 1926 *coup d'état* the government passed laws which prohibited the existence of similar industries in the colonies and the metropole. The production of sugar was designated a colonial enterprise, which meant that it could not be produced in the metropole; metropolitan capital through BESCL and international capital exercised this monopoly (20, p.132).

The Companhia Geral dos Algodoes de Angola (COTONANG), which was granted a monopoly to buy all the cotton from the concessionary zones, was also dominated by foreign capital. The Portuguese capital initially came from the Banco National Ultramarino which was replaced by Banco de Angola. The Banco Burnay represented both Portuguese and Belgian capital in COTONANG, which bought all the cotton produced by Africans in the concessionary zones at very low prices. For instance, in 1957, Angolans received 6$50 and 7$00 while the Junta de Exportacão do Algadão (a corporate entity) sold it to the government at a fixed price of 18$30 per kg for the high quality and 13$10 per kg for the poor. The world market prices for cotton stood at 23$60 kg. Since the company did not engage in direct production, it incurred no risks in its pillaging of the Angolan peasants. The partnership between foreign and metropolitan capital co-existed and persisted in the pillaging of Angola (39, p.53).

In the area of mineral prospecting and exploitation, the presence of foreign capital continued unabated; if anything the foreign capital component increased. An examination of the operation of international capital in this sector, not only attests to its preponderance but much more to the partition of the Angolan subsoil by foreign capital. DIAMANG, which controlled 390,000 square miles for diamond exploitation, continued to be foreign-owned. The Copper Company of Angola (Empresa de Cobre de Angola) was granted a concession of 60,000 square kilometres in the district of Congo in 1944. This concession was for the prospecting and exploitation of minerals other than diamonds, and hydro-carbons. This company was dominated by American, English and Belgian capital.[10] In the area of mineral resources, in 1949 yet another concession for the exploitation of manganese and iron ore was granted to the Companhia Louise A. Thérèse Berman. Again, this company was owned by American, German and Swiss capital. Most of the manganese produced in Angola went to the United States of America (12, p.98).

The prospecting and exploitation of petroleum of Angola was also ceded to foreign trusts. Belgian interests in this branch of the Angolan economy manifested themselves through CARBONANG. By 1932, CARBONANG, which had adopted the name of Companhia de Combustiveis do Lobito, used to supply coal, oil and petroleum to ships at Lobito, Angola's biggest port (38, p.7). In 1952, the company received a concession for the prospecting of petroleum in an area of 40,000 square kilometres. In 1955 the contract was modified and the concerned parties agreed to share the profits in the following proportions: the state was to take 50 per cent, Petrofina 44 per cent, and the remaining six per cent was to be left for administrative expenses for the whole enterprise. Petrofina also had shares in Portugal (Companhia de Petroleos de Angola). Sixty per cent of the total assets belonged to the Belgians in the following proportions: Petrofina 45 per cent and the Belgian Société Générale 15 per cent.

The Cabinda Gulf Oil Company was granted an oil and derivatives exploitation monopoly in the enclave of Cabinda in 1957. The following American companies – Gulf Oil Company, Mexican Gulf Oil, Chase National Bank and the National City Bank of New York – constituted the major subsidiary shareholders with a social capital of 1.5 million dollars (12, p.96). American interests in the Cabinda Gulf Oil have persisted to this date despite the advent of the MPLA – the People's Republic of Angola. This discussion of foreign companies involved in the exploitation of Angolan resources has not been exhaustive, but does suffice to prove the point.

In Mozambique, the control over the production of raw materials was more concentrated than in Angola. The Estado Novo's stand on the already established foreign companies was that it would allow them to work in a purely Portuguese atmosphere and to be subjected to conditions which would secure nationalisation and the conveniences of a colonial economy (66, pp.663–7; 74, p.248). Although the Niassa and Mozambique companies lost their charters, this did not signify the demise of foreign capital in Mozambique. Rather, the agricultural economy of Mozambique continued to be dominated by the same foreign companies as before, with the exception that they lost their former privileges which went with the *prazo* system.

It is particularly remarkable that the sugar industry of Mozambique was dominated by foreign capital. British capital was present through the Sena Sugar Estates Limited and the Companhia Colonial de Buzi which was a subsidiary of the Mozambique company. The Sociedade Agricola de Incomati Ida originally belonged to foreign capital but was later bought by a group of Portuguese capitalists among which was the BESCL. These three companies controlled more than 95 per cent of the total sugar production in Mozambique, 70 per cent of which was produced by Sena Sugar Estates by 1957. As already noted for Angola, the product was exported to Portugal at lower prices following the quota system. Portugal bought sugar from Mozambique at 2$50 per kilogramme while the same commodity retailed at 4$20 per kilo in Mozambique by 1957 (20, pp.290–1).

Almost half of the total number of coconut trees in Mozambique (about 10 million trees) belonged to European producers, 40 per cent of the latter consisting of four foreign capitalist companies, namely the Zambezi Company (French), Boror Company (French), the Madal Agricultural Company (British), and the Angoche Colonial Company with Swiss capital. These companies experienced a period of retrenchment in the 1930s owing to two factors: the falling copra prices in the 1920s and 1930s, and the Estado Novo's reduction of monopsonistic privileges exerted over local labour along with purchases of African-produced copra. Besides controlling the production of copra, these foreign companies spread their tentacles into the production of other raw materials such as sisal, tea, salt and many more. Their subsidiaries operated in the commercial sector as well.

Three of the above companies participated somewhat significantly in the development of the tea industry. The Sena Sugar Estates through its subsidiaries, the Oriental Tea Company (Sociedade Chá Oriental) and the Milange Agricultural Company (Sociedade Agricola de Milange), played an important role in this sector. Competition between these companies, through price wars aimed at dominating the industry, delayed the formation of a tea gremio until 1959. This clearly demonstrated that the Estado Novo could be manipulated by international capital.

The extractive industrial sector of Mozambique followed the same pattern of development as in Angola. Most of the mineral prospecting and extracting undertakings were joint ventures between international and Portuguese capital, with the former holding the majority of the shares. The mining sector of Mozambique was much smaller than Angola's. The value of all Mozambique's mineral exports by 1957 stood at 30,000 contos, while the value of diamond exports alone from Angola stood at almost 350,000 contos (15 million dollars) in 1961 (20, pp.290–1).

The mining of coal in the Zambezi valley was carried out by the Companhia Carbonifera de Mozambique with its social capital standing at 40,000 contos. The Mozambique Company and Banco Burnay were some of the shareholders representing international capital. In the energy industry, the American Gulf Oil company formed Mozambique Gulf Oil for the prospecting of oil. Another American company, the Mozambique Pan American Oil Company, participated in this venture. These two American-dominated companies were granted the exclusive right for prospecting and exploiting Mozambique's petroleum resources (20, pp.291–2).

In manufacturing, just as in Angola, metropolitan capital dominated. The Sociedade Algodeira de Fomento Colonial, a property of Portuguese textile industrialists and the Companhia União Fabril, the leading Portuguese financial group, dominated the colonial textile industry. Despite allowing the existence of a colonial textile industry, the colonies continued to function as markets for Portuguese textiles. The manufacturing sector geared to cater for internal consumption of commodities such as beer remained in Portuguese hands.

The commercial sector in both colonies merely reflected the structure of the two economies. The export trade in minerals was largely in foreign hands through subsidiaries of the mining companies. DIAMANG sold its diamonds to a sister company, the Diamond Corporation Company Limited. The Mozambique Company had many subsidiary companies which dominated commercial activities in Manica and Sofala. Portuguese capital, through financial groups such as CUF and BESCL, controlled many trading companies. The colonial bourgeoisie had long flourished on trading with Africans. In Mozambique the trading network in the interior was done by Indians just as in the rest of East Central Africa. In Angola, the Portuguese settler farmers often combined agricultural and commercial activities. The state, through marketing boards, coordinated production, marketing and the export of agricultural products throughout the colonies.

The above discussion has largely focused on the role of capital in the two colonial economies. The expansion of these economies especially after the end of the Second World War was due to the infusion of foreign and Portuguese private capital. The explanation for this phenomenon is not far-fetched as the changed global balance of power played an important part. Public investment in the colonies was constricted by the austerity measures imposed by the Estado Novo. The Portuguese colonies beginning from 1930–1 were required to finance their own budgets without recourse to the metropole for assistance. The overriding concern for balanced budgets financed from local resources did not allow much room for either public investment or actual development.

The coordination of colonial development only commenced in 1953 with the First Development Plans. These development plans were also financed largely from local resources. In the 1953–58 Development Plan of Angola, 95 per cent of the expenditure was local while the rest was obtained as a loan from Portugal (4, pp.38–9). The plans concentrated on the development of the infrastructure so as to facilitate the exploitation of the raw materials. In Mozambique the state financed two new railways, the Limpopo railway, inaugurated in 1956, and the Tete railway which was completed in 1950 (20, p.62). Other projects involving public investment were the purchase of the Beira railway, the construction of dams for hydroelectricity and geological surveys. Expenditures on education and health were very small (for Angola only 10 per cent was budgeted for the 1953–58 Plan).

ENTRENCHMENT OF DEPENDENT CAPITALISM 1960–1974

The outbreak of revolutionary wars, challenging Portuguese surrogate colonialism in the 1960s, was catalytic in the further entrenchment of Portugal's dependence on foreign capital for colonial economic development and for its continued presence in Angola and Mozambique. The backwardness of Portugal's home economy, insufficient metropolitan capital, the commitment to military activities and the exigencies of maintaining minority white settler regimes in Southern Africa greatly influenced the pattern of investment and economic activities in both colonies in the period under discussion. The boom conditions of the 1960s in the mining, manufacturing and construction industries and in the commercial farming of coffee, cotton, maize, rice, cashew and other crops made Angola and Mozambique attractive for foreign investments. Although Portuguese Africa became a haven for foreign private investment, both colonies experienced serious difficulties with their public finances.

In the 1960s and early 1970s Angola and Mozambique experienced a spurt of late colonial development. Portugal's abandonment of protectionism and the encouragement of foreign investment in the colonies generated boom conditions in both countries. The change in Portugal's colonial economic policies came as a result of the mounting pressure on its resources which were being stretched out by the liberation wars in the colonies. The diminishing economic utility of the colonies to Portugal should not only be sought in the new opportunities in continental Europe for her products and population, but should also be traced to the increasing role played by foreign capital. The repatriation of profits on foreign investments meant that Portugal was no longer the sole beneficiary of the colonial plunder.

The nationalist challenge forced a shocked Portugal to devise schemes of increased white immigration and settlement in the colonies as a way of propping up colonialism. Commenting on the increased white population in Angola Bhagavan observed that 'The immigration had been actively encouraged by the fascist regime in Lisbon, as a way of increasing the stake of Portuguese civilian population in retaining the colony, thus countering the successes of the MPLA' (8, p.7). Between 1960 and 1974 the immigrant white population rose from 172,000 to 335,000 which was about 5.7 per cent of a total of 5.9 million (8, p.7). By 1974 Angola had become a settler colony.

The reformulation of rural settlement strategy was greatly patterned by the Portuguese response to the revolutionary wars. The encouragement of white immigration to the colonies fitted the strategy of establishing a network of predominantly European paramilitary settler communities *(colonatos)* in the war zones. To implement the new strategy, provincial settlement Boards were set up (6, p.109). In Mozambique the plan envisaged settling one million Portuguese along the banks of the Zambezi river by the year 2000 (42, p.101). In Angola the Portuguese undertook multi-racial settlements which also brought in Cape Verdians as colonists.

Despite the attractive incentives such as free passage, housing, agricultural equipment and choice tracts of land, the settlement plans were dogged by high absentee rates. The majority of the colonists ran away from planned settlements. They trekked to urban centres where they swelled the ranks of the unemployed and underemployed. The new settlers came from the smallholder peasantry, the urban and industrial working class and the petty bourgeoisie who were escaping the hardships of the crisis-ridden and falling economy of Portugal. Once in Angola, the new colonists were not willing to undertake the hard agricultural work. Besides, they lacked the knowledge of tropical agriculture. Although Portugal made large investments in the settlement schemes they were characterised by low economic yield.

The strategy of utilising white settlement schemes to raise Portugal's stake in the colonies received great impetus under Caetano's revived colonial dynamism. In both Angola and Mozambique the emphasis was placed on developing irrigation schemes which could support the expansion of white farms and ranches. Thus in 1969 Portugal inaugurated the Cunene River Basin Scheme for Angola and the Cabora Bassa dam in Mozambique (27; 42, passim). The projects were expected to pave the way for increased economic activity. Portugal, lacking sufficient capital for these developments, turned to advanced Western countries for financial support. South African capital also played a leading role in financing these projects. South Africa was so concerned about Portugal's waning ability to maintain control over Angola and Mozambique that it committed its financial resources to these projects in an attempt to enhance Portugal's stake in the colonies. South Africa's own future would only be secured if white domination to its north could be maintained. The participation of foreign capital and particularly South African, French, German and Italian meant that Angola and Mozambique were now inescapably shackled by colonialism as never before.

The Portuguese strategy for counter-insurgency which involved the forced relocation of African peasants had serious repercussions for African productive capacity. African peasants were relocated into two types of settlements: the strategic resettlements *(aldeaments)* and rural resettlements *(re-ordenamentos)*. The strategic resettlements were envisaged to be military posts against guerilla attacks. They were usually large villages of formerly dispersed persons organised by the military and often surrounded by barbed wire (6, p.160). Rural resettlements occurred outside the immediate fighting zones. In Angola over a million peasants were relocated into these settlements (6, p.195). Although Portuguese propaganda claimed that the relocation of Africans was aimed at improving their social and economic conditions in the rural areas, the elimination of all contacts between the nationalist forces and the civilian population was the overriding consideration.

Forced relocation of African peasants in both Angola and Mozambique grossly affected their productive capacity. To begin with, forced relocation meant the abandonment of a stable and viable economic organisation which had provided for their subsistence. The reorganisation of economic life in the strategy zones was compounded by the fact that the new areas were badly chosen and lacked sufficient land for farming and pasture. The loss of African lands to incoming settlers under the grandiose schemes of white settlement undermined African productivity. In northern Angola the coffee lands, abandoned by Africans during the Portuguese counter-insurgency campaigns in 1961, were not all returned, if anything they were ceded to new Portuguese settlers in search of the coffee wealth. The resettlement schemes and the resulting loss of revenue from the abandonment of their previous economic activities could not easily be offset in the strategic hamlets and this greatly disadvantaged Africans. Instead of the schemes winning over Africans to the Portuguese side, thousands of Africans were herded into the nationalist camp of the MPLA and FRELIMO by Portuguese brutality.

By the late 1960s a new economic counter-insurgency policy which aimed at creating black rural capitalists was promoted by the military. The policy of restoring prosperity to the black peasantry focused on the north-eastern plateau in Angola. Here again the aim was to prevent a nationalist breakthrough counteracting with a peasant-oriented and government-financed development scheme. Producer cooperatives were set up and agricultural extension services were created to advise small and medium-sized coffee farms. It is this group of African capitalist farmers who were allowed to recruit paid migrant labour from the South. This move, however, was belated and inadequate and therefore could not forestall the nationalist advance. It was yet another experiment in dividing the people of Angola along class lines.

Although the outbreak of the liberation war in Angola in 1961 led to the abolition of the forced labour system, the reforms were merely a change in form rather than in substance. By the time of the reforms, the mobilisation of African labour for European enterprises did not require the use of naked force (12, passim). The necessity of having to pay tax and buying a bare minimum of essential food items (salt, sugar, edible oil, etc.) and clothing, the involvement in cash crop farming and its accompanying low prices and the devastation of African food production compelled African men to leave the land to seek employment as rural wage earners. Furthermore, the forced relocation of Africans into strategic settlements which had inadequate land for farming needs and limited opportunities resulted in Africans opting for wage employment. It is these circumstances which generated the much needed army of wage-earners during the boom years of the 1960s.

The pattern of labour utilisation remained the same. In both colonies the plantation economies continued to be supplied through migrant labour within the territories. The drift of Mozambicans to the Rand continued unabated. The swelling of urban centres with the unemployed and underemployed Portuguese immigrants fleeing from the hardships of their home country meant that new semi-skilled jobs arising from the late colonial development were taken up by this group. This inability and unwillingness to modernise the backward and inefficient methods of production and surplus extraction precluded the amelioration of the inhuman working and living conditions of African labour. The methods of coffee production in Angola and the coconut plantations in Mozambique serve as examples of the rigid methods of production (8, p.374). Despite an increase in the number of educated Africans, the pattern of labour utilisation was determined more by colour than economic opportunities.

African labourers continued to be underpaid, making Angola and Mozambique among the leading countries which yielded the highest profits on capital invested. 'The average daily wage for an African agricultural worker was 20 escudos i.e. 60 US cents' (8, p.10). The abysmally low income spelt lower purchasing power and this forced agricultural workers to grow their own food. Bhagavan estimated that 72 per cent of the total labour force in Angola were subsistence peasants with a poor nutritional standard (8, p.10). It may be concluded that though the system had grown and reforms been introduced, there was no change in the black and white relationship of power and opportunities because Africans continued to be organised within a white-dominated economy and for white profits. For the majority of the Africans the amelioration of their working and living conditions lay not in Portuguese reformism but in revolutionary change.

SPURT IN INDUSTRIAL GROWTH

The spurt in industrial growth during the 1960s was in part a product of a process set in motion by the liberation wars. Financial pressure caused by the African wars and the urging of its foreign partners forced Portugal to take the unprecedented step of allowing foreign investors to enter colonial sectors previously reserved for Portuguese domestic capital. From the Portuguese perspective the aim was two-fold. First, it hoped that Western countries would be expected to protect the capital risked by their nationals and in the process render political support for Portugal's colonial wars. Second, Portugal expected the new investments to generate wealth with which to modernise the country's economy, infrastructure and transport, which would invigorate its counter-insurgency campaigns.

Although industrial output had begun to rise from 1962, a year after the outbreak of the revolutionary war, the turning point came with Portugal's abandonment of the protectionist policies in 1964. In both colonies, foreign multinational corporations seized the new opportunity and moved into high risk, high cost and high technology mining operations. It is in this high profit yielding area that Portugal found herself dependent on foreign capital and technology. The absence of substantial Portuguese capital in the mining industry exposed Portugal's own neo-colonial plight.

Angola's economic boom lay in the foreign exploitation of its mineral resources. Between 1965 and 1970 mineral exports doubled, reaching a total of US $425 million (27, p.315). Oil production rose from 58,000 tons in 1958 to 7.4 million tons in 1973. Iron-ore production went up from 106,000 tons in 1958 to 7 million tons by 1973. Between 1960 and 1973 diamond production doubled from one million carats to 2.1 million carats (8, p.16). The dramatic increase in the exploitation of minerals and the subsequent outflow of foreign dividends under liberal terms transferred wealth from Angola to Portugal's NATO allies. The most powerful multinationals were the American Gulf Oil which invested in the Cabinda oil fields, the South African companies of Anglo-American and De Beers in the diamond mines and the West German giant, Krupp, which operated the iron-ore mines at Cassinga in the south. All these companies, with many more, participated in the plunder of Angola's mineral resources.

The involvement of foreign capital in the extraction of minerals in Mozambique was not as dramatic as in Angola. By 1974 Mozambique's mineral wealth had been largely untapped. Although the territory was potentially rich in mineral resources such as chalcopyrite, bentomite, authrophyllite, mica, potash, columbo-tantalite, manganese and asbestos, the numerous uncertainties created by the liberation war limited their exploitation. The large American oil companies of Gulf Oil and Texaco and small ones such as Clark Oil and Refining Company and Skelly Oil Company were granted concessions for petroleum exploration. The Mining Company of Tete, Mozambique Diamond Company, Mozambique Mining Company and Mozambique Uranium Company held exclusive prospecting rights; however, by 1974 production was not significant (49, p.41). In Angola, foreign companies concentrated on the exploitation of the minerals while in Mozambique the focus was on prospecting.

Substantial growth in the manufacturing sector took place between 1960 and 1973. The number of manufacturing enterprises in Angola rose from 2,490 in 1961 to 5,561 in 1972. The total investment rose from 2,561 million escudos to 7,336 million escudos during the same period (8, p.17). This expansion was made possible by the metropolitan state's abandonment of its policy of limiting colonial industrialisation. From 1965 it encouraged import substitution industries in the colonies. The metropole, however, only allowed light industries to operate, primarily to produce for the sizeable domestic markets, provided by the increased number of settlers.

Considering that the purchasing power of 95 per cent of the African population was about 25 escudos per head, the manufacturing industries ended up catering to the luxury consumption of the settlers. The vast majority of manufacturing industries were small establishments owned by white settlers. Angolan capital raised from the export of crops continued to find outlets in the manufacturing industry. The collaboration between metropolitan capital and settlers, which had been observed earlier, persisted in the manufacturing sector. Big Portuguese capitalist groups such as União Fabril, Champalimaud, the Espirito Santo Group, Banco Portugues de Atlantico, the Banco Nacional Ultramarino and the Banco de Angola combined manufacturing activity with banking, insurance, trade, transport and plantation agriculture.

In Angola and Mozambique foreign involvement in manufacturing was modest. In Angola German capital went into sisal fibres, wood products, pulp and paper, the British into textiles, the South African into meat processing and the Belgians went into the manufacture of rubber tyres (8, p.16). In Mozambique Firestone, General Tyre, Compagnie

Générale d'Entreprises d'Électricité and others financed tyre plants and built textile, paper and pulp factories. Foreign capital did not invest much in manufacturing for two major reasons. First, since the manufacturing industry was oriented towards meeting the small domestic markets in Angola and Mozambique, the low profit margins did not attract foreign capital. Second, the provision by law that at least 55 per cent of the shares in each manufacturing firm had to be in Portuguese hands contributed to limiting foreign investments.

Manufacturing industries in both colonies concentrated on production of consumer goods and processing of export crops. Food, beverages and textiles tended to be the predominant consumer items. In Mozambique these items comprised 53 per cent of local production and 63 per cent of total investments (49, p.41). In both colonies the processing industries of export crops such as sugar, tea and coffee were dominated by a few large firms. By looking at Portuguese and foreign investments in manufacturing, it becomes apparent that domestic production of intermediate and capital goods was not developed. Thus the focus was on the plunder of the colonies' resources.

By 1974 Angola earned almost all its foreign exchange through the export of a concentrated number of unprocessed or semi-processed primary products. 'Oil at 55.4 percent of total exports dominated followed by coffee with 23.2 percent, diamonds 9.1, sisal 4.7, iron ore 4.5, raw cotton at 1.9 and sugar at 0.1 percent of total exports' (8, p.15). The principal importers of Angolan products were the United States, Portugal, the UK, the Netherlands, West Germany, France and Italy. By 1974 the United States had emerged as the major Angolan market and Portugal fell to second place. Portugal, however, continued to be Angola's major supplier, though its share had declined from 31.6 per cent of all imports in 1971 to 25.4 per cent in 1973. This was a direct product of the import controls introduced in 1971 (33, p.11).

Mozambique's export trade was characterised by a concentrated number of products, namely cashewnuts, cotton, and sugar which contributed 74.3 per cent of total exports in 1973 (33, p.25). The major importers of Mozambique's exports in order of importance were Portugal with 24.9 per cent, followed by the United States with 18.2 and South Africa with 9.6 per cent of the total. Portugal's share of Mozambique's imports had been declining continuously until it reached 17.3 per cent in 1974. South Africa replaced Portugal as the main exporter to Mozambique with 19.7 per cent of total imports (33, p.26). This development underlined Mozambique's increased dependence on South Africa in yet another area.

Between 1961 and 1973 Mozambique suffered from an adverse balance of payments situation. Since 1956 Mozambique's balance of payments continued to be negative throughout the period to 1973. Angola's record was much better and from 1969 to 1973 it enjoyed a positive balance of payments. The difficulties experienced in maintaining sound balances of payments within the Escudo Zone compelled the Portuguese authorities to introduce import controls, in 1971, for both Angola and Mozambique. These regulations prohibited the authorisation of Portuguese imports without foreign exchange cover as a means of reducing the trade deficit with the Escudo Zone. It is largely this measure that contributed to the decline of Portugal's share of the colonial imports.

Mozambique's chronic balance of payments deficits were alleviated by its invisible exports. Port and railway charges on international traffic, transfers and deferred pay from migrant workers in Witwatersrand, together with the tourist trade, helped to reduce the deficits. Mozambique earned about 63 per cent of its foreign exchange from invisible exports to South Africa (50 per cent) and Rhodesia (13 per cent) (49, p.44). Rhodesia's use of Mozambique's railway and port facilities, at the time of an international trade embargo against it, made the Portuguese colony serve as the principal sanctions-buster. In this way Mozambique became more dependent on the white minority regimes of Rhodesia and South Africa and its role perpetuated their resilience against international pressure.

The public finances of both colonies were riddled with difficulties in the period after 1961. They were characterised by rapid increases in expenses caused principally by the rising military costs for counter-insurgence campaigns and the development of the infrastructure. In Angola the cost of Portuguese counter-insurgence campaigns against the nationalist guerillas' incursions escalated from US $7.5 million in 1960 to US $28.7 million in 1967 (4, p.123). The development of the infrastructure, transport and communications was spurred by two important events. Late colonial economic development required improved road transport and communication systems. For Portuguese military strategists, an expansion in transport and communications networks was considered to be necessary for their operations. In both instances the onus fell on public finances.

Since revenue could not cover expenditure the Portuguese turned to their NATO allies for military and financial support. Western countries led by the United States provided Lisbon with aid and loans which helped to finance the war and thus alleviate Portugal's financial strain.[11] As indicated earlier, the financial support served as a *quid pro quo* for Western involvement in Angola and Mozambique. Despite the rhetoric supporting the principle of self-determination, Portugal's NATO allies were pitted against the African people of Angola and Mozambique.

This involvement prompted the Western countries and South Africa to continue to be embroiled in the Angolan and Mozambican affairs even after the attainment of independence in 1975.

CONCLUSIONS

The plunder of resources, through violent means, characterised the Portuguese presence in both colonies. From the time of their incorporation into the Portuguese seaborne trade Angola and Mozambique were ravaged by the slave trade and slavery until the second half of the nineteenth century. Before 1890, events in the colonies evolved around their own inertia owing to Portugal's inability to exercise its authority effectively. Mozambique's occupation was achieved through grants of large areas to foreign concessionary companies as from the 1890s. As a result Mozambique became fragmented and subordinated to foreign capital. In Angola this approach was applied on a much smaller scale.

From the 1890s to 1928 the colonies were plagued by financial and economic instability owing to the fluctuating commodity prices and fraudulent practices of the Banco Nacional Ultramarino. Through export of labour and transit trade Mozambique was drawn into South Africa's orbit. In Angola metropolitan and colonial capital, together with foreign capital, was invested in the agricultural and mining sectors. From 1930 a corporatist framework was imposed on the colonies and through it imperial autarky, based on coercion, was achieved. Colonial industrialisation was thwarted for fear of competition with the metropole. Foreign capital continued to be allowed in the extractive sectors of the colonial economies despite the corporatist rhetoric repudiating foreign capital. Moreover, under corporatist protection metropolitan capital found investment outlets.

The outbreak of the liberation wars, in the early 1960s, openly exposed the failure of the corporatist framework to harmonise opposing and antagonistic social forces in both colonies. Portugal responded by reforming social and economic policies and by turning to its NATO allies for military and financial support to maintain the *status quo*. The abandonment of its protectionist policies and the encouragement of foreign investments generated boom conditions, turning Angola and Mozambique into a haven of foreign private investment. Western involvement in the colonial economies diminished Portugal's dominant role and allowed the United States of America and South Africa to assume a leading place in Angola and Mozambique respectively. The continuation of the United States' and South Africa's embroilment in post-colonial Mozambican and Angolan affairs is, therefore, not surprising.

71

NOTES

1. The Africanised Europeans who had married and settled among the African communities.
2. For a discussion of the nineteenth-century slave trade see References (2) and (3).
3. See References (74, p.63). This concession was later revoked due to the protests of the British interest in the Lake Malawi area. The British wanted the Zambezi to be opened to foreign trade.
4. See References (56, Vol.2, p.29). Oliveira Marques has shown in his work that the number of the proletariat proper was estimated at 100,000. This was only 30% of the total number of workers engaged in industry and crafts.
5. The army rebellion of 1926 was not a fascist movement. It was not directed against parliamentary institutions. In fact, the Republican constitution was only abrogated in 1933. See References (15, pp.24–35) and (56, Vol.2, p.179).
6. The establishment of an agricultural research station to disseminate information for the plantation economy in 1907 was an indication of this approach.
7. State corporatism derived from a deliberately articulated ideology emphasising an organistic-unitary and harmonistic conception of the state and society. Thus it emerged from the top to the bottom. Corporatism of association, in contrast, assumes the evolution of such structures historically and thus voluntarily. It implies that since the grass-roots are organised corporately, the state and society will be structurally influenced in the same way. Portugal's corporatism embodied both conceptualisations.
8. By 1950, the agricultural sector absorbed 73.9% of the total labour force in Mozambique. In Angola the proportion was slightly higher, by 1960 amounting to 75.7%. See References (20, pp.130–4).
9. The term has been used in literature to indicate the vast powers enjoyed by the concessionary companies, namely the Zambezi, Mozambique and Nyasa companies.
10. Portuguese interests in the copper industry were represented by CUF, the privileged Portuguese monopoly. See References (20, p.161).
11. See References (42, p.105). The authors have shown that West Germany gave Portugal US$90 million in direct financial aid and the United States supplied a $100 million loan to upgrade the Portuguese army; Nixon, through the Export-Import Bank, paid out US$435 million. Most of the financial support was secret and thus these figures represent only a fraction of the financial assistance rendered to Portugal by its NATO allies.

REFERENCES

1. Abshire, D.M. and Samuels, M.A., *Portuguese Africa: A Handbook*. London 1969
2. Alpers, E.A., 'Trade, State and Society among the Yao in the Nineteenth Century', *Journal of African History*, Vol.10, No.3, 1967
3. —, *Ivory and Slaves in East Central Africa*. London 1975
4. Andrade, Mario de, and Olliver, Marc, *The war in Angola: A Socio-economic Study*. Dar es Salaam 1975
5. Anon., *Amboim: Subsidios para history de desbravamento e da ocupação*. Luanda 1938
6. Bender, Gerald J., *Angola under the Portuguese: The Myth and the Reality*. London 1978
7. Berman, Bruce, 'Structure and Process in the Bureaucratic States of Colonial Africa', *Development and Change*, Vol.15, No.2, 1984
8. Bhagavan, M.R., *Angola's Political Economy 1975–85*. Research Report No.75, Scandinavian Institute of African Studies, 1985
9. Bhila, H.H.K., *Trade and Politics in a Shona Kingdom: The Manyika and their African and Portuguese Neighbours 1573–1902*. London 1982
10. Birmingham, David, *Trade and Conflict in Angola*. Oxford 1966
11. —, 'The Coffee Barons of Carengo', *Journal of African History*, Vol.19, No.4, 1978
12. Boavida, Americo, *Angola: Five Centuries of Exploitation*. Richmond 1972

13. *Boletim oficial de Governador da Provincia de Angola* (22 July 1865), 'Contrato Celetrado com o Citadão Americano Augusto Archer Silva'
14. Boxer, C.R., *The Portuguese Seaborne Empire 1415–1825.* London 1969
15. Bruce, Neil, *Portugal: The Last Empire.* Toronto 1975
16. Burns, Bradford, *A History of Brazil.* New York 1970
17. Cabral, Manuel Villaverde, *O Desenvolvimento do Capitalismo em Portugal no Seculo XIX.* Lisbon 1981
18. Cadbury, W.A., *Labour in Portuguese West Africa.* London 1910
19. Capela, Jose, *O Imposto de Palhota e a Introdução do Modo Produção Capitalista nas Colonias.* Porto 1977
20. Castro, Armando, *O Sistema Colonial Portugues em Africa: Meades do Seculo XIX.* Lisbon 1980
21. Chilcote, Ronald H., *Portuguese Africa.* Englewood Cliffs, New Jersey 1967
22. Clarence-Smith, W.G., *Slaves, Peasants and Capitalists in Southern Angola 1840–1926.* Cambridge 1979
23. ——, 'The Myth of Uneconomic Imperialism: The Portuguese in Angola 1836–1926', *Journal of Southern African History*, Vol.5, No.2, 1979
24. Correia, A.A.S., *Historia de Angola,* 4 vols. Lisbon 1937
25. Correia, Jose de Araujo, 'Possibilidades Economicas de Angola', *Boletim de Direscão dos Servicos de Agricultura e Comercio de Angola* 3, 1, 1926
26. Cunha, Leal, *Subsidios para o Estudo do Problema do Credito em Angola.* Lisbon 1930
27. Davidson, Basil, *In the Eye of the Storm: Angola's people.* New York 1973
28. Derrick, M., *The Portugal of Salazar.* London 1938
29. Dias, Jill R., 'Black Chiefs, White Traders and Colonial Policy Near the Kwanza: Kabuku Kambilo and the Portuguese 1873–1896', *Journal of African History*, Vol.17, No.2, 1976
30. Diniz, Ferreira, 'A Evolução de Politica Colonial Portugues', *Boletim de Agencia das Colonias*, Ano 4, 34, 1928
31. Duffy, James, *A Question of Slavery.* Oxford 1967
32. Egerton, Clement F., *Salazar, Rebuilder of Portugal.* London 1943
33. Economist Intelligence Unit, 'Angola, Mozambique', *Quarterly Economic Review: Annual Supplement.* London 1975
34. Ferreira, Vincente, *O Sistema Monetario de Angola: Explanação simples da sua Organização e Funcionamento e dos Principios e Experiencias Alheias que o Justificam e Apoiam.* Luanda 1927
35. Figueredo, Antonio de, *Portugal: Fifty Years of Dictatorship.* New York 1976
36. Freund, Bill, *The Making of Contemporary Africa.* Bloomington, Indiana 1984
37. Fryer, Peter and Pinheiro, Patricia M., *Oldest Ally: A Portrait of Salazar's Portugal.* London 1961
38. Great Britain, Department of Overseas Trade, *Report on Economic Conditions in Angola, 1932.* London, HMSO, 1932
39. Guerra, Henrique, *Angola Estructura Economica e Classes sociais: Os Ultimos Anos do Colonialismo Portuguese em Angola.* Lisbon 1979
40. Heintze, Beatrix, 'Angola nas Garras do Trafico de Esclavos', *Rivista Internacional de Estudos Africanos*, Vol.1, No.1, 1984
41. Henrikson, Thomas, *Mozambique: A History.* London 1978
42. Isaacman, Allen and Isaacman, Barbara, *Mozambique: From Colonialism to Revolution, 1900–1982.* Boulder 1983
43. Konczacki, Zbigniew A., 'Portugal's Economic Policy in Africa: A Reassessment', in Z.A & J.M. Konczacki (eds.), *An Economic History of Tropical Africa*, Vol.2. London 1977
44. Lanning, G., and Müller, M., *Africa Undermined: Mining Companies and the Underdevelopment of Africa.* Penguin Books 1979
45. Lara, Sousa, 'Crise Agricola e Comercio em Angola: Sua Causas oque tem, oque urger Fazer'. *Congresso Colonial Nacional*, 1901
46. Matos, Jose Mendes Norton de, *A situação Financiera e Economica da Provincia de Angola.* Lisboa 1914
47. Matos, Pires, *A Questão Monetario de Angola.* Luanda 1927

Studies in the Economic History of Southern Africa

48. Miller, J.C., 'The Paradoxes of Impoverishment in the Atlantic Zone', in Birmingham, D., and Martin, P. (eds.), *History of Central Africa*, Vol.1. London 1983
49. Mittelman, James H., 'Mozambique: The Political Economy of Underdevelopment', *Journal of Southern African Affairs*, Vol.3, No.1, 1978
50. Montalvao, Anibal Coelho de, 'Breve Consideracões sobre O Comercio de Cafe', *Boletim da Direcção dos Servicos de Agricultura e Comercio de Angola*, Vol.5, No.3, 1928
51. Moreno, Mateus, 'Corporativismo e Propaganda Colonial', *Portugal Maior*, 11, 1974
52. Neil-Tomlinson, Barry, 'The Nyassa Chartered Company: 1891–1929', *Journal of African History*, Vol.18, No.1, 1977
53. Nevinson, H., *A Modern Slavery*. London 1906
54. Newitt, M.D.D., *Portuguese Settlement on the Zambezi*. New York 1973
55. Newitt, Malyn, *Portugal in Africa: The last Hundred Years*. London 1981
56. Oliveira Marques, A.H. de, *History of Portugal: From Empire to Corporate State*, Vol.2. New York 1975
57. *Relatorios e Informações: Apenso de Boletim Oficial da Provincia de Angola*, 'Dados Estatisticos para o Estudo das Pautas de Angola – Exportação pela Alfandega do Circulo e do Congo nos Anos de 1888 a 1913'. 1918
58. Relatorio de Conselho de Administração, 1927–28, *Fomento Geral de Angola, Publicações Diversas I–XVI, 1924–33*
59. *Relatorio de Banco Nacional Ultramarino*, 1, 1876
60. *Relatorio de Banco Nacional Ultramarino, 1900–1.*
61. *Relatorio de Banco Nacional Ultramarino, 1905*
62. Ross, E.A., *Report on Employment of Native Labour in Portuguese Africa*. New York 1975
63. Seleti, Y.N., 'Portuguese Colonialism, Capitalism and the Angolan Coffee Industry: 1850–1950', Ph.D. dissertation, Dalhousie University, 1987
64. Sideri, S., *Trade and Power: Informal Colonialism in Anglo-Portuguese Relations*. London 1970
65. Small, R.T., *Economic Conditions in Angola*. London: Department of Overseas Trade, HMSO, 1929
66. Smith, Alan K., 'Antonio Salazar and the Reversal of Portuguese Colonial Policy', *Journal of African History*, Vol.15, No.4, 1974
67. —, 'The Indian Ocean Zone' in D. Birmingham and P. Martin (eds.), *History of Central Africa*. London 1983
68. Teixeira, Alberto de Almeida, *Angola Intangivel: Notas e Comentario*. Porto 1934
69. Thornton, John K., *The Kingdom of Kongo: Civil War and Transition 1641–1718*. Madison 1983
70. Trancoso, F., *Angola*. Lisbon 1920
71. —, *Angola nos Ultimo Anos: Alguns Numerous*. Lisbon 1936
72. Vail, Leroy, 'Mozambique's Chartered Companies: The Rule of the Feeble', *Journal of African History*, Vol.17, No.3, 1976
73. Wheeler, D., and Pelissier, R., *Angola*. New York 1971
74. White, L., and Vail, L., *Capitalism and Colonialism in Mozambique*. London 1980
75. Wiarda, H., 'Towards a Framework for the Study of Political Changes in the Iberian-Latin Tradition: The Corporate Model', *World Politics*, Vol.25, 1973
76. —, *Corporatism and Development: The Portuguese Experience*. Amherst, Mass., 1977

3

Industrial Development in Zambia, Zimbabwe and Malawi: The Primacy of Politics

MARCIA M. BURDETTE

INTRODUCTION

Orthodox texts in economics posit that the preconditions for industrial development are plentiful raw materials, labour, skills, infrastructure and a sizeable market. However such common sense does not demonstrate how political factors have come to influence economic decisions as well as vice versa. Central Africa as a whole is rich in many minerals, has extensive agricultural potential, hydroelectricity and adequate labour supplies. But of three states – Zimbabwe, Zambia and Malawi – only one, Zimbabwe, has developed an integrated industrial base.[1] The roots for early differentials in industrial development lay in the interplay between the colonial politics of the settlers and the British Colonial Office, the workings of the imperial system and existing material conditions. In much of the colonial period these three economies were linked together so that one was the beneficiary and the other two were distinct losers. With self-rule, the new leaders introduced forms of import substitution but with varying degrees of success. Although all three countries have disarticulated economies, heavily dependent upon the colonial metropole of Britain and secondarily on the largest regional economy of South Africa, the degree is much greater in Zambia and Malawi than in Zimbabwe.

The reasons for the continuing position of Zimbabwe as the more industrialised economy have to do with the nature of the material base established under settler colonialism, the early appearance of a national bourgeoisie, and the interests of the evolving imperial system. The interplay of politics between the metropole and the settler classes determined the greater degree of manufacturing in Rhodesia, which is the key to industrial development. Ultimately, the endurance of Zimbabwe's superior position will rest on the class composition of the new governing class and its alliances with local capitalists.

To support this argument, I will examine the industrial evolution of the region up to 1986. In particular, I will focus on the strategy of import substitution which evolved in Zambia, Zimbabwe and eventually Malawi[2] from informal origins to the status of an integral part of a national development strategy. The analysis begins with the early economic changes which introduced capitalist mining, one of the key aspects of modern industry, at the turn of the twentieth century. Then I describe how aspects of industrial development began in all three territories. The next section outlines efforts at import substitution industrialisation which came with self-rule. I conclude with a brief restatement of the original argument of how the appearance, or non-appearance, of a national bourgeoisie interacted with the interests of foreign capital to launch industrialisation to a much greater degree in Zimbabwe than either mining-centred Zambia or the poor cousin, Malawi.

EARLY COLONIALISM AND ECONOMIC CHANGES

As early as the 1830s, various British and Boer adventurers had looked north of the Limpopo River to lands that they hoped would be rich in diamonds and gold. In the fifty years leading up to the Congress of Berlin (1884–85), individuals and countries claimed the land. The Belgian King took personally what became known as the Belgian Congo, the Germans claimed the territories along the coasts which later became known as Tanganyika and South West Africa and the Portuguese held Mozambique and Angola and had claim to the lands around Lake Malawi. Scots missionaries came to the lands south and west of Lake Malawi and imposed a form of church rule over many of these peoples, while the Catholics established a bridgehead in Barotseland and elsewhere.

Concerned about aggressive land grabs and also intra-African warfare, various African leaders such as Mzilikazi and Lobengula of the Matabele and Lewanika of the Lozi entered into what they thought were mutual defence pacts with the Europeans. But, over time, the capitalists and adventurers stripped Barotseland, Matabeleland, Mashonaland and the chiefdoms of Lake Malawi of their political sovereignty and then their mineral wealth and lands, while the missionaries introduced Christianity and their notions of the proper way of life which altered the social system. First, the Europeans claimed vast tracts of lands despite their occupation by others. Second, they asserted physical control over the area to the degree that they could then dispense the mineral and land

76

rights as they saw fit and profitable or proselytise freely. Finally they introduced new economic systems, commercial farming and mining and later manufacturing.

Modern mining and manufacturing (the core of industry)[3] were introduced in Central Africa under different forms and periods of colonialism. Basically, these activities were promoted, along with settler agriculture, in order to reduce the costs of administering the region while the local wealth of raw materials was extracted. In Malawi, commercial agriculture was meant to pay taxes to underwrite the administration along with hut taxes extracted from the local people. The traditional economies were destroyed directly and indirectly by the intrusion of capitalism. Later the British Colonial Office became the sole governing authority.

THE COMPANY COLONIES: 1890 to 1923/24

The first company in the region was the Africa Lakes Company, established in 1879 by the missionaries located in the lands around Lake Malawi in order to stimulate 'legitimate' trade as an alternative to the prevailing slave and ivory commerce (71, p.129). Just over a decade under the leadership of Cecil John Rhodes, the British South Africa Company (BSACo. or the Company) became the immediate agent of capitalism in Northern and Southern Rhodesia. Under its aegis, Company representatives established claims through the technique of treaties signed by chiefs and headmen in the areas concerned: the Moffat treaty and the Rudd and Lippert concessions for Matabeleland and Mashonaland, and the Sharpe, Lochner and Thomson treaties for Barotseland and Bembaland. Harry Johnstone, the British consul in Mozambique, collected treaties in 1889 from the Mambwe, Lungu and Tabwa chiefs between Lake Malawi and Tanganyika on behalf of the Company. These treaties gave a dubious legality to BSACo claims over the minerals in the ground and, later, to the land itself, a far cry from the expectations of the local African authorities who had signed in good faith for collective security.

Missionaries to the west and south of Lake Malawi were unwilling to be governed directly by the BSACo. 'Early in 1891 it was agreed that the British government should be directly responsible for a new Nyasaland Protectorate . . .' (56, p.162). However, when Johnston was Commissioner for Nyasaland, he operated with a dual mandate: he spoke for both the colonial power and the BSACo. His efforts to end the slave trade benefitted both the local people and the foreigners who could then begin to do more business in the fertile lands around the lake. When the missionary-sponsored Africa Lakes Co. was liquidated in 1893, its concessions of lands and minerals in Nyasaland were passed on to its

77

major shareholder, the BSACo (71, p.180). So although the BSACo did not directly rule Nyasaland, it had substantial financial interests there.

Having claim to the lands by the end of the nineteenth century was one thing, but actually establishing European-owned farms and businesses was another. In order to infuse this new political and economic system, the old ones had to be destroyed or undermined. As an example of how this was done, one can look at what happened in Mashonaland and Matabeleland. Claiming that the concessions granted by Ndebele King Lobengula also covered Mashonaland, in 1890 the BSACo's 'Pioneer Column' occupied the northern and eastern parts of what became known as Southern Rhodesia. Land and cattle seizures which followed precipitated several wars of resistance from the local people (the first Chimurenga) but the Africans were suppressed by the Company's superior fire power. In 1893 Dr. Jameson organized an invasion of Matabeleland which ended up with the death of King Lobengula and the seizure of much of the cattle of the Ndebele as loot. Again the Ndebele and Shona rebelled in 1896–7, but Company police and settlers suppressed the rebellions with great brutality. By 1898 Mashonaland and Matabeleland were joined in the Colony of Southern Rhodesia; by 1911 the territories of North-East and North-West Rhodesia were amalgamated into Northern Rhodesia. From the turn of the century until 1923, in the Rhodesias 'the Company was the State' (9, p.19). Thus the new political system was imposed.

Next came the new economic system. The directors of the British South Africa Company had anticipated a 'Second Rand' in Southern Rhodesia with vast mineral wealth of the sort they had exploited in South Africa. When they did not find such plentiful and accessible gold and diamonds, Company agents and police encouraged commercial farming by European settlers. Between 1901 and 1911 the European population in Southern Rhodesia doubled from 11,000 to over 23,000 (2, p.337). Eventually the BSACo permitted other prospectors and mining companies to look for gold and copper and later for base minerals. The railway, which had reached just south of Victoria Falls in 1904, was extended into Northern Rhodesia; by 1910, it connected Livingstone to Elizabethville (now Lubumbashi), the capital of Katanga (now Shaba) province of the Belgian Congo (now Zaire), linking together the north and south by the railway.

The successful suppression of the preexisting peoples and introduction of capitalist mining and farming did not immediately financially benefit the BSACo for its administrative expenses were not adequately offset by revenues from the railways, forestry, gold and coal mining, banking and financial services, insurances, and land exploited for commercial farming purposes (2, p.337; 9, p.19). Towards the end of the first quarter of the twentieth century, the Company turned over the role of direct administrator for the Rhodesias to the British government while retaining claims to the minerals and vast tracts of lands. Nyasaland continued in its status as a British protectorate.

EARLY INDUSTRIALISATION UNDER FORMAL COLONIAL RULE:1923–63

The Regional Economy Until The Depression

In the 1920s Britain became the legal custodian for all three colonies, endowing each with its own colonial government. The transfer of power in Southern Rhodesia was complex, both because of the diverse economic interests and because of the presence of an influential group of white settlers. The Company shed its administrative responsibilities for Northern Rhodesia more easily, although it carefully held on to claims of mineral rights. When both economies began to undergo early industrial development in the late 1920s, Northern Rhodesia took the lead because of its rich veins of high grade copper ore. Foreign capital's interest in Southern Rhodesia became more diversified and complex. Nyasaland remained the weak sister behind the Rhodesias, attracting few settlers, having no major mineral finds and almost no manufacturing. However, this protectorate played an important role as a reservoir of labour for the capitalist development in the other two regions.

Immigration patterns varied considerably between the three territories, with different colonial plans and material possibilities. Drawn by Company and colonial policies, a substantial number of white farmers, merchants and small prospectors/miners settled in Southern Rhodesia. By 1923, 35,000 whites lived in this southern territory. Unlike the northern territories, the future of Southern Rhodesia was bound up with farming and small-scale mining, especially gold mining, by owner-workers. Arrighi argues that the immigration and subsequent land policies were the direct result of efforts by the Company to establish a white rural bourgeoisie which would develop the country and raise the value of Company assets in the area, viz. the railway system, the mine claims and especially the land: (2, p.336). Indeed, towns developed to service farming and mines, thus introducing a small commercial petty bourgeoisie; a percentage of the administrators for the area also became permanent residents. Southern Rhodesia was becoming a colony for white settlement on the model of Kenya.

These settlers had rejected union with South Africa in 1922, so when the rule of the Company ended in 1923 Southern Rhodesia was made a

British colony with internal self-government. The British gave a certain amount of power to the white settler classes who in turn had to cooperate with the more powerful interests of the metropole and international capital. As Clarke pointed out, 'this must be understood as something less than a major defeat for external investors . . . if only because in the main the shift to local white political control never seriously damaged foreign firms, certainly at least up until 1965' (9, p.20). These settlers wanted access to the better land; already in 1919 they had challenged BSACo rights to the land. In the 1930s the government passed legislation which allowed the settlers to annex the best African land and crush any African attempts to compete in the marketplace. A second goal for the settlers was to gain state aid to make the smaller mines viable. The government also introduced important infrastructure which made small-scale mining profitable and laid the base for a small manufacturing sector. As a result the economy of Southern Rhodesia was based on commercial farming, small- and medium-scale mining and some retail business up to the Second World War.

In 1924 the BSACo relinquished control over Northern Rhodesia to the British Crown but retained the mineral rights. The territory became a protectorate, although the peoples and their economies were hardly 'protected' under formal colonial rule. Ironically, the turnover of sovereignty to the British occurred almost simultaneously with the discovery of a flotation process which made possible and profitable the extraction of copper from the sulphide ores of the Copperbelt. From the 1920s through 1930s two major mining groups – the subsidiary of the Anglo-American Corporation of South Africa Ltd., Rhoanglo, and the Rhodesian Selection Trust (RST), a British concern with substantial American financial and technical backing – consolidated their control over the copper-bearing minerals of the territory. The people of Northern Rhodesia and immigrant labour from the nearby territories worked for subsistence wages (in some cases below subsistence) in order for the mining companies to export copper ores to the industrialised world at a considerable profit. A small white working class was drawn to the mines, living a relatively privileged existence from the high wages for skilled manpower. Other whites came and developed commercial farms to feed the mining towns, and eventually a small commercial petty bourgeoisie developed. Yet their numbers were few; by 1921 there were still only 3,634 resident whites.

Basic social and economic infrastructure was established, reluctantly, by the administrators and the mineowners, while missionaries provided some limited schooling to the African population. In general the modern economy of Northern Rhodesia was limited to a mining enclave and a strip of land on either side of the railway linking Livingstone to the Copperbelt and was occupied by a small number of whites and a large army of low-wage African workers. Until 1935, according to Alistair Young, the only manufacturing establishment listed in the annual Blue Books was a sawmill belonging to Zambezi Sawmills Ltd. (78, p.4). Mining almost exclusively dominated the modern economy.

As a symbol of its marginality, Nyasaland was not included in the central rail system until 1922. Even then, passengers and freight had to cross the Zambezi River by ferry to connect to the Shire River. It was not until 1935 that a bridge was built connecting the rail lines. Thus Nyasaland remained a backwater in the capitalist development of the region. In this agricultural colony, the small white population was divided between civil servants and missionaries. The major fact of economic life for the local people was a serious shortage of land. The population per acre was much higher than in the rest of the region.[4] The traditional techniques of cultivation based on shifting agriculture became impossible with the population pressure. By the late 1920s many adult male Nyasalanders migrated in search of work. Remaining African smallholders turned to producing tobacco for export as well as maize and cassava for consumption while the white-owned planations began tea and sugar production using local labourers. Wages were low and life was hard for the people of the colony and there were no plans for the industrial development of Nyasaland.

From the Depression to the Second World War

In the 1930s the economies of Central Africa were drawn further into the Western capitalist system as their primary products were in demand despite interruptions from the Depression and briefer recessions. Initially, as A.G. Frank described in Latin America, the disruptions in trade during wartime and depressions created an artificial protection and some new factories sprang up producing consumer goods (7, passim). However, by the 1940s Europe's demands for raw materials and food reestablished the strong commercial ties with Central Africa.

In the late 1920s the economy of Southern Rhodesia was diversifying. The mining industry included many small- and medium-scale mines, involved in a variety of different base and precious metal mining. Commercial agriculture, with tobacco as the major export crop, was augmented by an African peasantry producing maize and cattle. There were some incipient retail and manufacturing businesses. This more complex economy was reflected in a more stratified class system. Although most of Southern Rhodesia's white population was involved in farming or small-scale mining, a growing number were white wage workers – artisans, semi-skilled workers, foremen, clerical workers, administrative employees working for the railway or the colonial administration (2, p.338). International capital also had a presence. The Chrome Trust under Sir Edmund Davies had existed since the 1920s when Foote Minerals and Union Carbide began mining chrome; Turner and Newall controlled the marketing of asbestos in Britain in the mid-1920s and the forerunner of today's Lonrho expanded its agrarian and mineral base (9, p.20). These corporations were influential in the political corridors of Salisbury, the capital of Southern Rhodesia. One thing both international and local capital were agreed upon was the need for more cheap labour. When restrictive legislation took its bite in the 1930s, many local rural cultivators were undermined. This, in turn, supplied more cheap, unskilled labour to the mines and commercial farms, the beginnings of the proletarianisation of the indigenous people.

The internal and international upheavals of the 1930s changed the political economy of Southern Rhodesia and brought more direct state intervention in the economy. After the general election of 1933 augmented the power of the settlers, the Southern Rhodesian government began to take steps which later proved central in the development of modern industry as well as the success of large-scale commercial farming. Government services to the mining industry were instituted or augmented, 'most notably the establishment of a state-financed roasting plant at Que Que for the treatment of refractory sulphide ores and the provision of regular, cheap power through the Electricity supply Commission. Many small mines were thus able for the first time to undertake the extraction of sulphide gold ores, while simultaneously electric power contributed to lower working costs' (47, p.36). For the commercial farmers, the Tobacco Marketing Act helped strengthen the bargaining power of the Rhodesian farmers against the United Tobacco Company; a Cotton Marketing Board sponsored that area of commercial agriculture.

The Southern Rhodesian government fostered local manufacturing – by 1938 there were 299 industrial establishments in the colony (9, p.26). The state also became more actively involved in infrastructure. A road-building campaign was begun in the 1930s; after the partial nationalisation of the railway in 1938, spur lines crisscrossed the land. One should not overstate this local capitalist power however. As Stoneman points out, 'both the railways, and the colliery at Wankie remained under the control of the British South Africa Company . . .' (63, p.30). At most a 'weak and intermittent economic nationalism' characterised the policies of the new settler government (63, p.40). Southern Rhodesia was still a mining and farming colony with British civil servants governing although influenced by the settlers.

Economic changes were coming, brought about partially by the action of the settlers and partly by policy changes. Although most manufactured goods were imported from Britain or South Africa, some consumer goods were supplied locally. The initial stages of an agricultural implements industry had appeared through the efforts of local white capitalists. The state supplied the roasting plant, electricity, roads, dams, veterinary services which aided the expanding economy of the settlers as well as foreign capital. Of course, the state gained by more taxes from more enterprises. Yet the initial infrastructural costs were paid for by taxing the larger mining concerns such as the Wankie colliery, owned by Powell Duffryn, and the large foreign-owned companies involved in asbestos, coal and chrome. The low wages paid to the African work force indirectly provided capital for these local investments. Despite a more diversified economy, the mining sector in Southern Rhodesia responded to the same economic laws as those in Northern Rhodesia – the minerals were extracted and processed and then shipped abroad in an unfabricated state. Although a more balanced economy, Southern Rhodesia was still a dependent colony with external actors heavily influencing its health and direction.

Northern Rhodesia's modern sector was more narrowly based on mining and underwent boom and bust cycles along with the fortunes of copper, lead and zinc. 'By 1930 mines were either in production or under development at Bwana Mkubwa, Roan Antelope (now Luanshya), Nkana (Rhokana), Mufulira, Nchanga (Chingola), Chambishi and Kansanshi' (10, p.6). The lead and zinc mine at Broken Hill (now Kabwe) was prospering. This expansion collapsed when the Great Depression hit the Copperbelt in 1931; the mining houses temporarily closed down several of the bigger mines. This contraction ended the era of smaller prospectors and companies and gave full rein to the two major mining groups, RST and Rhoanglo. When in 1933 the fortunes of the Copperbelt turned again, RST and Rhoanglo reopened several mines. The Rhokana Corporation began construction of an electrolytic refinery at Nkana Mine that same year. By 1937 the protectorate was fourth amongst world producers of copper, turning out 210,000 tons per annum (5, p.60).

In this protectorate where copper was king, the power of the white settlers was very constricted. Occasionally, the white mineworkers flexed their muscles by holding a strike. In general white politics revolved around the relationship with the larger white populations of the south (Southern Rhodesia and South Africa) on the one hand, and with the Company and later the British Colonial Office on the other. RST and Anglo-American were the most important entities outside the colonial administration; they essentially ruled the Copperbelt in these early years and their desires were readily transferred into legislation until 1953.

The expansion of war industries in Europe from 1935 onwards increased worldwide demand for copper and the other base metals. The international mining companies, in alliance with the colonial officials, designed and determined the features of the newly expanded enclave to service the needs of the Allies. In general, this expansion meant more shafts and more underground miners. The whole protectorate of Northern Rhodesia served the needs of the mining enclave of the Copperbelt. Taxation, education, urban stabilisation, welfare policies, all suited the demands for a skilled and relatively permanent black labour force for the mines. The spine of the country from Livingstone to the Copperbelt was developed by a limited number of white commercial farmers who supplied food for the towns. Outlying Bembaland supplied labour to the Copperbelt; Barotseland provided men for the mines of South Africa and Rhodesia. The overall welfare or interests of the majority of the population were of little concern to either the mining officials or the colonial administrators except insofar as Africans remained a key source of cheap labour and thus of primitive accumulation for the farmers and more sophisticated extraction of variable capital by the mineowners.

New investment in mining coupled with the economics of transport led the mine owners in Northern Rhodesia to refine and smelt at the mine sites, an early form of manufacturing. Copper refineries at Ndola and Nkana, the first step of downstream integration of the copper industry, had been set up to save money. However, the mineowners never intended to continue the downstream process onto semi-manufacturing. Northern Rhodesia was to be an exporter of base minerals, not a source of fabricated copper goods. Under the Customs Agreement signed in the early 1930s, Northern Rhodesia's growing market for consumer, intermediate and capital goods was supplied from South Africa and Southern Rhodesia.[5] The proximity and openness of the territory to these larger economies which were already involved in manufacturing had a backwash effect on local infant industries. The colonial state would not intervene to protect or sponsor the development of secondary industry. So Northern Rhodesia remained a mining enclave.

Nyasaland in many ways was the least affected except insofar as the peasant economies had to reabsorb manpower when their foreign employers sent them home. With a large population on the remaining land, Nyasaland continued to export labour. The colonial government was most interested in lessening the costs of administration. The collapse of cotton and tobacco prices hurt the peasant farms and plantation owners.

Too few Europeans were resident to press for representation on the Legislative Council, so they focused their attentions on the agricultural marketing boards established from 1923 onwards (41, pp.240–262). The prevailing racism excluded the African majority from politics until the creation of the Native Authorities in 1933 which gave traditional leaders minimal and indirect access to the central government. A report in 1939 said that Nyasas[6] were the most literate people of any British tropical dependency, but the local economy did not benefit much from this important human resource. Missionary-trained men from Nyasaland provided skilled labour, especially clerkships, to the industries and commercial farms in the whole region. Nyasa clerks were the first literate local manpower on the Northern Rhodesian Copperbelt for example. There was no government-sponsored development of industry in Nyasaland and the private sector had just begun processing plantation crops (sugar and tea) while one firm had a small soap factory. Intensification of industry came with the Second World War and primarily to the Rhodesias, especially Southern Rhodesia.

The Period from 1939 to 1953: Import Substitution Begins

Wars in the industrial world encouraged import substitution in Central Africa in two ways. Military uses stimulated production of raw materials in Central Africa especially of base metals. Commensurately, interrupted supplies from foreign sources tended to protect all three economies, which began to produce more of their own consumer goods. In Southern Rhodesia, increased foreign purchases of agricultural commodities poured money into the government's coffers and the pockets of the commercial farmers. With new-found income, the Southern Rhodesian government expanded infrastructure and provided direct and indirect state subsidies both for small-scale mining and for manufacturers. Both Northern and Southern Rhodesia began to produce domestically goods previously imported, which is the basic definition of import substitution industrialisation (ISI). Entrepreneurs started with manufacturing consumer goods, and in both Rhodesias the factories were established by private parties. A major difference in the period from 1939 to 1953 was that ISI in the south was part of government policy whereas in the north it occurred coincidentally with activities of private capital and some new interest of the mining groups.

Over these years the Nyasa workforce was drawn further into the money economy of the Rhodesias, with more mineworkers migrating to the regional mines and other workers going to the factories and plantations. Nyasaland even experienced some domestic manufacturing growth under the protectionism of the war years, granting further support for André Gunder Frank's thesis about the possible development that occurs when a periphery is cut off from the core. In general, however, the industrial evolution of the region continued to be uneven, as the description below of the experiences of Northern Rhodesia, Southern Rhodesia and Nyasaland attests.

In 1939 the Copperbelt mines produced 212,000 long tons of copper per year (10, p.6). By 1943 Northern Rhodesia's production peaked at 251,000 long tons or nearly four times the 1932 output (45, p.22). The boom on the Copperbelt deepened the presence of another key underpinning of industrial society, a construction industry. More shafts were opened and more refineries and smelters were built; this meant more housing and roads as well. Importantly, manufacturing also grew. The most important sector was food processing followed by the timber and wood industries. Most local needs, however, were still supplied from outside, especially from Britain, Southern Rhodesia and South Africa (78, p.11). 'Roughly speaking Southern Rhodesia was [Northern Rhodesia's] largest single supplier of the simpler manufactured goods (like processed food, cigarettes and nonmetallic minerals), while South Africa had already reached the stage of being able to supply the products of the more advanced industries' (78, p.11).

The exigencies of the war years encouraged the growth of local secondary industries. Efforts were made to produce munitions in the workshops of the mines and the railways, while some establishments were set up to carry on the simpler manufacturing processes with a view to replace scarce imports. The first *Census of Industrial Production*, taken in 1947, revealed 79 establishments engaged in 'Factory and Workshop Industries' (78, p.5).

After the Second World War ended, there was a brief contraction on the Copperbelt as the demand for base minerals dropped off dramatically. Also the coppermines, which had produced to the limit of capacity during the war period, were in need of refurbishment. New developments in technology had passed by Northern Rhodesia. The mines now required a double infusion of capital: for retooling and for rebuilding. In the post war era, the initial competition between the Anglo and RST group had given way to basic cooperation. Still some differences between the mining groups persisted as with the issue of whether to invest in secondary industry. Anglo-American promoted some factories around the Copperbelt to manufacture inputs; its subsidiary Rhoanglo set up companies to manufacture cement and ball bearings in this period. RST, by contrast, remained focused on mining alone and, except for a joint investment in a hotel and farm, remained almost exclusively a mining house. These differences reflected some variation in the interests of foreign capital in the Copperbelt. The South African-based group had a longer term vision of their role in the region while the managers of the British/American RST were more narrowly focused on immediate returns.

When the Copperbelt again revived in the late 1940s, private capitalists began to produce a wider range of consumer goods for the growing local market. Asian and European merchants were drawn by the high wages of the Copperbelt; by 1951 there were 37,097 Europeans in Northern Rhodesia (45, p.17) and 2,524 Asians (13, p.51, Table 3). The African mineworkers were the highest paid on the continent. Local capital financed a new wheat-flour mill in Ndola in 1951 (78, p.6). The same year the settler politicians finally stimulated the government to make some basic infrastructural investment: Chilanga Cement was opened near Lusaka as a joint venture involving government capital. This project remained unique. In general, the Northern Rhodesian government worked on the basis of *laissez faire* and was opposed to direct government involvement in the economy. The external imperial masters continued their vision of Northern Rhodesia as a mining enclave and were not willing to invest in the manufacturing sector or commercial agriculture.

Expansion of the mines and introduction of more skilled people and a larger domestic market in Northern Rhodesia did not inspire more self-sufficient industrial development. Most of the capital generated by the copper mines was either extracted in dividend or interest form, sent as taxes to Britain or royalties to the BSACo or reinvested into the enclave. Outside the mines, the development of commercial agriculture and secondary manufacturing was very restricted. In 1954 the percentage contribution of manufacturing to the GDP was only 3 per cent (78, p.6). There was no large-scale import substitution or government-backed diversification away from the heavy focus on the extractive industry. The capital was there but not the political will. A major reason for this lack of political will was that the settlers in Northern Rhodesia were not a bourgeoisie or even in the process of becoming a bourgeoisie, and the mining companies and imperial powers' interests were served well with the territory continuing as a raw materials supplier only.

In marked contrast, stimulated by high export demands and substantial capital inflows, Southern Rhodesia's industrial sector expanded rapidly (63, p.38). The Second World War resulted in a sharp, 50 per cent rise in export values for Southern Rhodesia's products. The allied powers demanded more and more essential raw materials, especially copper, chrome, tungsten and asbestos found in the region. Imports were reduced or cut off by the war. These changes protected Southern

Rhodesia's infant manufacturing industry which thus steadily increased its percentage of the GDP to 16 per cent by 1952 (see Table 1).

After the war, British immigrants flooded into Southern Rhodesia providing new manpower and skills; they were joined after 1948 by an outflow of whites from South Africa, fearful of what the Afrikaner government might mean. Labour and land laws made tobacco farming and citrus growing more profitable. Finally, considerable amounts of foreign capital were invested in Southern Rhodesia (63, p.34). Foreign companies saw South Africa and Southern Rhodesia as secure outposts of capitalism. For this reason they were willing to invest more capital and bring new technology into Southern Rhodesian manufacturing while few were willing to invest outside mining in Northern Rhodesia. Thus national and international capitalists coexisted in Southern Rhodesia, joined in their desire to make money in the low-wage colony.

Faced with these advantageous conditions and aided by foreign investment, the Southern Rhodesian government shifted the economy away from heavy reliance on exports of only raw materials, to one considerably more internally oriented. Essentially, its strategy emphasised import-substitution of consumer goods with some investment in intermediate goods. It left export diversification to the private sector. The government introduced economic planning and price controls, controlled the direction and cost of labour, imposed rationing and higher taxes and actually nationalised central industries. As already mentioned, being cut off from the European suppliers facilitated this industrial evolution by protecting the smaller, less competitive, industries of Southern Rhodesia. More actively, the government continued to expand and deepen the infrastructure, benefitting both the raw materials producers and incipient

TABLE 1
SOUTHERN RHODESIAN INDUSTRIAL ORIGIN OF THE GROSS
DOMESTIC PRODUCT: PERCENTAGES

	1946	1948	1950	1952
Non-African Agriculture	–	19.1	18.3	–
African Agriculture	–	7.8	5.1	–
Mining and Quarrying	10.4	10.0	9.9	10.5
Manufacturing	13.3	13.0	14.7	16.0
Electricity, Water, etc.	(1.6)	1.3	1.6	(1.4)
Building and Construction	(4.1)	7.2	8.8	(9.2)
Distribution	–	14.3	13.7	–
Other Services	–	27.3	27.5	–

Source: Colin Stoneman, 'Foreign Capital and the Prospects for Zimbabwe', *World Development*, 1976, vol.4, no.1, p.30. Table 2.

manufacturing. Public works, especially road building, were carried out on a large scale. The government nationalised the already existing but small-scale iron and steel industry in 1942, and moved it to Redcliffe, adding foundries and mills. It also developed cotton spinning mills and established a Cotton Research and Industry Board (9, p.25) to encourage both cotton farmers and local textile manufacturers. In 1944 it nationalised the Triangle Sugar Estates and placed the plantation under the local Sugar Industry Board to bolster south-eastern lowveld agriculture. In 1947 Rhodesia bought the railway from the BSACo, via a stock option in London. By 1953, the government had invested over Rh$29.0 million in three commissions, two industrial boards and a roasting plant, besides supplying funds to small industries through the Industrial Development Commission (29, p.40). This form of state capitalism benefitted both the settlers and international capital, but particularly the former.

The effects of these government policies were dramatic. The 459 industries existing in 1945 (29, p.39) had expanded to 700 industrial establishments by 1953 with a gross output worth nearly £62 million (9, p.26). A large part of this expansion was in local food processing, but some simple intermediate goods were being produced. An important new subsector was the textile industry. In 1947 the newly independent Indian Government placed an embargo on trade with South Africa, a measure which primarily affected textiles. Southern Rhodesia received Indian piece goods and reprocessed them for sale to South Africa. In 1949 Southern Rhodesia signed an agreement with South Africa allowing the duty free import of textiles, giving a further push to that subsector (76, p.154). The Land Apportionment Act, which continued to squeeze the land available for African settlement, provided cheap labour for all these newly expanded enterprises.

Towards the end of the Second World War, the Southern Rhodesian government recognised that the local factories were too small and too technologically simple to compete internationally once the big industrial economies revived. So a Commission of Inquiry was set up to explore ways and means to protect the secondary manufacturing sector. 'It proposed protection of domestic industry, provision of subsidies and export incentives to deserving enterprises, confirmed the wisdom of duty free imports of industrial plant and machinery and raw materials from the British Empire, and advocated search for reliable external markets' (29, p.40).

Although not all of these suggestions were transferred into policy, a coalition of owners, small retail businesses and artisans in the metal production area pushed for the import substitution which was to become the base for the next twenty years of industrialising. This was important because although international capital saw Southern Rhodesia as an important outpost of capitalism, foreign investment still favoured the primary sector rather than manufacturing and considerable profits were externalised. One of the reasons for this was the lack of an expanding internal market in the 1930s which put a natural limit to the size of consumer goods industries and thus unit costs of production and profit margins. The marginalisation of the African peasants and the low wages for the non-white workforce meant that they could not provide effective demand despite continued population growth.

This situation changed in the 1940s and early 1950s. The war stimulated all sectors of the economy, drawing more Africans into wage employment. In Southern Rhodesia the number of Africans in wage employment rose from 254,000 in 1936, 377,000 in 1946 to more than 600,000 in 1956 (2, p.351). White commercial farmers now had a large foreign market for all food crops as well as a reliable domestic one; manufacturers could make and sell cheap wage goods which previously had been imported and retailers could make money as well. The typical industrial unit had grown in size from the small family shop stage to the large-scale, mechanised, corporate owned factory (2, p.353) and manufacturing was well entrenched.

These conditions made some outsiders, for example Anglo, willing to take a chance. In addition to Anglo's mining interests (expressed through four corporations – the Tanganyika Concessions, De Beers, British South Africa Company and AAC itself), it became a major plantation owner (Hippo Valley estates), was involved in banking and insurance, and controlled coal and iron pyrites mining, the ferro-chrome and cement industries. Together with RST, it dominated iron and steel production and, through the Argus Group, the Rhodesian daily press as well as major investments in citrus and sugar estates, forests, clay products, financial houses, etc. This diversification by Anglo in Southern Rhodesia reflected the same original political sense that it had demonstrated in Northern Rhodesia: this South African company intended to have a long future in the Rhodesias.[7] So foreign capital began to invest in secondary and tertiary activities as well as the primary sector, sometimes in competition and sometimes in cooperation with local capitalists.

In summary, by 1953 the industrial sector of Southern Rhodesia had reached the stage of a mining industry with a multitude of products, export-oriented and foreign-dominated, and a more internally-oriented manufacturing sector heavily reliant on consumer goods and more dominated by local capitalists. Diversification into intermediate goods and capital goods production to feed the consumer goods industries and also other sectors such as commercial agriculture was the next logical step for Southern Rhodesian manufacturers. This stage of industrial development, however, is expensive, technologically and organizationally demanding and relies on a large market, both for the consumer goods and also for the intermediate and capital goods. There was not sufficient capital in the hands of local Rhodesian businessmen for such investments. Large-scale international entrepreneurs still concerned with the limited nature of the markets which would inhibit new manufacturing efforts, kept their investments in the primary product sector, agriculture and mining and in consumer goods fabrication. It seemed that Southern Rhodesian manufacturing would halt at the consumer goods stage.

In this decade and a half, Nyasaland was not industrialised on a par with its two neighbours. Agriculture continued to dominate with the small-holders producing tobacco and cotton and the plantation owners controlling tea and the marketing boards. No large-scale mining was developed, but a flour mill was set up in 1941 to join the tobacco and cigarette factories located along the corridor between Blantyre and Limbe. By the 1950s several firms manufactured food containers for local produce and some factories produced soap and clothing for domestic consumption. Despite this limited ISI, the bulk of manufactured goods, especially all investment goods, had to be imported. Symbolically, the capital at Zomba remained exclusively an administrative centre, untouched by industry. The growing population intensified land pressure, so more and more able-bodied men migrated outside the country for work.[8] Another important stimulus for migration was the low wages paid in Nyasaland. The dominant economy was agrarian, divided between small-scale African producers and large plantations, with a manufacturing fringe dependent on agriculture, and a portion of the national income coming from migrants' remittances.

The social structure of the protectorate was equally distinctive. A tiny African professional class had emerged along with a larger salariat connected to the colonial government. The vast proportion of the people were impoverished peasants, many tenant farmers on the estates of white owners or corporations. The small resident European group was divided between civil servants, missionaries and landowners with a sprinkling of businessmen while the Asians were primarily in commerce and agricultural marketing. No real national bourgeoisie existed, either African or settler, and the colonial government operated primarily on the advice of Whitehall.

The existence of a local bourgeoisie became vital in the diversification of these economies and in particular the evolution of a manufacturing base. Northern Rhodesia and Nyasaland lacked a national bourgeoisie (either settler or local) and were dominated by foreigners in contrast to Southern Rhodesia where a small but vocal settler bourgeoisie had

Studies in the Economic History of Southern Africa

formed and linked its economic interests to control over the state. Prominent Southern Rhodesian industrialists pushed the government to extend infrastructure and even to establish important intermediate goods industries. International capital had considerable power in all three territories, but its overall power was more untrammelled in Northern Rhodesia where RST and Anglo essentially called the shots. On the Copperbelt, the mining firms were not interested in investing their copper profits into manufacturing. All they wanted were certain firms to produce vital inputs for the mines such as diamond headed drills, timber and mine workers' clothing. With improved transportation, all other inputs could be obtained from their subsidiaries in South Africa, facilitated through the preferential trade agreements. The settler population (now over 35,000) felt aggrieved at the domination by the mineowners and the failure of the parsimonious colonial government to support industry directly with investment or indirectly through tariffs.[9] They organised opposition to the plans of the foreign magnates when their interests diverged. Without the political weight of a resident national bourgeoisie, the colonial authorities and the mineowners continued to develop almost exclusively the mining sector while the commercial farmers developed, to a lesser degree, the line of rail. Since the Northern Rhodesian government, by and large, reflected corporate mining interests, there was no integrated industrial development of significance in Northern Rhodesia despite the considerable revenues from the commodity boom of the 1940s and 1950s.

Southern Rhodesia, on the other hand, had expanded its manufacturing, mostly under the leadership of the local national bourgeoisie. Although still a colonial economy, dependent on sales of raw materials to the metropole, the latter was more diversified and more internally focused. Nyasaland, lacking a mining industry and also a local bourgeoisie, lagged further and further behind the Rhodesias in terms of industrial development. The unevenness of regional development was compounded by the events of the postwar era and the creation of a new political organisation, the Federation of Rhodesia and Nyasaland.

The Federation Period, 1953–1963

By 1953 the uneven industrial development in the region meant considerably more manufacturing in the south than in the north. The federation between the two Rhodesias and Nyasaland crystallized this regional imbalance as the new political institutions were controlled by the settlers in the south. The Federation was promoted as a way to expand the market, widen the resource base, enlarge employment and investment and augment income through integrating the region economically. Politically, it was said to lay the base for rule by a racial 'partnership' between African

92

and European. In reality, free access for Southern Rhodesia's stronger manufacturing sector into Nyasaland and Northern Rhodesia undermined possibilities for competitive secondary industry in the other partners. The mines of Northern Rhodesia provided massive infusions of capital into the coffers of the south, paying for the deepening of industry and infrastructure in Southern Rhodesia. Nyasaland supplied cheap labour to its more industrial neighbours but particularly to the tobacco industry of Southern Rhodesia. As Colin Stoneman succinctly put it, 'Southern Rhodesia in effect acquired two colonies' (63, p.40).

Politically, the multiracial 'partnership' turned out to be one 'between the rider and his horse' (remark attributed to the first Federal Prime Minister). Not surprisingly, the African peoples of all three territories resented their continued (and some would say enhanced) exploitation. The first area to experience real opposition was Nyasaland. The racism experienced by many Nyasa workers in Southern Rhodesia fuelled their resistance to federation in the first place and continued exclusion from power within the federal government only deepened the determination of the African nationalists to both end federation and establish an independent state. Resistance by the African people in all three areas to the imposition of federation was the core element in the development of nationalism which eventually destroyed the federation and led to majority rule for Malawi and Zambia and a long painful war between black and white in Rhodesia.

The negative economic aspects of the Federation were not so apparent in its early years, which were ones of considerable growth in all sectors, especially for manufacturing. The output of textiles, clothing, footwear, foodstuffs, drinks, tobacco, metal and metal products and chemically based products expanded rapidly. A boom in mining drew more Africans and Europeans into employment at relatively high wages. External funds flowed in and new companies came to do business in the Federation. Construction projects began throughout the federal territory with a federal budget of Rh$243,454 million for capital expenditure in the 1957–61 Development plan (29, p.49). But the benefits and investments were allocated very unevenly, with Southern Rhodesia receiving the lion's share and Northern Rhodesia contributing much of the capital. The fiscal distribution was so uneven that in 1959 the Northern Rhodesian Minister of Finance, a British civil servant, publicly complained at the grossly uneven distribution of wealth between the territories (56, p.214). By 1963 it was estimated that over £97 million had gone from Northern Rhodesia to the Federal treasury. Northern Rhodesia received only a small proportion of that capital back in the form of investment and services. The remainder went to pay for the federal bureaucracy in Salisbury and development projects in Southern Rhodesia and Nyasaland. Under the federal arrangement, Northern Rhodesia could no longer determine its own rate of income tax and could do nothing about the massive flow of mining dividends and royalties out of the country (c.£260 million after tax for the decade) (56, p.214). Crudely put, ten years of federation fed the manufacturing industry in Southern Rhodesia with an infusion of federal funds from taxes on the Copperbelt and provision of infrastructure which in turn attracted more foreign investment to the south, enhancing the uneven development between the territories.

In addition to the loss of income and sovereignty over fiscal measures, domination by Southern Rhodesia's manufacturing sector undermined possibilities for industrial diversification in Northern Rhodesia. Copperbelt facilities expanded and more consumer goods industries were introduced. Two new mines were opened at Bancroft (Chililabombwe) and Chibuluma and in 1958 a new refinery was opened at Ndola. Increased output as well as high prices meant that the value of Northern Rhodesia's base metals went from £50,000,000 in 1950 to £95,000,000 in 1953 (56, p.212), swelling the coffers locally as well as providing great profits to the foreign owned companies, including the old rentier, the BSACo. Food, beverages and tobacco production were growing: a sugar refinery was set up at Ndola in 1959; a large brewery was established at Kitwe in 1961; and in the same year, a new wheat-flour mill was opened at Broken Hill (Kabwe) (78, p.19). An overall effect of this new investment was that manufacturing did grow in these years, moving from contributing only 3.3 per cent to the GDP in 1954 to 6.1 per cent in 1963 (15, p.299). Yet that growth was limited to consumer goods and a few feeder industries for the mines, as the Southern Rhodesian and South African factories were supplying the rest of Northern Rhodesia's needs.

The settlers, allied with some portions of the Northern Rhodesian Territorial civil service, forced the government to create the Northern Rhodesian Development Corporation in 1960 but by then it was too late to capture enough taxes to use to diversify and expand Northern Rhodesia's secondary industry. By the end of Federation in 1963, only 46 investments had been approved, involving a total of £658, 087 (78, p.23). In general RST and Rhoanglo had carried the day, as they did when they broke the colour bar on the mines in the 1950s in order to cheapen the costs of labour (45, p.24). Despite the massive profits of the war years and good markets throughout much of the 1950s for base metals, little development took place in Northern Rhodesia outside the mines and the line of rail. What manufacturing development there was was too little, too late. The settlers in Northern Rhodesia could not force their conservative territorial administration to use that capital for state-sponsored industrial integration or for extending commercial farming. In addition, now under Federation they had to contend with the southern-dominated Federal Parliament and bureaucracy.[10] Within the Federation, Northern Rhodesia was clearly subordinated to Southern Rhodesia. 'In the Federal Parliament, out of the twenty-six members elected on a franchise that excluded most Africans, fourteen came from Southern Rhodesia and only eight from the north . . .' (56, p.212). The Federal government dealt with all matters concerning Europeans and economic development, and the preponderance of southern interests in these fields shortly became very clear.

Southern Rhodesia gained the lion's share of manufacturing during federation. Almost all secondary industry that developed under the 'partnership' was established in Southern Rhodesia where federal funds modernised Salisbury and intensified infrastructure for future investors. Under optimal economic conditions – protection for industry by the federal tariff and free access into Northern Rhodesia and Nyasaland under federal free trade – Southern Rhodesian manufacturing took the lead. Although mining remained export-oriented, a larger percentage of its products were absorbed locally. Mining's overall percentage contribution to GDP shrank (see Table 2) as manufacturing now had expanded markets, especially from the high wage Copperbelt.[11] Secondary industry intensified and diversified. The state promoted intermediate and producer goods industries directly and by supplying indirect subsidies through the provision of such items as cheap electrical power. Meanwhile, the Federal tariff protected the infant factories.

TABLE 2
SOUTHERN RHODESIAN INDUSTRIAL ORIGIN OF THE GROSS
DOMESTIC PRODUCT: PERCENTAGES

	1953	1955	1957	1959	1961	1963
Non-African Agriculture	–	13.2	12.5	12.8	15.1	14.3
African Agriculture	–	8.1	7.3	6.4	6.6	6.6
Mining and Quarrying	9.1	8.4	7.4	6.5	6.4	5.1
Manufacturing	15.3	14.4	15.0	15.8	16.8	17.4
Electricity, Water, etc.	(1.3)	2.5	2.7	2.6	3.5	4.3
Building and Construction	–	8.3	9.7	8.0	6.1	4.7
Distribution	–	14.5	13.6	14.6	14.5	14.3
Other Services	–	30.5	32.2	33.2	31.0	33.3

Source: 'Foreign Capital', p.30, Table 2.

95

Despite some rumblings of political discontent throughout the Federation, foreign capital continued to flow into Southern Rhodesia. Between 1953 and 1963 it is estimated that there was a net increase of foreign capital inflows of $Rh 700 million, a 250 per cent increase over the previous 10 years (29, p.49). Of course, large amounts of profits produced by foreign-owned companies were repatriated, but some funds went into factories connected to the primary sector. Also now the growing number of companies owned by residents in the manufacturing sector were making profits and these monies were mostly not exported. Their net profits were re-absorbed by the domestic economy, an indication of the growth of a national settler bourgeoisie. Such an infusion of funds meant more expansion, diversification and technological breakthroughs, especially in those subsectors dominated by local capitalists. Both foreign and domestic capitalists benefitted greatly from the Federal government's infrastructure programme. Large sums went to build the Kariba Hydroelectric Power Project, to invest heavily in the jointly-owned Rhodesia Railways, roads, bridges, posts and telecommunications, housing and civil aviation. The mass of expenditure by the Federal government was allocated to Southern Rhodesia to finance projects such as the Southern Rhodesia Electricity Supply Commission, the Dairy Marketing Board, the Grain Marketing Board, and the Sabi–Limpopo Irrigation Pilot Scheme (29, pp.49–50). In the decade of the Federation, state capitalism was conducted by the federal administration, primarily to the benefit of Southern Rhodesia.

Nyasaland was the Cinderella of the Federation, beautiful but poor. The territory gained some large infrastructural investments such as the Shire Valley Project to regulate the flow of the Shire River. This project lessened flooding, developed hydroelectricity and provided irrigation to the farmers of Southern Province. This meant that sugar plantations became major economic ventures in this decade, dominated by foreign companies. Yet the free trade regulations meant the flooding of the local market with Southern Rhodesian wage goods and investment goods, rather than local products. Low wages and the lack of industrial development meant that the GDP per capita in 1957 averaged £11 per year as opposed to £51 in Northern Rhodesia and £54 in Southern Rhodesia (21, p.195). Migration continued to be a main feature in social and economic life. Migrants' remittances constituted 12 per cent of African money incomes in 1957 and the number of Nyasalanders outside the territory was about equal to the number in paid employment domestically. Three-quarters of these were in Southern Rhodesia (21, p.221). Rather than develop industries at home to absorb these workers, the territorial government emphasised projects to promote agriculture, especially export-oriented, and tried to control peasant farming through marketing.

Behind these industrialisation policies and practices lay a realignment of political and social forces throughout the Federation. In Southern Rhodesia, the old coalition between white capital, white workers and white farmers was slowly being replaced by an alliance between domestic and foreign capital, whose political interests were expressed through the United Federal Party (63, p.42). Still the white workers and middle class (wage workers, small-scale merchants and farmers), especially in Southern Rhodesia, remained a force to be reckoned with politically. Their numbers continued to expand in this era by the postwar emigration from Britain and South Africa and the high wages and opportunities of the Central African Federation. The white population in Southern Rhodesia went from 157,000 in 1953 to 220,000 in 1963 (43, p.3). The bulk of these new emigrants were not bourgeois or even petit bourgeois; they were sometimes antagonistic to the interests of foreign capital, as when the MNCs tried to end the colour bar and apprenticeship restrictions. In this particular battle, the white working class won the day, to the disgust of the owners. The white workers later allied to a white petit bourgeoisie and smaller farmers and, as a block, they stymied many attempts by large-scale capital to rationalise its labour pool through the development of a stable and skilled African labour force (Industrial Conciliation Act for example). In 1962, a coalition of white farmers, mineowners, shopkeepers and workers brought the Rhodesian Front Party to victory, overthrowing the big-business sponsored United Federal Party. So the old racial solidarity of the colony was under strain as the economy evolved into a more complex and diversified one in the 1960s.

In Northern Rhodesia, the white working class was unable to block the ending of job reservation which reflected the greater political power of the mining groups. It was their newly organised African unions which confronted the mineowners most militantly, with strikes in 1952, 1955 and 1956. The racial and occupational barriers between the mineworkers made it impossible for them to join in pressing the mines to reinvest more locally, however, which would have produced more jobs for all. In many ways the industrial imbalance between south and north continued, augmented by the trading effects of the Customs Union, with Southern Rhodesia benefitting rather than South Africa (78, p.22). Despite many years of boom on the Copperbelt (drawing more Africans and Europeans into wage employment, increasing output and profits from abroad and supplying a large market), most benefits of the superprofits went south. Symbolic of this financial focus on Southern Rhodesia was the decision by Anglo-American and RST to move their original headquarters to

Salisbury. Some development of intermediate goods industry did take place on the Copperbelt but it was largely from private sources when the copper companies began to farm out some manufacturing processes to other firms. Despite these minor developments, the politics of federation meant that important investment from the state almost always went to Southern Rhodesia (with some expenditures in Nyasaland) and this had a long-term effect on industrial development.

Several reports such as that of Gibb in 1960 attributed the resultant uneven development to 'natural causes and not as a result of Government policy or action'. However, the positioning of the Kariba Hydro-Electric project draws such a statement into doubt. The Kariba Dam's main power station was supposed to have been built on the Northern Rhodesia side of the gorge. Instead it was put, at far greater cost, on the south bank, under the control therefore of the settlers in that territory. The political significance of this was hidden until years later when Northern Rhodesia became the independent nation of Zambia under majority rule after the break-up of the federation.

The first to opt out of the Federation was Nyasaland in 1962, becoming the independent state of Malawi in 1964. In October of 1964 Northern Rhodesia became the Republic of Zambia with intentions of continuing economic cooperation with its southern neighbour. Instead of following suit, in November of 1965 the settler government in Southern Rhodesia staged a unilateral breakaway from Britain and went on its own regressive path, antagonistic to its former northern 'partners'. At this point the regional dependency on the manufacturing sector of Rhodesia and some key areas of infrastructure (hydroelectricity, railways) became most apparent. Both of the northern nations now began their own development strategies to try to become self-sufficient. Zambia took an aggressive approach of developing both its infrastructure and secondary industry, while Malawi emphasised large-scale commercial agriculture with some minimal manufacturing to supply agricultural inputs. Under the white settlers, Rhodesia moved into a more complex phase of ISI, producing capital goods and investment goods. The divergence of their industrial bases widened yet further in the next two decades.

INDUSTRIAL DEVELOPMENT IN INDEPENDENT ZAMBIA

As indicated already, Zambia inherited from the colonial era, a severely distorted economy, overwhelmingly dependent on the mining sector. Within industry as a whole, manufacturing was seriously underdeveloped. The new government led by President Kenneth Kaunda wanted to diversify the economy and in particular to build the manufacturing sector while retaining the primacy of the mines. Initially, they had hoped that the private sector would set up the needed industries. As this was a period considerable boom for mining, the new leaders expected that foreign investors would be attracted to Zambia and would build factories and workshops throughout the nation. The state, for its part, would build the infrastructure.[12] In general the idea was that the drive towards industrialisation would be a market-led affair. Later on it became clear that this strategy would be a non-starter and the regime began a more active policy of import substitution which, unfortunately, was neither clearly defined nor carried out.

A short-term advantage was that the government of the Republic of Zambia (GRZ) started with considerable funds for its development policies. Revenues to the government were very high following independence (changes in the tax structure, royalty payments, etc.). In a deft move, on the eve of independence the Zambian leaders negotiated an end to the long period of payment of royalties to the BSACo. A serious disadvantage came when the Rhodesian Front government, led by Ian Smith, declared itself unilaterally independent of Britain, the (in)famous UDI. The former and dominant federal partner now was not only economically dominant but hostile to Zambia. Transport links to the south were in doubt; supply of electricity from the Kariba Dam could be cut off overnight and Zambians had to find new sources of consumer goods and mining inputs (78, p.112). However, even this cut-off Rhodesia did not have to harm the economy in the long run, for it could effectively protect local manufacturers who previously had to compete against settler industrialists in Rhodesia.

Partly because of UDI and partly because foreign capital did not flow into the country (and in fact mineral revenues continued to flow out), in 1968 the political leadership took a more interventionist path, based on import substitution and state ownership of key industries. Basing many actions on President Kaunda's philosophy of Humanism, a new era of social welfare and state participation began for Zambia. Following the suggestions of the developmental experts of the early 1960s, especially those affiliated with the ILO and UN, in the First National Development Plan (1966–1971) the planners used much of the capital from the copper-bottomed treasury to build the national infrastructure as well as to expand services to the neglected population. Some expansion by private firms in manufacturing occurred but this was almost exclusively light industry. As Michael Faber pointed out in 1971, most of the industries which were established after 1964 confined their activities to two aspects of the manufacturing sector: the production of 'components of the building industry' and the production of 'African household goods' (15, p.300). An exception to this generalization was the basic metal products and fabricated metal products industry which had developed on the Copperbelt and served the needs of the mines, railways and government public works. Although few in number and using technologically simple processes, these companies represented the nucleus of a capital goods industry, a very important advantage to the country if fostered properly (68, pp.1–30).

As the new governing class settled into power in the first decade of independence, its class character became more apparent. As there was no African bourgeoisie in the country to speak of, the regime was staffed by people Poulantzas refers to as the new petty bourgeoisie. Unlike the traditional petty bourgeoisie of shopkeepers, artisans and small peasants, this new petty bourgeoisie consisted of clerical workers, supervisors and salaried personnel in modern industry and commerce (50, passim). Their ranks were swelled by a large number of political workers and a few technocrats and, with backing from a rural peasantry, they formed the political backing for the new governing class.

In order to meet many of the demands of its constituency, the UNIP government embarked on an active social welfare policy and also a series of economic practices which essentially made some businesses available to African capitalists. Before the planning period ended in 1971, the government undertook more aggressive actions through nationalisation in order to direct existing industry to invest in factories and agricultural projects, and to satisfy its constituency in the petty bourgeoisie and aspirant bourgeoisie. The GRZ then established a large parastatal network to manage their acquisitions. With the Mulungushi reforms of 1968, President Kaunda announced the takeover of twenty-six firms, mostly foreign-owned, in retail, commercial building materials, construction, road transport and breweries. In August of 1969 (Matero Reforms), Kaunda demanded (and received) a majority share of the two mining companies, reorganising them into two joint venture companies, NCCM and RCM. In 1970 the state attempted to nationalise major financial institutions. This failed, but the GRZ did obtain control over local insurance companies and building societies. Again in 1973 the government took greater control over the mines. The state's shares in these diverse sectors were put under three separate parastatal organisations: MINDECO (for mining), INDECO (for manufacturing) and FINDECO (for financial institutions) and they were all eventually placed under an umbrella parastatal ZIMCO with President Kaunda in the chairman's seat. To staff these parastatals, the numbers of civil servants and technocrats expanded, and these elements became major fractions within the evolving governing class of Zambia.

100

The first decade of independence was an exciting one. In many ways the FNDP was quite successful in meeting its goals. By 1972 much of the infrastructure begun in the early periods was established or nearly so. Stage two of Kafue Dam Hydroelectric project was near completion; the Victoria Falls generating station was operating and the second station under construction. The principal cities, industrial centres and the majority of towns along the line-of-rail were now supplied with cheap electric power. For transport, 3000 kms of tarmac had been laid by the end of 1971. The Great North Road (822 kms to the Tanzanian border) and the Great East Road (430 kms to Malawi) were completed. A K10 million railway workshop at Kabwe had started operation in October 1971. An oil pipeline was completed; a petroleum refinery was almost done and the Lusaka Airport was now receiving international flights.

Although manufacturing was the weak sister behind mining, it too had expanded. Its overall contribution to the GDP had gone from K28.2 million (6.1 per cent) in 1964 to K162.7 million (11 per cent) in 1972. Although many of these parastatal firms had been privately owned and profitable ones, which by definition meant consumer goods industry, some large-scale intermediate goods industries were now functioning. These included the Zambia Clay Industries (1969), Truck Assembly Plant at Luanshya, Chilanga Cement Ltd. expansion, Dunlop Zambia Ltd. (1969), Kafue Textiles Ltd. (1970), Kabwe Industrial Fabrics Ltd. (1970), Nitrogen Chemicals of Zambia Ltd. (1970), and Kafironda Explosives (1970) (52, pp.21–23). Most of these new companies were set up by the state and run as subsidiaries by the parastatal INDECO.

Encouraged by these results, the new governing class planned further expansion and diversification of secondary industry, including the first attempt to fabricate copper into an end product within Zambia (Zamefa) and for state companies to do local metal work and engineering (Monarch

TABLE 3
ZAMBIAN GDP BY KIND OF ECONOMIC ACTIVITY (IN PRODUCERS'
VALUES AT CONSTANT 1970 PRICES) (K MILLION)

Kind of Econ. Activity	1975	1977	1979	1981	1983
Agriculture	157.0	168.2	160.0	180.0	172.3
Mining	427.9	469.7	390.8	433.3	469.6
Manufacturing	165.4	152.4	163.0	180.0	181.9
Total GDP	1435.5	1446.5	1369.9	1484.0	1476.5

Source: Republic of Zambia, *Monthly Digest of Statistics*, vol.20, nos.4 to 6 (April/ June), 1984 (Central Statistical Office: Lusaka, 1985), Table 51, p.48.

Zambia Ltd. and Lenco). In the period of the Second National Development Plan (1972–1976), state-owned companies were to take over more existing firms and set up new factories to provide other consumer and intermediate goods. Investments in roads, railways, schools and clinics continued as the country remained short of such human and physical resources. State capitalism in Zambia had a populist face, for its focus was to lessen the power of external capital, to diversify the economy and also to provide base needs for the mass of the population. The reality was more inequitable. According to World Bank income distribution statistics, by 1976 the top 10 per cent of the population controlled 46 per cent of household incomes and the top 20 per cent controlled 60 per cent of household incomes.[13]

The bottom fell out of the copper market, beginning in 1974 and continuing into the late 1980s. Since the whole high cost industrialisation effort rested on the ready supply of foreign exchange (FOREX) from the mines, the FOREX shortage weakened secondary industry too. Factory production fell back to the level of the early 1970s, wage employment stagnated. The contribution of manufacturing to the GDP grew slowly until becoming completely static in the early 1980s while the value of mining in 1983 was fractionally less than in 1977 (see Table 3). Between 1975 to 1983, the GDP barely grew at all when measured in 1970 constant prices, and with the constantly increasing population, per capita income shrank too. Agricultural production expanded but slowly, affected by a serious regional drought. A cycle of shortage of FOREX and declining production set in as so many of the big parastatal firms were heavily import-dependent. By the time of the Fourth National Development Plan, capital to develop the more risky areas of intermediate and capital goods was just not available. With high costs and only a national market to service, these later stages of import-substitution were never launched. Zambia got stuck at the early phase 1 of 'easy' consumer goods import substitution.

The implications of some of the early choices about industrialisation came home to roost. As Ann Seidman pointed out in the early 1970s, the new and nationalised parastatal companies were heavily concentrated in the consumer goods area, using capital-intensive technology and often oriented towards luxury production for a few rather than necessities for the many. She argued that the value of local production was declining in these boom years as parastatal firms relied heavily on imported materials, technology, skilled expatriate manpower and, of course, machinery and spares. In some industries (e.g. wood and wood products, paper and paper products, chemicals, chemical petroleum and plastic products, basic metal products and non-metallic mineral products) import intensity was growing rather than declining despite the overall strategy of import substitutions (60, p.101).

Other critics, such as Taffare Tesfachew, argued that the state over-looked an important advantage that it inherited at independence. 'Then the state should have concentrated on developing the capital goods sectors while leaving consumer goods and service industries to private capital. In particular, the mining sector should have been utilised as a market or stimulus for developing locally based engineering industries. This could have been achieved by encouraging the establishment of local engineering industries through direct and indirect incentive and redirecting the purchasing pattern of the mining companies from external to internal sources' (68, p.19). Instead for the fifteen-year period from 1964 to 1979, the amount of foreign exchange spent on capital goods imports (including inputs for the mines) had increased fourfold (68, p.20).

An important addition to these arguments about Zambia's failed import substitution industrialisation is that many of the choices undertaken were predetermined by the inherited economic base, the events just after independence and by the class character of the new regime. Without adequate human and physical infrastructure, any development is impossible, so the regime began with these major projects. UDI derailed the early industrialisation plan as the government had to emphasise delinking from Southern Rhodesia as quickly as possible and trying to develop alternatives to the Southern trade route. Without a true local or even settler bourgeoisie, it was not possible to leave the development of many consumer goods industries to private capital, yet these wage goods were greatly in demand and the traditional supplies came from Southern Rhodesia and South Africa. Finally, emphasising capital goods through state control would have required managerial and technical skills that the new government did not have. To allow these factories to continue in private hands would have required the new regime to rely on a small group of white capitalists on the Copperbelt and on some firms such as the Anglo-American Corporation of South Africa Ltd., an unpalatable alternative.

In many ways, the industrialisation path that Zambia took suited the evolution of its petty bourgeoisie, but the strategy was based on a con-tinued availability of FOREX. This kind of import substitution shifted the vulnerability of the Zambian manufacturing sector from the stage of fin-ished consumer goods upstream to dependency on imported inputs and technology and machinery. Foresight was sadly lacking about integrating the industrial sector as a whole and providing inputs to agriculture. For example, little attention was given to producing or growing important raw material inputs for the factories. In 1979 the General Manager of ROP (1975) (Refined Oil Products – a parastatal which produces cooking oil, bath soap, detergents and toiletries) estimated that 70 per cent of the raw materials in RPO's processing was imported.[14]

By the early 1980s, this economy, like others in Africa and elsewhere, was in a serious economic crisis. Implementation of development plans had largely ceased; corruption had become widespread at all levels of economic and political life; the country was now heavily in debt; and the mining and manufacturing sectors were in bad straits.[15] In desperation, the Zambian government undertook both an IMF-suggested structural readjustment programme and an IMF-sponsored system of allocation of FOREX through an auction. This involved a general opening up of the economy both for any new foreign investors and for local companies which could now charge 'economic prices' for their scarce commodities. Because the parastatal companies had to bid with all the others for FOREX, there has been a rapid inflation in prices of goods from government-owned firms as well as gouging by private merchants. The price of fuel increased by over 100 per cent at the end of the first week following the start of auctioning. The Zambian Sugar Company and soap manufacturers raised prices between 50 and 100 per cent on 22 October 1985 barely two weeks after they had been raised last.[16] This rapid inflation was particularly difficult for the lowest income groups in the urban areas which had become common users of these commodities. Important social services such as free health care and free secondary schools were being terminated.[17] Still the economy did not respond, primarily because the mines were now in a serious internal crisis of production themselves. In January 1986, following a World Bank sponsored rationalisation scheme, the government announced a five-year production and investment plan for the mines which meant the closure of seven mining operations and the loss of 5,000 jobs.[18] The manufacturing sector, so dependent upon FOREX from the mines, contracted as well. With capacity utilisation rates averaging below 50 per cent in many INDECO firms, shortages worsened. Despite the explicit purpose of beginning import substitution with wage level consumer goods, more and more luxury goods (many of South African origin) appeared on the shelves, well beyond the income of the average Zambian, while many necessities were hard to find (7, passim).

Another step in the sad decline of Zambia's industrial sector is that various of the parastatal companies are now up for sale, a further response to IMF terms and local conditions. In 1987 INDECO announced the sale of 49 per cent of its shares in the Lusaka ROP edible oil and soap factory to the American food processor, H.J. Heinz and Company.[19]

Other firms which have not been able to find a buyer or investor are just going to the wall. In many ways, Zambia in the 1980s is becoming deindustrialised and denationalised. On 1 May, 1987, following riots on the Copperbelt, President Kaunda announced his intention to stop following the IMF directives and to start a more domestically-oriented development strategy. It is difficult to see how that can occur with no reserves, little ability to attract foreign capital, a demoralised civil service and a population struggling to cope with high inflation and frequent shortages. No coherent alternative development strategy had been announced and it is likely that Zambia will return to the IMF for yet another round of economic punishment. And the situation worsens. On 2 October, 1987 the IMF declared that Zambia is not eligible for further recourse to IMF funds until the government repays some US$300 million in arrears.[20]

What went wrong with Zambia's industrialisation strategy? In general the petit bourgeois leadership seemed unable to design a plan to integrate the industries by maximising backward and forward linkages. Choice of final products and individual takeovers were done in haphazard isolation and the investments were neither vertically nor horizontally integrated. The whole economy suffered heavily when the price of base metals collapsed, for it was the foreign exchange earnings from copper and cobalt which paid for infrastructure, manufacturing and a comfortable lifestyle for the new leaders of business and government.[21]

For Zambia, ISI did not significantly alleviate the balance of payments constraint nor did it launch a strong (though protected) manufacturing sector. Rather, it led to a growing dependence in manufacturing on import- and capital-intensive technology which did not create extensive employment opportunities or lead to indigenous technological development. In short, the new local ruling class's path to industrial development, based primarily on the creation and expansion of secondary consumer goods industries, did not work. When the mines' income collapsed, so did the industrial development plan. The future in the urban areas seems to be one of denationalisation and deindustrialisation, increasing income inequality and misery for the poor.

MALAWI: INDUSTRY IN AN AGRICULTURAL ECONOMY

When discussing Malawian industry, it is tempting to dismiss its industrial profile as "not very much". Yet this would be an understatement, as manufacturing, mining and construction have expanded since independence although at a much slower pace than estate agriculture. In 1984 12.3 per cent of its GDP arose from manufacturing, with an additional

2.0 per cent from utilities and 3.9 per cent from construction (14, p.3). This is despite the fact that most investment has not been in industry but rather in tobacco and sugar: an export-oriented, agriculturally-based strategy. As John McCracken notes, 'Malawi's record of economic growth and agricultural self-sufficiency in the 1970s led some researchers, particularly those connected with the World Bank, to cite Malawi, as an example of a successful "free market" economy' (33, p.3). In the second half of the 1980s, this positive image began to crack. The export sector went into a decline and the Malawi people carry a heavy debt burden to pay for new estate companies and for some large prestige and infrastructural projects. How has industry evolved in the modern Malawian economy and what has been the strategy for this sector?

At independence in 1964 the Malawian economy consisted of three interdependent subeconomies: the estate economy, the peasant cash-cropping economy and the labour reserve economy. These economies were connected, as it was the peasant sector which supplied most of the manpower both to the large national plantations and to other nations in the region. The first two economies were agricultural, and not surprisingly agriculture contributed around 55 per cent of the GDP in that year. There was almost no mining and a very limited manufacturing sector.[22] In addition there was processing of tea, grading and packaging of tobacco and ginning of cotton (69, pp.44–45), along with some construction, water and electricity. The modern sector was almost completely owned by Europeans (the large-scale enterprises) or Asians (distribution and transport).[23]

As with Zambia, the new leadership demanded access to the modern sectors of the economy – the estates, commerce and manufacturing. It also attempted to tackle the chronic problem of land shortage and to increase national overall economic growth. Unlike Zambia, however, the Malawi Congress Party (MCP) and President Dr. Hastings Kamuzu Banda approached development from an explicitly capitalist vantage point. Three phases of post-federation policies can be distinguished. First is the period from 1962 to 1965 which coincided with the first national development plan and was characterised by the continuation of many of the trading links of the federation days. Second, from late 1965 to the end of the 1970s, was the beginning of pragmatic moves to speed economic growth, dictated by President Banda. In this period the state encouraged a degree of import substitution industrialisation, and new corporations appeared in estate agriculture producing tobacco and sugar. This expansion was largely conducted by parastatals and financed from within by squeezing the peasant economy and by drawing cash from the commercial banks. Finally, in the period since the early 1980s, Malawi's indebtedness had led to more and more of its economic planning being tailored to suit the demands of the World Bank and the IMF. By the mid-1980s a slow opening up of marketing had taken place through liberalisation measures which have also incorporated an end to the minimal protectionism of domestic manufacturing.

A radical theorist within the MCP, Dunduza Chisiza, designed the first National Plan (1962–65) to stimulate production within agriculture and industry, with the goals of providing income for the masses and reducing inequities in the distribution of income, wealth and economic power (42, pp.53–56). Chisiza died in 1962 and thereafter President Banda's conservative pragmatism became the guiding force behind state actions. As Simon Thomas had put it, 'To a considerable extent, Malawi's economic policies are those of Banda himself' (69, pp.32). Banda did not seem to have any strong ideas about industrialising the country. Rather his attentions were divided between gaining hegemony over the MCP, dealing with the crisis of land shortage for the peasantry and increasing export earnings. Malawi entered into a formal trade agreement with Southern Rhodesia in 1964 which allowed the free entry of Rhodesian products into Malawi to be compensated by an intergovernmental payment (21, p.243). This undercut any stimulus for new weaker manufacturing and also ensured the availability of many goods to agriculture and commerce. In many ways, such an agreement extended the trading arrangement of federation.

TABLE 4
MALAWI: ANNUAL GROWTH RATES FOR MANUFACTURING AND CONSTRUCTION (VOLUME AND EMPLOYMENT) AND FOR ELECTRICITY PRODUCTION

Item	Period	Annual Growth Rate %
Total Manufacturing Volume	1970–1980	9.4
of which:		
Food, beverage and tobacco		11.3
Footwear, clothing and textiles		14.1
Other goods		10.0
Intermediate goods for construction		4.2
Export industries		7.2
Manufacturing employment	1968–1979	7.6
Construction real value	1973–1980	6.9
Construction employment	1968–1979	6.8
Electricity production	1969–1980	11.7

Source: Kydd and Christensen, Table 3, p.361.

107

After Banda suppressed the Cabinet Revolt of 1964, he turned to extract unused land from the plantations, redistributing it to the land-hungry peasantry and increasing his political backing in the countryside (69, passim). He also began the Gwelo No.2 Plan which involved the construction of a new capital at Lilongwe, the building of a lakeshore road and a university. Despite such expenditures, another of his intentions was to eliminate the budgetary deficit which was being bridged by U.K. grants-in-aid. In order to do so, he had to maximise economic growth and limit government recurrent expenditures. Expenditures were reined in by a limit set on health, education and defence budgets, the three largest items in most African state budgets. In order to expand economic growth and gain more foreign exchange, the focus was on expanding estate agriculture, especially tobacco.

From late 1965 through the 1970s a series of changes can be seen in the initial approach, some of which involved industry. After the Rhodesian UDI in November 1965, the Malawi government abrogated the Rhodesian trade agreement and began to encourage private investors while supplementing their activities by state participation in the Malawi Development Corporation. Encouragement took the form of improved industrial sites, liberal tax regulations, financial incentives for capital investments, tight regulation of the labour market and tariff barriers against Rhodesian goods. An effect of these policies was that more consumer goods industries were established within Malawi. Imports of consumer goods declined as a share in Malawi's total imports from 42 per cent in 1964 to 21 per cent in 1973 (69, p.44). The new protectionism reduced Rhodesia's share of Malawi's imports from 39 per cent at independence to 15 per cent in 1973 (69, p.44). After the establishment of a small-scale industry unit within the Industrial Division of the Ministry of Trade, Industry and Tourism in 1977, a trickle of small entrepreneurs in manufacturing appeared.

Manufacturing as a whole experienced a very rapid growth rate, averaging 16 per cent from independence to 1973 and 9.4 per cent from 1970 to 1980 (28, pp.355–375), but these figures must be considered in the light of the very small base. This expansion was mostly import-substitution led by the consumer goods sector, yet intermediate goods for construction and manufacturing by the export industries also grew. Although the new factories absorbed some workers, in general the scale was too small to lessen the unemployment problem for the country or to make much of a dent on migrant labour (see Table 4). The policy was predicated on attracting foreign investors who often brought with them capital-intensive technology. In cases where private capital was reluctant, Banda nationalised or established new industries via state-owned corporations and these

108

tended to be capital-intensive as well. Most small African businessmen stayed in the retail side of business.

The construction industry also boomed in this decade as 30 per cent of the development budget went to improving transport, upgrading existing roads, construction of the Lakeshore Road and building a new rail link with the Indian Ocean (69, p.45). Its rate of expansion averaged 20 per cent from 1968 to 1973. Electricity, another component of modern industry, also expanded at the rate of 11.7 per cent from 1969 to 1980. In addition to this growth, there was a considerable localisation of ownership in the modern economy. The government took shares in the larger economic enterprises; individuals (mostly the president and other senior members of the MCP) bought into many firms and established estate companies. In the 1970s many Europeans on leasehold estates had their licences cancelled and later on Asians in distribution and transport suffered the same fate (69, p.44).

The class nature of the regime was manifesting itself with these changes. A very small land- and capital-owning class of Africans and Europeans sat at the top of the social pyramid, above a traditional and new petit bourgeoisie of shop owners and civil servants. A minuscule working class existed in and around Blantyre while a much larger stratum of landless rural poor (a rural proletariat) laboured on the estates and the farms of the capitalist small-scale farmers. Dr. Banda personally owns large tracts of plantation lands and commerce and industry. State capitalism was paralleled by private capitalism, led by Banda's party. Unlike Zambia, the group at the top was a very exclusive set indeed. In response to the political pressures of the peasantry, the government purchased underutilised lands on the tea plantations and redistributed them, but the problem of land shortage persisted, aggravated by the new accumulation by the ruling class.

To finance its policy of export promotion, the government took a two-pronged approach. Recurrent expenditures, especially education and health, were squeezed as a proportion of the government budget.[24] A surplus was extracted from the peasant agriculture through the state monopoly exercised over the marketing organisation ADMARC. Tobacco prices were high in the 1970s, so when ADMARC paid the peasant producers a low, fixed price (most of the estates were permitted to market their own produce), the agency gained large profits which were then used for state-directed investment. The commercial banks were also drawn upon to supply capital to the new export-oriented companies, especially Press (Holdings) Ltd., 90 per cent owned by Dr. Banda. In many ways, the Malawian case is a striking one, for the government turned the terms of trade dramatically against its own population, not to build industry, but

Studies in the Economic History of Southern Africa

to use the surplus to expand estate agriculture and to enrich the new bourgeoisie which held shares in these companies. To enforce such unpopular policies, the regime became progressively more authoritarian in the 1970s.

The social and international trade effects of these policies manifested themselves in the 1980s. The heavy tax on peasants through the state crop marketing board eventually led to declining average return to labour in peasant agriculture (28, p.370). The government promotion of tobacco estate development at all costs caused a misallocation for financial resources which in the era of low prices for tobacco meant a financial crisis in that agroindustry in 1980 onward. The costs of Gwelo 2 Plan largely had to be reimbursed in foreign exchange, causing a heavy drain on the national export earnings. Malawi's public foreign debt went from $229.6 million in 1974 to $718.6 million in 1983 and the debt service ratio from 7.8 per cent in 1974 to 20.3 per cent in 1982. Although such a debt service ratio is not high in the light of some other low income debtors, the escalation from a modest to a considerable draw on export earnings is remarkable (see Table 5).

TABLE 5
MALAWI'S FOREIGN DEBT SERVICE RATIO,
1974–1983 ($ MILLIONS AND PERCENTAGE)

Item	1974	1976	1978	1979	1980	1981	1982	1983
Public Foreign debt	229.6	294.6	504.1	510.6	646.9	682.0	705.6	718.6
Debt service ratio(%)	7.8	8.5	17.0	17.7	21.8	27.8	20.3	–

Source: Economist Intelligence Unit, *Quarterly Economic Review of Zimbabwe, Malawi*, no.1, 1986, p.33, Appendix 2.

Malawi's expansion of agriculture and industry did not lessen the regional imbalance of its economy. By 1983 it had replaced its old dependence on Rhodesia (now Zimbabwe) with South Africa. Although the U.K. remained the principal destination of exports (28% in 1983), imports now mainly came from South Africa (39 per cent of imports in 1983 as compared to 13 per cent from the U.K. and 8 per cent from West Germany) (14, p.3). Domestic production had replaced many consumer goods, so imports were now more and more industrial inputs, machinery and transport equipment and intermediate goods rather than consumer goods, but the balance of trade was now chronically in deficit.

By the mid-1980s Malawi, one of the international donors' few 'success

110

stories', had become a regular World Bank recipient and thus subject to Bank and Fund policies. In 1986 the Malawian government was seeking a new structural adjustment loan (SAL) from the World Bank ($70 million over two years) to be matched by co-financing from the USA, West Germany and Japan, to make a total package of $114 million (14, p.28). In order to get this loan, Malawi's politicians and planners had to promise to tackle problems in agriculture and industry. It is hard to guess what overall effect this 'liberalisation' will have on agriculture as some policies seem contradictory. For example, Malawi is supposed to phase out smallholder fertiliser subsidies, a plan guaranteed to drive down productivity of the peasant yet further. However, it is also supposed to lessen the monopoly of ADMARC, a step which could help many smallholders increase their returns from farming.

What effects will 'liberalisation' have on industry? Malawi is committed to abolishing price controls, ending the sheltering of monopolistic firms behind industrial licensing regulations by lessening tariff protection, and allocating foreign exchange to imports that compete with domestic production. These free trade policies, if invoked, are likely to destroy the fragile industrial component of national income. On the other hand, new mining legislation and involvement of foreign donors have resulted in prospecting and even the development of coal mines in Malawi, adding a new element to the overall industrial picture.[25]

For international capital, industrialisation was never a goal for Malawi, from colonial times to the present. Malawi's role was to be an exporter of cheap agricultural produce and labour. With independence, however, basic economic nationalism and regional politics dictated that the politicians try to supply more consumer goods domestically and to develop the nation's infrastructure beyond the rudiments inherited in 1964. Another goal was to diversify agriculture away from a limited number of plantation crops by introducing new ones. Banda's economic policies always had a strong pragmatic streak and so the orientation away from trade dependence on Rhodesia was replaced with a strong industrial dependency on South Africa. Although very much a proponent of foreign investment and free enterprise, Banda was willing to nationalise and expropriate as it suited his political and personal interests. Out of this mixture of motivations, a simple secondary industrial sector grew along with construction and electricity, and now supplemented by mining. That industrial kernel is threatened, however, by the free trade policies of the World Bank. It is most likely that the next decade will see Malawi return to its agricultural roots, albeit a more diversified sector now.

IMPORT SUBSTITUTION INDUSTRIALISATION
IN ZIMBABWE: AN UNFINISHED STORY

Zimbabwe has had quite a different experience with import substitution from that of its two neighbours. This is in part due to the different starting point, in part the peculiar economic circumstances of UDI, and finally in part because the settler bourgeoisie cooperated with the state although its immediate interests were not expressed in UDI. In many ways, the Smith government, with the help of the private sector, deepened import substitution in an era of relative isolation. Whether the Mugabe government will continue this adventurous kind of import substitution is unclear while under heavy pressure from the World Bank for more economic liberalisation and without a strong constituency in a national bourgeoisie.

The economy under UDI had two distinct phases: the first decade was one of boom (1965–1975) while the war economy (1976–1979) was one of contraction. The Smith regime inherited an economy fattened from the good years of Federation, with the basic industrial infrastructure completed, and balanced with its reliance on agriculture and manufacturing as well as mining. However, the first two and a half years after the end of Federation showed how rapidly these conditions could change. When the protectionism and privileged markets of the Federation disappeared in 1962, investment income flowed out of the country while new capital failed to come in. UDI came at an important stage – capturing much of the foreign capital and forcing the private capitalists and state into close cooperation to build the manufacturing sector, especially in the intermediate and capital goods areas.

In the first decade of UDI, the whole economy expanded. From 1964 to 1974 the annual growth rate in real terms was 7.4 per cent while per capita growth was 3.8 per cent (29, p.55). For Zimbabwe (and Zambia), official estimates of manufacturing production tend to be underestimates because no satisfactory solution has yet been found to account properly for manufacturing activities of the mining companies. Still, it is clear that the manufacturing sector boomed under this form of protectionism. Between 1966 and 1974 the overall annual growth rate of manufacturing by volume was 9.6 per cent (76, p.156). Textiles, basic metals and metal products subsectors expanded rapidly. The number of products produced by manufacturing went from 1,059 in 1966 to 3,837 in 1970 with the number of units employing more than 10 workers going from 665 to 1,036 (65, pp.1–3).

Capital goods, that precious and fragile sector, grew in these earlier years of UDI. Developmental orthodoxy argues that capital goods are

112

difficult to establish in low income countries because they require a large scale, much capital intensity, a large market, and technological complexity. In the face of these opinions, local capitalists with the backing of the government made significant strides in the development of machinery and spares. Cut off from many foreign suppliers (and also from inhibiting patent laws!), Rhodesian companies began to manufacture a wide variety of machinery and equipment for the mining sector, including switch gear, conveyor idlers, ventilation ducting, mine cars, hydraulic equipment, ball mills, and rail and rolling stock (37, p.149). Many of these firms were medium or small in size and a large proportion of them were locally owned (37, p.149). The engineering industry began to service factories and other priority sectors such as commercial agriculture, construction, transport, mining, energy and telecommunications. This capital goods subsector provided backward linkages for the steel industry as these small firms used steel products. Under extensive government/private sector cooperation, skills were developed and local researchers augmented and introduced new technology to provide appropriate processes for the other plants.

In the long run, therefore, whether an economy will develop local capital-goods capacity or not will depend on the extent to which the state protects the economy from perpetual dependence on foreign skills and technology, and also prepares to forgo short-term political, social and economic gains in order to divert investment to institutions and industries that will augment local skill formation (68, p.5).

Mining remained highly concentrated and with government help in breaking sanctions, it continued to remain export-oriented. Local integration increased with more smelting of ores done domestically. Chromium, for example, which had been exported in its raw form, was now exported as the far more valuable ferrochrome alloys. Mining grew through 1977 with foreign investment for expansion and rehabilitation projects in chromium, copper, nickel and iron and steel. The mining sector also used more locally produced inputs, although the manufacturing sector absorbed only a small proportion of the minerals produced in Rhodesia.

An important indicator of the degree of industrialisation of any country is the existence of an iron and steel industry. In Rhodesia, that industry provided semi-finished and finished steel products for the capital goods sector, accounted for much of the rapid overall expansion of metal and metal products subsectors, and demonstrated the cooperation between the state, and large-scale foreign and domestic capital. During UDI, the Rhodesian Iron and Steel Company (RISCO) plant at Que Que (now KweKwe) was expanded in three phases, raising total capacity from 400,000 tons to 1 million tons of castings per year (43, p.13). A sanctions-busting foreign company (Voerst Alpine from Austria) supplied the latest technology and involved the state in steel producing joint ventures with large companies, both local (Morewear), South African (Anglo-American, Stewarts & Lloyds), and British (John Brown, British Steel and many others) (65, p.283). Since the Rhodesian market could only consume between one quarter and one third of the output of RISCO (38, p.15), the regime then had to aggressively market its raw steel, mostly to South Africa. The result was 'a large iron and steel industry, fed by local raw materials, which in turn feeds a large mechanical engineering industry, well-integrated with other industrial sectors' (76, p.151).

Whether or not these policies were thoroughly conscious is not clear from the literature, but the kind of gut-level economic nationalism of the white regime in rebel Rhodesia led them to undertake the more difficult and perilous stages of ISI. Deepening import substitution worked for Rhodesian industry because the international regulations closed the economy to much external involvement yet sanctions-busting allowed the regime to sell its minerals and tobacco abroad to obtain FOREX. Further, the country could obtain vital materials such as petroleum and technology via its ally South Africa as well as sell textiles and steel to South Africa. Most importantly, the government followed an industrial integration plan which it enforced with an iron fist and, after an initial period of opposition, gained the cooperation of much of the local white bourgeoisie and foreign capital.

However, the overall picture was not so rosy. Much of the cost of this economic miracle was paid for by the African population whose real wages dropped. The consumer goods sector was distorted away from the production of cheap wage goods to the production of luxury goods for the very narrow white market. The chemicals and petrochemicals subsectors remained underdeveloped, which has serious implications for continued import dependency in the commercial, agricultural and manufacturing sectors. The nation became more and more economically dependent on South Africa. Finally, the arrogance of the Smith regime exacerbated conditions locally, fuelling the war for liberation by the African people in the second half of the 1970s.

This growing and seemingly internally self-reliant economy took a serious downturn in the period from 1974 to independence in 1980. The economy was negatively affected both by the world recession and by the stepping up of the war for independence. Davies and Stoneman argue that the economy would have declined anyway because it had passed the easy first phase of import substitution. Manufacturing production (measured by volume) went down 27 per cent from 1974 to 1978 (11, pp.95–126). While the Rhodesians now had large stockpiles of iron and steel, the government had to loan RISCO large sums to keep it afloat. Company liquidations increased (29, p.65), and agriculture experienced a serious deterioration, mostly because the war was being fought in the countryside, driving many commercial farmers off the land and forcing peasants into subsistence agriculture. Despite these inauspicious features, the Smith government continued to invest in infrastructure, perhaps because of the pervasive belief that the white regime would last at least to the end of the century. For example, the government began a major overhaul of the railways and a very expensive coal thermal complex at Wankie Colliery (76, p.157).

As the war wound down in late 1979, the economy was in serious recession. Agriculture was not producing as much as it had a decade earlier; aging capital machinery in most of the country's factories meant that productivity was low; the policy of protecting white living standards and profits at the expense of black living standards made for an inadequate domestic market. Depressed prices for many base metals resulted in inadequate foreign exchange to service debts, buy key inputs and purchase new machinery. The Mugabe government inherited an economy whose industrial sector was worn out by the war and whose white skilled manpower was poised for flight.

INDUSTRIAL POLICIES IN INDEPENDENT ZIMBABWE

In the seven years since independence, the Zimbabwean economy has experienced three distinct phases in terms of economic growth. First was boom and reconstruction in the years of 1980/81. Second was a recession which was at its deepest from 1982 through 1983. In 1985 a third phase of slow recovery began, whose pace has been threatened by a severe and deepening shortage of FOREX. From 1986 through mid-1987 some sectors (manufacturing) stagnated while others (mining) experienced selective expansion.

Three non-industrial factors have contributed to this uneven pattern of economic growth. The region has experienced severe drought four years out of the seven since independence. The Zimbabwean economy is quite reliant on its agricultural sector to export raw materials and to feed itself. The commercial farming sector is also a central market for many of the goods of the manufacturing sector, and indirectly, for products from mining, for example phosphates for fertilizers. The second factor is external and that is the unsteady condition of the international economy, whose brief recoveries seem to be followed by ever deepening recessions. Connected to the health of the international political economy, are the

115

variable prices for many of Zimbabwe's traditional exports, which has affected FOREX earnings. Finally, tensions in the region over sanctions and countersanctions against the racist regime in South Africa spill over into the economic arena with uncertainties about key inputs, transport routes and a major market.

Mining, as a whole, has been hardest hit within the wider industrial sector. Although basic mining only contributes around 7.6 per cent to the GDP, it is a crucial source of FOREX. If one includes mining and refining of major metals such as ferrochrome and iron and steel, the contribution to total exports is around 43 per cent (74, p.417, Table 4). The devaluation of the Zimbabwe dollar, which renders the country's exports more competitive, decreases the actual value of the commodities in hard currency terms. From 1979 to 1984 while the local value of mineral production increased (from 315 $Z million to 546 $Z million – 54, passim), the actual value decreased. Also the devaluation makes the costs of inputs higher. In the non-ferrous metals subsector alone, 'between 1979 to 1984, the average value per ton ... increased by 65 per cent in Zimbabwe $ terms but decreased by 26 per cent in US$ terms and it should be noted that real (deflated) value of the US$ also decreased substantially over this period meaning that the real loss in value was well above this' (24, p.69).

In such a weak market, there is little incentive to expand production, so overall volume of minerals exported has remained below the 1980 level.[26] Fortunately the gold industry receives high prices and the increased sales of coal (domestically to Wankie Thermal) and chrome (in the form of ferrochrome alloys) have kept the sector from a serious recession. Very little new investment has come into mining; only gold mining seems to attract the eye of the foreign entrepreneur (an exception is Cluff Minerals). In general, a depressed outlook for base metals and state controls over repatriation of profits have not made the mining sector attractive for foreign capital. Also the costs of production (particularly for wages and electricity) undercut profitability so that local owners cannot (or choose not to) reinvest.

The Mugabe government has developed a complex strategy for dealing with this sector. The government has intervened directly in cases of marginal operations because of the negative effects on communities from large-scale unemployment with the closure of a mine; in the cases of the Messina copper mine and Kamativi Tin it has recognised the economic importance of the mines and given loans to hard pressed firms. A mining continuation fund was set up to supplement normal FOREX allocation to mines to help replace obsolete machinery and buy spares. In the crucial area of gold, the Reserve Bank introduced a gold price support scheme (Nov. 1984 Z$ 500 per fine ounce; Jan. 1987, Z$ 650) which has kept many small producers in business. The Zimbabwe Mining Development Corporation (ZMDC) promotes joint ventures in the mining area and the Mineral Marketing Corporation of Zimbabwe (MMCZ) sells all the minerals (except gold and silver) and thus exerts government policies without having to become directly involved in mining (54, p.130). In the crucial area of coal mining, the government expanded its ownership of Wankie Colliery, and took a large investment stake in the Hwange Thermal Power Station (42%) in partnership with foreign capital and the Anglo-American Corporation. This multilateral partnership was expanded further when a World Bank facility was used by the Zimbabwe Electricity Supply Commission (a parastatal) to purchase $5 million in spares to keep Hwange Power Station operating and thus to provide the key market for the colliery.[27] Although there continues to be friction between the big mines (represented by the Chamber of Mines) and the government (mostly through the person of the Minister of Mines and his Permanent Secretary), their mutual concern to keep this sector operating and exporting (e.g. the finance package for exporters) to supply the crucial funds for the rest of the economy has been uppermost.

Manufacturing has fallen on bad days since its early good performance in 1980–81 when it experienced an average 9.8 per cent growth. From 1982 through 1984 growth averaged only 0.4 per cent per year (54, p.3); from 1985 to early 1987, the growth rate has slightly increased. According to the Secretary for the Ministry of Industry and Technology Cde. Sam Geza, the volume of industrial production during the first six months of 1987 rose by only 1 per cent compared with the corresponding period during 1986.[28] In general manufacturing was stagnating in the mid-1980s.

Droughts, inflation in the costs of inputs, foreign exchange constraints are all cited for the lacklustre performance of this sector. The structural features of the sector are also responsible. First is the heavy import dependency of manufacturing. Despite its considerable degree of intersectoral links, manufacturing used about 45 per cent of all the commodities imported and is a net user of FOREX (72, vol.1, p.1). Second are the characteristics of the key subsectors. Metals and metal products are heavily dependent on non-ferrous metals and iron and steel, neither one of which is in good shape at the moment (1987). Foodstuffs and textiles are the most rapidly expanding subsectors, but these consumer goods industries are intimately linked to wages and inflation. Fortunately the textiles industry has undertaken a very aggressive export promotion strategy and is using its advantages in the region and links to the EEC to supply the country with a new leading export sector which is not based on the export of a primary commodity as with metals and tobacco. Finally, chemicals, a vital subsector to many other parts of the economy, absorbs on average 35 per cent of the FOREX allocations within manufacturing as a whole.[29] Because this subsector is technology- and capital-intensive, the likelihood of real import substitution is small.

Government policy for manufacturing was laid out in the Transitional National Development Plan and the First Five Year Development Plan. In general the emphasis in the industrial area has been more on the export promotion side than import substitution. A UNIDO study took up the current state of ISI and made some recommendations. It felt that ISI had to be extended into those intermediate sectors which had not been well-developed before, specifically, chemicals and non-metallic minerals. Also, further development of metals and transport equipment is vital. It pointed out that the potential of an expanded regional market, through the PTA and SADCC, might allow reasonable unit costs of production and reasonable economy of scale in plant size and technology. Underutilisation of existing capacity had to stop and the private sector should be given incentives to use local raw materials as the sector now imports 25 per cent of its raw materials (72, p.14). Finally, it emphasised the importance of protecting and fostering the capital goods industry.

On industrial integration, the government states its intentions to increase value addedness locally and to augment the linkages of mining with manufacturing. These goals, while admirable, face serious difficulties. First is the fact that while the mining industry produces a vast quantity and variety of minerals, the bulk of these are not likely to be consumed locally. Over 90 per cent of Zimbabwe's minerals are exported and this percentage is not likely to be altered in the near future, especially with the lack of expansion of the manufacturing sector. Second, the attempt to add value locally by increased local beneficiation is problematic. Certain moves, for example processing chromium ore into ferrochrome alloys, were very beneficial to the whole industry. There is talk of diversification into stainless steel, which would consume ferrochrome, steel and nickel – all locally mined. At present technological issues as well as finances and market size constrain this possibility. Conditions are even less positive for other base minerals or simple metals. For example, the regional market for copper semi-fabricated products is quite limited and the international market is currently contracting as copper is being replaced by fibre optics in many of its industrial uses. Iron and steel faces the same depressed international conditions and the greater scale and technological advancedness of the South African industry limits possibilities there. Producing a wider range of steel goods would meet with acceptance locally but the high cost of these inputs might price them out of the market. In the current market situation, further downstream processing of the widely diversified Zimbabwean mining sector is unlikely.

However, if sanctions and countersanctions come into force in the region, then the calculus changes. Research continues into stainless steel, nickel wire, spinning asbestos fibre, a coal-based chemical industry, upgrading magnesite, the production of tin plate and the manufacture of refractory products.[30] Although downstream integration for Zimbabwean mining is limited, possibilities remain for the industry to absorb a larger amount of goods from local manufacturing, especially if the capital goods industry can expand into the area of mining equipment and inputs. At the moment, the mines use a variety of locally manufactured products, estimated at about 47 per cent of the total. Being cut off from the South African market makes the economics of such upstream integration more attractive, even for the foreign mining groups.

By mid-1987, movement towards extending import substitution in manufacturing had been slow. The subsector of chemicals and drugs has been plagued with serious production problems, mostly connected to FOREX shortages for purchasing raw materials. The inadequacy of the plastics industry has had a ripple effect throughout the economy, with chronic shortages of packing materials affecting most consumer goods industries. Seemingly permanent shortages of rubber compounds have undercut the tyre and rubber components industry and the frequent shortage of types of tyres has affected the efficiency of transport. The metal products industry continues to remain strong, mostly because of a strong market for ferrochrome and steel exports. Aggressive regional marketing has extended the potential for textiles, steel, and various consumer goods, but the structural problems of regional trade and nationalistic behaviour of some of the participating states make these markets a bit unreliable and rather small. According to a recent financial press report, there is an overall lack of business confidence in Zimbabwe. Still, investment plans continue, although more towards replacement than expansion.[31] This is probably most strongly expressed in the locally-owned businesses. But capacity remains underutilised in many subsectors because of the complex problems of shortages of raw materials, inadequate markets and obsolescent and frequently out of commission capital machinery.

119

CONCLUSION

The industrial development of the region began with mining, and only in Zimbabwe has it truly deepened into a strong, diversified manufacturing sector. This is not accidental, but rather the result of interaction between material conditions, colonial inheritance, the interests of foreign capital, the class nature of those owning production and their alliances with those controlling the state. The continued agricultural focus of Malawi is perhaps to be expected given its particular colonial history, its overpopulation problem and the advantages of soil fertility and water around the great lake. Zambia's bold attempts to expand and diversify away from mining and build a modern infrastructure were doomed by the collapse of the copper price after 1974, the weaknesses inherent in Zambia's own planning, and the lack of a nationally directed bourgeoisie. Both Malawi and Zambia had to allocate major portions of their development capital to build the infrastructure which was so extremely underdeveloped under colonialism. Zimbabwe, in contrast, was the winner in the regional sweepstakes. Its more balanced economy attracted more foreign capital and its vocal settler population successfully pressured the government to lay the groundwork for modern industry.

When all three territories were bound together in Federation, the inequities intensified and Zimbabwe once again emerged as the chief recipient of investment, a considerable proportion of which went into manufacturing. These beneficial conditions did not extend into the 1980s, however. Now an independent Zimbabwe has to face the cold shoulder from international capital, declining terms of trade for its major exports, and a disjuncture between the interests of the domestic and foreign owners of industry and those of the new governing class.

The politics of industrialisation are as important as the physical resources. When the pre-existing economies were destroyed or distorted, international capital installed extractive mining and agricultural enclaves in Zambia and Malawi. In Colonial Rhodesia, however, a settler rural bourgeoisie was evolving into a truly national bourgeoisie with a base spread between mining, commerce and agriculture. It jostled for power with foreign capital and, under the particular circumstances of self-rule in 1923, was able to influence government to invest in infrastructure and undertake policies necessary for the next fifty years of industrial development.

Independence allowed the new petit bourgeoisies of these African nations to try their hands at industrial development, beginning with import substitution, partial nationalisation and various attempts at

120

developing human and physical infrastructure. Malawi's new ruling class quickly observed that the path to wealth lay with estate agriculture and so continued many of the colonial policies to extract wealth from the peasantry and the rural proletariat. Policies to develop industry were secondary, especially as most capital, intermediate and consumer goods could be obtained cheaply from Rhodesia or South Africa. Zambia's new governing class had grander plans – to obtain access to the foreign-owned sectors of the economy, both for its own traders and manufacturers, and to use the state to obtain control over the mines and large companies. The idea of lessening import dependency through the promotion of parastatal companies was not backed with an integrated industrial plan, however. When the copper revenues dried up, the manufacturing sector began to contract. Now even the mines are on hard times.

In Zimbabwe the local settler bourgeoisie appears to want to stay; international capital, while not investing, is at least not divesting rapidly. Many of those in power, despite the socialist rhetoric of the ZANU(PF) government, want to gain access to farms, shops, and trade. Others see the importance of protecting and sustaining the manufacturing sector. Large-scale international mining companies are not pouring into Zimbabwe, but existing mining groups are reinvesting and some local concerns have managed to profit from the boom in gold. Will the new leadership make an alliance with white capital, and act in a manner that will be politically unpopular (cutting education and health expenditures, for example) in order to extract capital for re-investment in this sector? Or will the state undertake a more socialist path to industrialisation, despite the capitalist nature of its economy?

NOTES

1. Integrated industry means that various industrial sectors – consumer, intermediate and capital goods – are interlinked and that the manufacturing sector has backward linkages, to a considerable degree, with the local mining industry. A well integrated economy also requires forward linkages to agriculture for both mining and manufacturing and for agriculture to supply for many inputs into industry.
2. Malawi in 1986 and 1987 is having to review this Import Substitution Industrialisation (ISI) emphasis under pressure from the World Bank.
3. For this chapter, industrial means divisions 1 to 5 of the International Standard Industrial Classification which includes mining and quarrying (division 1); manufacturing (divisions 2 and 3); construction (division 4); and electricity, gas and water and sanitary services (division 5).
4. By 1953 some 2.5 million Africans were living in Nyasaland and while Northern Rhodesia had an average population density of six people to the square mile and Southern Rhodesia had about ten, Nyasaland had over 60 (71, p.247).

5. 'Northern Rhodesia [was] divided into two areas for customs purposes: the Zambezi Basin area, south of a line drawn from the south-east corner of the Katanga pedicle to Fife on the Tanganyika border, which contains all the important industries in the Territory, and the area north of this line, which is included in the conventional Congo Basin area but which is of negligible importance from the commercial point of view. In the area within the Congo Basin no preference can be granted and customs duty is charged at the Empire rate on all goods whatever the country of origin.' Colonial Office, *Report of the Commission Appointed to Enquire into the Financial and Economic Position of Northern Rhodesia* (the Pim Report), Colonial No.145 (London: HMSO, 1938), par. 202 cited in A. Young p.13, note 42 to chapter 1. 'In 1935 the Customs Agreement between the two southern territories (South Africa and Southern Rhodesia) was replaced by a Trade Agreement. Under the new Agreement South African imports were subject to a preferential system of tariffs that were in many cases less than the low 'United Kingdom and Colonies' rates' (78, note 43 to Chapter 1).

6. In colonial days, all people from Nyasaland were called Nyasa despite their actual ethnicity.

7. A more typical major foreign company, Turner & Newall, handled approx. 90% of the territory's asbestos output as well as dominating the asbestos cement product industry, while a company like Lonrho limited its large investments to gold mining, cattle and later an oil pipeline.

8. In the 1950s Tindall estimated that 100,000 migrated per year (71, p.254).

9. Debates in the Legislative Council by the unofficial members especially Welensky exemplified this issue (78, p.14).

10. Northern Rhodesia remained under the Colonial Office and there was no significant increase in settler power in the Legislative Council (56, pp.211–12).

11. 'The Federation increased the [market] size of Southern Rhodesian industry from 2.95 million in 1952 to the Federal market of at least 8.73 million people in 1953' (29, p.48).

12. See the *Transitional National Development Plan* (Jan. 1965 to June 1966).

13. *World Development Report, 1985* (Oxford: O.U.P. 1985), p.228, Table 28.

14. Mr M.S. Nyirongo, General Manager of ROP (1975) Ltd. 'Industry in Zambia – Intentions versus Performance', *UNZA Business and Economics Journal* 1, 3 (June 1979), p.9.

15. The essays in Klaas Woldring (ed.), *Beyond Political Independence: Zambia's Development Predicament in the 1980's* (Berlin, 1984) detail many of these issues.

16. *Africa Research Bulletin*, Economic Series 22, 10 (30 Nov. 1985), p.7970 B-C.

17. *Financial Gazette* (Zimbabwe), 4 Sept. 1987, 'Fees will be introduced in all hospitals in Zambia. . .', p.13.

18. *Times of Zambia*, 31 Jan. 1986, p.1.

19. *Financial Gazette* (Zimbabwe), 13 March 1987, p.13.

20. *Financial Gazette* (Zimbabwe), 16 Oct. 1987, p.1.

21. Not all of Zambia's industry has failed, however. Those areas that have an inbuilt form of vertical integration have survived even those trying times. For example, Kafue Textiles has over the years of its operations managed to encourage the growing of cotton by a large number of smallholders in Central and Southern Provinces. The parastatal ginnery successfully supplies most of the needs of raw but cleaned cotton to the textile firms and a goodly portion of cotton seed to ROP for processing into vegetable oil. Perhaps one conclusion from this case is that successful industrial development for most newly independent countries cannot be separated from agricultural development. Textile development, however, has been the exception rather than the rule for Zambia and, even with this linkage effect, the cost of machinery, spares and skilled manpower has meant the end cost of cloth is far beyond the reach of most citizens. The company has countered with an aggressive export promotion drive, which makes economic sense but rather less human sense in such a core consumer goods industry.

22. At independence, there was 1 cigarette factory, 1 oil expression plant, 2 clothing factories, 2 blanket factories, 1 cement mill, 2 sweet factories, 1 soap factory, and 1 vehicle assembly plant which produced 20 vehicles in 1964.

23. In 1961 there were 8,750 Europeans and 10,630 Asians compared to approximately 5.5 million of African descent (13, p.48, Table 21).
24. Education and health had fallen from 23.3% in 1964 to 12.8% in 1973 despite a growing population (69, p.46).
25. Mr Fairbairn (Chief Mining Engineer, Lilongwe, Malawi), 'Small-Scale Mining in Malawi', paper presented to a SADCC Seminar, 3 Sept. 1987, Harare, pp.1–3.
26. *Financial Gazette* (Zimbabwe), 20 March 1987, p.4.
27. *Financial Gazette* (Zimbabwe), 23 Jan. 1987, p.1.
28. 'Business Herald', *The Herald*, 8 Oct. 1987, p.3.
29. Cde. Sam Geza, 'Business Herald', 8 Oct. 1987, p.3.
30. *Financial Gazette* (Zimbabwe), 26 Sept. 1986, P.16.
31. *Financial Gazette* (Zimbabwe), 19 Dec. 1986, p.7.

REFERENCES

1. African Economic Development, *Special Report on Zimbabwe*, April 1986
2. Arrighi, Giovanni, 'The Political Economy of Rhodesia' in *Essays on the Political Economy of Africa*, Giovanni Arrighi and John Saul (eds.), New York and London, 1973
3. Bank of Zambia, *Report and Statement of Accounts for the Years Ended 1984 and 1985*, Lusaka 1984 and 1985
4. Barber, William J., *The Economy of British Central Africa: A Case Study of Economic Development in a Dualistic Society*, London 1961
5. Burdette, Marcia M., 'The Dynamics of Nationalization Between Multinational Companies and Peripheral States: Negotiations between AMAX Inc., the Anglo-American Corporation of South Africa Ltd., and the Government of the Republic of Zambia', unpublished Ph.D. thesis, Columbia University, 1979
6. —, 'Were the Copper Nationalizations Worthwhile?' in *Beyond Political Independence: Zambia's Development Predicament in the 1980s*, Klaas Woldring (ed.), Berlin 1984
7. —, *Zambia: Between Two Worlds*, Boulder, Co., 1988
8. Chitala, D. Chintu-Ndya, 'Zambia's Import Substitution Industrialization and Its Role in the International Division of Labour', Mimeo, dated March 1982
9. Clarke, D.G., *Foreign Companies and International Investment in Zimbabwe*, London 1980
10. Daniel, Philip, *Africanization, Nationalization and Inequality: Mining Labour and the Copperbelt in Zambian Development* (University of Cambridge, Department of Applied Economics, Paper in Industrial Relations and Labour, No.4). Cambridge 1979
11. Davies, Rob and Stoneman, Colin, 'The Economy: An Overview' in *Zimbabwe's Inheritance*, Colin Stoneman (ed.), London 1981
12. Dickinson, Neal J., 'Performance and Prospects in Rhodesian Manufacturing Industry', *The Rhodesian Journal of Economics*, Vol.5, No.4, 1971
13. Dotson, Floyd and Dotson, Lillian, *The Indian Minority of Zambia, Rhodesia and Malawi*, New Haven, 1968
14. Economist Intelligence Unit, *Quarterly Economic Review of Zimbabwe, Malawi*, No.1, 1986
15. Faber, Michael, 'The Development of the Manufacturing Sector' in *Constraints on the Economic Development of Zambia*, Charles Elliot (ed.), Nairobi 1971
16. *The Financial Gazette* (Zimbabwe), 1985–86
17. Frank, A.G., *Capitalism and Underdevelopment in Latin America: Historical Studies of Chile and Brazil*, New York 1967
18. Franklin, Harry, *Unholy Wedlock: The Failure of the Central African Federation*, London 1963
19. Gann, Lewis H., *A History of Northern Rhodesia: Early Days to 1953*, London 1964
20. Good, Kenneth, 'Settler Colonialism: Economic Development and Class Formation', *The Journal of Modern African Studies*, Vol.14, No.4, 1976
21. Hazlewood, Arthur, 'The Economics of Federation and Dissolution in Central Africa' in *African Integration and Disintegration*, Arthur Hazlewood (ed.), London 1967

22. *The Herald* (Zimbabwe), 1985–86
23. The Institution of Mining and Metallurgy, *African Mining*, London 1987
24. Jourdan, Paul, 'The Non-Ferrous Metals Industry of Zimbabwe', Paper for presentation to UNIDO, December 1985
25. Kabuwa, B.W., 'The African Industrialists? The Prospects in Malawi', Paper presented at the conference *Malawi: An Alternative Pattern of Development*, Centre of African Studies, University of Edinburgh, May 1984
26. Kemp, Tom, *Industrialization in the Non-Western World*, London 1983
27. Kydd, Jonathan, 'Malawi in the 1970s: Development Policies and Economic Change', Paper presented at the conference *Malawi: An Alternative Pattern of Development*, Centre of African Studies, University of Edinburgh, May 1984
28. Kydd, Jonathan and Christiansen, Robert, 'Structural Change in Malawi since Independence: Consequences of a Development Strategy Based on Large-Scale Agriculture', *World Development*, Vol.10, No.5, 1982
29. Makoni, Tonderai, 'The Rhodesian Economy in a Historical Perspective, Part II', in *Zimbabwe: Towards a New Order. An Economic and Social Survey*, UNCTAD and UNDP Working Paper, Vol.II, 1980
30. *Malawi: An Alternative Pattern of Development*, Proceedings of a conference held at the Centre of African Studies, University of Edinburgh, May 1984
31. Mandaza, Ibbo (ed.), *Zimbabwe: The Political Economy of Transition, 1980–1986*, Senegal 1986
32. McCracken, J., 'Planters, Peasants and the Colonial State: The Impact of the Native Tobacco Board in the Central Province of Malawi', *Journal of Southern Studies*, Vol.9, No.2, 1983
33. —, 'Introduction', *Malawi: An Alternative Pattern of Development*, Seminar Proceedings No.25, Centre of African Studies, University of Edinburgh, May 1984
34. Ministry of Finance, Economic Planning and Development, *Socio-Economic Review of Zimbabwe, 1980–1985*, Harare, 1986
35. Morris-Jones, W.H. (ed.), *From Rhodesia to Zimbabwe: Behind and Beyond Lancaster House*, London, Cass, 1980
36. Mosley, Paul, *The Settler Economies: Studies in the Economic History of Kenya and Southern Rhodesia, 1900–1963*, Cambridge 1983
37. Ndlela, Daniel B., 'Problems of Industrialization: Structural and Policy Issues' in *Zimbabwe: The Political Economy of Transition*, Ibbo Mandaza (ed.), Senegal 1986
38. —, 'Prospects for an Integrated Development of the Iron and Steel Industry and Capital Goods: East and Southern African Countries', UNIDO paper, ID/WG, 458/8, 12 Dec. 1985
39. —, 'Technology Imports and Indigenous Technological Capacity Building: The Zimbabwean Case', Working Paper in the World Employment Programme Research, WEP/2–22/WP 173, March 1987
40. Nixson, Fred, 'Import-Substituting Industrialization' in *Industry and Accumulation in Africa*, Martin Fransman (ed.), London 1982
41. Ng'ong'ola, Clement, 'Malawi's Agricultural Economy and the Evolution of Legislation on the Production and Marketing of Peasant Economic Crops', *Journal of Southern African Studies*, Vol.12, No.2, 1986
42. *Nyasaland Development Plan 1962–1965*, Zomba 1962
43. Nziramasanga, M., 'Major Trends in the Rhodesian Economy, 1955–1977', paper presented at the Symposium on Zimbabwe's Economic Prospects, co-sponsored by Columbia University's Research Institute on International Change and Seven Springs Center at Mt. Kisco, New York, 31 Jan. – 2 Feb. 1980
44. Palmer, Robin, 'The Nyasaland Tea Industry in the Era of International Tea Restrictions, 1933–50', *The Journal of African History*, Vol.26, 1985
45. Parpart, Jane, *Labor and Capital on the African Copperbelt*, Philadelphia, 1983
46. Pearson, D.S., 'Industrial Development in Rhodesia', *The Rhodesian Journal of Economics*, Vol.2, No.2, 1968

47. Phimister, I.R., 'Gold Mining in Southern Rhodesia, 1919–1953', *The Rhodesian Journal of Economics*, Vol.10, No.1, 1976
48. —, 'Rhodes, Rhodesia and the Rand', *Journal of Southern African Studies*, Vol.1, No.1, 1974
49. —, 'The Structure and Development of the Southern Rhodesian Base Mineral Industry – From 1907 to the Great Depression,' *The Rhodesian Journal of Economics*, Vol.9, No.2, 1975
50. Poulantzas, Nicos, 'The Petty Bourgeoisie, Traditional and New' in *Classes in Contemporary Capitalism*, trans. by David Ferback, London 1975
51. Republic of Zambia, *Transitional National Development Plan (January 1965 to June 1966)*
52. —, Ministry of Development Planning and National Guidance, *Second National Development Plan, January 1972 to December 1976*
53. Republic of Zimbabwe, Ministry of Finance, Economic Planning and Development, *First Five-Year Development Plan, 1986–1990*
54. —, *Socio-Economic Review of Zimbabwe, 1980–1985*
55. Riddell, Roger C., 'Zimbabwe: The Economy Four Years After Independence', *African Affairs*, Vol.83, No.33, 1984
56. Roberts, Andrew, *A History of Zambia*, London 1976
57. Rotberg, Robert, *Black Heart: Gore-Browne and the Politics of Multi-Racial Zambia*, Berkeley, Calif., 1977
58. Rweyemamu, J.F. (ed.), *Industrialization and Income Distribution in Africa*, Senegal 1980
59. Seidman, Ann, 'A Development Strategy for Zimbabwe', paper for Department of Economics, University of Zimbabwe, 1982 (mimeographed)
60. —, 'The Distorted Growth of Import Substitution: The Zambian Case' in *Development in Zambia: A Reader*, Ben Turok (ed.), London 1979
61. Seshmani, V., 'The Manufacturing Sector of Zambia Since Independence: An Analytical Profile' (Mimeographed, n.d., c.1984)
62. Sprack, John, *Rhodesia: South Africa's Sixth Province: An Analysis of the Links Between South Africa and Rhodesia*, London 1974
63. Stoneman, Colin, 'Foreign Capital and the Prospects for Zimbabwe', *World Development*, Vol.4, No.1, 1976
64. —, 'The Mining Industry' in *Zimbabwe's Inheritance*, Colin Stoneman (ed.), London 1981
65. —, 'Industrialization and Self-Reliance in Zimbabwe' in *Industry and Accumulation in Africa*, Martin Fransman (ed.), London 1982
66. —, (ed.), *Zimbabwe's Inheritance*, London, 1981
67. Sutcliffe, R.B., *Industry and Underdevelopment*, London 1971
68. Tesfachew, Taffere, 'The Development, Growth Potential and Constraints of the Capital Goods Industry in Zambia', paper presented to the University of Zambia, Humanities and Social Sciences Seminar, 26 March 1985
69. Thomas, Simon, 'Economic Development in Malawi Since Independence', *Journal of Southern African Studies*, Vol.2, No.1, 1975
70. Thompson, C.H. and Woodruff, H.W., *Economic Development in Rhodesia and Nyasaland*, London 1954
71. Tindall, P.E.N., *A History of Central Africa*, London 1968
72. UNIDO, *Study of the Manufacturing Sector in Zimbabwe, Vol.I-III*. DP/ID/SER./631 12 Sept. 1985
73. Viewing, Keith, 'Mining and Development in Zimbabwe', Report No.C314, Sept. 1983, Institute of Mining Research, University of Zimbabwe
74. Viewing, Keith, Phimister, B., and Jourdan, P., 'A Review – Past, Present and Future of Zimbabwe's Mining Industry', paper presented at The Institute of Mining and Metallurgy conference on African mining held in Harare, Zimbabwe, 31 Aug. – 2 Sept. 1987
75. Waller, Peter P., 'The Structure of the Rhodesian Manufacturing Industry and Its Development Potential' in *Perspectives of Independent Development in Southern Africa: The Cases of Zimbabwe and Namibia*, Occasional Paper of the German Development Institute, No.62, Berlin 1980

76. Wield, David, 'Manufacturing Industry' in *Zimbabwe's Inheritance*, Colin Stoneman (ed.), London 1981
77. Woldring, Klaas (ed.), *Beyond Political Independence: Zambia's Development Predicament in the 1980s*, Berlin 1984
78. Young, Alistair, *Industrial Diversification in Zambia*, New York 1973
79. *Zimbabwe: Towards a New Order. An Economic and Social Survey*, Working Papers Vol.I and II, New York 1980

4

The Direction of Agricultural Development in Zambia, Zimbabwe and Malawi

KENNETH GOOD

Rising agricultural productivity in developing societies involves class formation among the peasantry, and requires for its greater success broad and active support from the state which itself grows stronger in the process. The formation of middle and rich peasantries and, recently, of smaller black rural capitalist classes of large-scale farmers, accompanied the growth of commercial agriculture in the region: in Zimbabwe slowly from the 1930s (and briefly earlier); intermittently in Zambia, then more steadily from the 1950s; and in Malawi mainly after independence in 1964.

Rising agricultural productivities represent a basic national resource: the achievement of food self-sufficiency; an export capacity earning revenue and foreign exchange; the basis for economic development and diversification; and a source of an investment surplus for the strengthening of the state. It also constitutes a lever for social and economic transformation in the long term, when established productivities provide a firm base for redistribution and greater equality. Zimbabwe, and even Malawi, much the smallest of the three, differ markedly from Zambia in the achievement of increased productivities. Banda's autocratic state has produced rapid economic development based chiefly on support for large-scale capitalist farming and the state-organised supply of cheap peasant labour. In Zimbabwe settler colonialism constructed a relatively advanced, integrated, and diversified economy out of the heavy exploitation of peasant land and labour, to the particular advantage of large-scale white farmers. But in Zambia a disinterested colonial and independent state produced no notable advances in agriculture in its long concentration upon the mining and urban sectors. The deepening impoverishment of the poor peasantry is not ameliorated by a growing capacity for possible structural change in the future. With abundant untouched land in the country and with labour that is unutilised in farming, the Zambian poor peasantry is the most abandoned of the region, if not its most exploited.

The formation of rich rural classes in peasant societies offers a smaller contribution to agricultural development if the state is inactive in the sector, as Zambia before and after 1964 generally indicates. But the struggles of rising indigenous farmers in the region over decades against colonial systems which favoured large-scale white-owned agriculture, constituted limited but significant economic gains. Though a racially biased interventionist state was particularly strong in Zimbabwe, weaker in Zambia, rich peasantries nevertheless actively arose in both countries under colonialism. Colonial opposition to peasant agriculture meant, however, that a true articulation of pre-capitalist and capitalist agricultural systems, one which encouraged the dynamics and hierarchies of the old societies, hardly occurred in the region. Exceptions were perhaps the early 'peasant prosperity' and the interrupted development among the Tonga in southern Zambia.

Despite the new inequalities which it inevitably subsumes, rural class formation is a force which can place demands on the state for investment in agricultural development. Indigenous class formation also serves to draw domestic resources out of the hands of large-scale white farmers – tasks in which a supposedly undifferentiated small peasantry faces well-nigh impossible barriers. It is also a force for economic indigenisation on a broad though long-term basis, since indigenous control over commercial agriculture is a more feasible and achievable proposition than is the case with other sectors of the domestic economy.

Rising agricultural productivity and the possession of a relatively strong and activist state has placed Zimbabwe, and recently Malawi to a lesser extent, in a special position regionally and even continentally, freed from the vicious and constantly debilitating nexus between backward agriculture and a weak state. By contrast the continuance of this interconnection characterises Zambia still.

But it is also significant that Zimbabwe's agricultural productivities rest today upon a narrow and unstable social base both in class and racial terms. Around 1980 Zimbabwe's large-scale farming sector produced almost 95 per cent of total marketed agricultural output, and contributed some 11 per cent to the country's GDP. This sector then comprised only some 4,700 large-scale farmers (3, pp.27, 35). Next in productivity were 9,500 rich peasants (called 'small-scale') who are titleholders to land – averaging in 1977 123 ha and ranging in size up to a largish 800 ha – in the former Purchase Areas, with further unenumerated sections located

128

in the so-called communal lands and the new settlement schemes. The productivity of these 9,500 established rich peasants was on average some thirty times greater than that of the peasantries in the backward communal lands totalling between 650,000 and 850,000 households (3, p.31; 4, p.11).

There are indications that the social base of Malawi's agricultural achievements is narrower still at its topmost level. In 1971 there were only about 104 large-scale farm units. Near the end of the decade there were in addition some 100,000 *achikumbe* ('progressive farmers') or middle-to-rich peasants (7, pp.79, 81). Other instabilities in the two countries turned on the fact that the majority of producers in the large-scale sectors were white or other foreign owners – probably less so in Malawi than Zimbabwe – with an inherent and serious impermanency in their positions. Since both countries also experience today critical shortages of good land, the maintenance of their productivities in the future is affected by deep uncertainties.

THE STATE

While other functions of the state are not absent or unimportant – in particular as a force towards class domination – its salient role in developing countries is as the main agency, positively or negatively, for development. Despite spectres of foreign bureaucratic systems and the realities of African authoritarian regimes, a viable state is essential for the self-determination and material advancement of a people (10, p.84; 32, p.19). A state's developmental capacity might generally be understood as an increasing capacity to create, plan, implement, and manipulate change towards specific goals (32, p.19), and as the new institutions and agencies necessary for these purposes. Given the prominence of agriculture in the economies and societies of Africa – as variously a large percentage of GNP, in exports employment, the way of life of the majority, etc. – the capacity of the state stands, it waxes or wanes, largely in relation to this sector. Hart summarised the relationship in West Africa: 'states must revolutionize their agricultural sectors if they wish to escape from permanent backwardness and poverty. No single factor is more important' (32, p.51).

The role of the state over a long period in Africa has been 'especially vital' (13, p.77) because of the lateness and weakness of capitalist development. At the same time colonialism usually established only 'the rudimentary elements of a modern state' (12, p.26), in its niggardliness and lack of interest in development broader than a very narrow range of commodities. With such an inadequate institutional inheritance, the

129

independent state is usually characterised chiefly by its inadequacies and weaknesses as a developmental instrument (15, p.30). Even where an autocrat holds sway or a proclaimed single-party system is prominent, what is most notable is 'the great constraint and incapacity' of the ruler and his clique 'to implement and enforce' their policies (15, p.79). Inertia, inaction, and decline may easily result, and perhaps the perversion of the state into a predatory instrument feeding the leader and his clique off the body of the nation.

But the inaction of the state in relation to a significant sector of the economy represents a policy choice with serious consequences. African governments, Iliffe has noted, 'have shown that they can prevent capitalism; they have not yet shown that they can replace it with anything else that will release their people's energies' (15, p.79). Those whose capacities are most in need of encouragement from the state are in fact the bulk of the peasantry. The problem which decolonisation left to its successor regimes, according to Hart, was 'how to build modern nation-states when the bulk of production remains in the hands of small farmers' (15, p.86).

The parameters of the weak state and undeveloped agriculture have constrained development in Zambia and Malawi no less than in most of the rest of Africa, in the former for far longer and more deeply than in the latter. But they are relatively absent in Zimbabwe. Settler colonialism in this country as in for example Kenya and South Africa, was characterised by its unusually strong drive towards domestic capitalist development. A notable feature of this developmental impulse was the gradual establishment of a comparatively strong and activist state. The settler state was the agency for a fairly broad economic development, wherein a growing commercial agriculture was a basic part. As Wield noted clearly, 'The impetus for industrial growth came relatively early in colonial Rhodesia. The most important reason for this was the semi-autonomous nature of the white settler "self-government" after 1922' (29, p.153).[1]

The settler state's developmental capacity in commercial agriculture originated before 1910. The country's Department of Agriculture was 'reorganised' in 1908, when its first director and specialists in fields such as botany, entomology, chemistry, and irrigation were appointed. An experimental farm-station was opened near Harare, and 'a wide range of extension facilities' was soon offered to the new white farmers. Over the period 1903–14 the annual average expenditure of the department more than doubled (21, p.231).

These early initiatives in the areas of research and extension services were soon extended to making credit available to commercial farmers. A Land Bank was begun in 1912, with an initial share capital of

£250,000, and it became of 'crucial importance' in the establishment of commercial agriculture. Land was reduced in price, simpler title introduced, and rebates offered for improvements. Between 1908 and 1914 over 5.5 m acres of land were sold, export markets for maize were obtained, and the number of occupied white farms rose beyond 2,000 in 1914 (21, pp.231–2). The annual expenditure of the Agriculture Department increased from some £33,000 in 1918 to about £76,000 a decade later, when Zimbabwe had already found markets for its exports, largely of tobacco, maize and cattle, in Germany and Britain, as well as in many regional countries including Northern Rhodesia. By the mid-1920s, according to Palmer, large-scale commercial farming was 'firmly established as a central sector of the Rhodesian economy' (21, p.237).

The quick advance of large-scale commercial agriculture in Zimbabwe was achieved through broad and active support from a state wherein farmers themselves were highly influential; all Prime Ministers with one exception and the majority of cabinet ministers, said Palmer in 1977, had been farmers (21, p.237). The close symbiosis of producers, state, and support for the centrality of agriculture in economic development, characteristic of settler colonialism in different places, was and is almost unique in Africa. The annual expenditure of the Department of Agriculture reached more than £260,000 in year 1936–37 (21, p.239) – more than three times the figure in the mid-1920s. But the significance of the close collaboration of commercial agriculture and the state was perhaps best seen with the establishment by the government of a number of key production and marketing parastatals in the 1930s. Control boards were then set up in tobacco, dairy products, and maize, as a result of the demands by white farmers for greater state participation (21, p.240). At independence four main parastatal marketing boards existed: the Cold Storage Commission, as residual buyer of cattle and sheep; the Grain Marketing Board, as exclusive buyer of maize, sorghum, groundnuts, soya beans, wheat, and coffee; and the Cotton and the Diary Marketing Boards, both as exclusive buyers. These four are subsidiaries of the Agricultural Marketing Authority which is appointed by the Minister of Agriculture in consultation with farming organizations.

In a continent where parastatals are often deemed to operate merely as exploitative parasites on a community and sector, Zimbabwe's inheritance is different. Its marketing boards, the Chavanduka report recognised, 'have not grown from the same roots' as similar organisations in most African countries. In Zimbabwe, 'the need for controlled marketing was recognised by producers and the boards were set up as a result of producers' initiative. Producers have considerable influence on both the policy and the general management of the boards.' In other countries marketing boards were established on the initiative of the state, where farmers' representation tends to be weak or ineffective. The efficiency of operation of the marketing parastatals in Zimbabwe, declared the Commission, 'derived to a considerable extent from the strength of producers' representation' (3, p.102). And the strength of such representation originated in the essentials of the settler state where, unlike in colonial Malawi, and in Zambia still today, commercial agriculture was of central importance.

The rise of commercial agriculture in Zimbabwe derived in large part, of course, from the heavy and systematic exploitation by the settler state of peasant land and labour: initially a crude and brutal seizure of the crops and cattle of African farmers, subsequently a methodical appropriation of their land and the transformation of once relatively independent peasantries into labourers working for very low wages on the farms and other establishments of whites. As in Zambia to a more limited and less systematic extent – for example, only 6.5 per cent of Zambian land was appropriated by the state – the underdevelopment of peasant agriculture causally accompanied the establishment of large-scale farming. In Zambia, however, the losses experienced by the peasantry were not succeeded by the rise of commercial agriculture, which was neglected by the colonial state in preference to copper production for export. An Agricultural Loans Board was established only in 1934 with a share capital of just £24,000, and a Land Bank did not begin until 1946 (22, p.17). Not one viable export crop as an alternative to maize was developed, and by 1952 only about 1,100 white farmers were located in the country (1, pp.5–6; 20, p.64). Such commercial agriculture offered few or no mitigations in the form of rising productivities or domestic food self-sufficiencies to set against the poverty of the peasantry.

The colonial state in Malawi brought even greater poverty to the peasantry in its efforts to support what nevertheless remained a very small estate sector, not through material investment, but mainly from the supply of cheap wage-labour. It only 'intervened fitfully' in the economy (28, p.41), its developmental capacities narrowly restricted by its lack of domestic revenue, the country's regional weaknesses, and Zomba's financial dependence on London. The colonial government was 'primarily concerned' with the white owned plantations (28, p.49) – numbering in 1900, for example, 100 estates, as many as the overall total of large-scale units in 1971; while the peasantry was forced to function as a labour pool for these and for the advancing settler colonies nearby, Malawi quickly became a place of 'atrocious working conditions and wretched wages' even by regional standards, while the plantations survived as 'parasites on the people' (28, p.50).

Cotton production by the peasantry was encouraged in certain areas and was 'enthusiastically embraced' by many Malawians in the early 1900s (28, pp.46–8).[2] A Department of Agriculture was set up in 1909 with support for peasant cotton growing as a chief task. But the First World War brought disruptions, and soon afterwards Zomba fell deeply into debt and lost the capacity to assist peasant production. With the 1930s the 'poverty of the state' worsened further (27, p.375; 28, pp.60–1). Agriculture received only three per cent of the government budget in 1935, but London ordered further economies to be made. 'No' extension work could be carried out, and in 1937 some two-thirds of the country's cotton crop was destroyed by insects in the fields (28, pp.60–63). Around this time the Zomba government became a 'conscious' exporter of its people to Rhodesia and South Africa.[3]

Malawian peasantries in favourable areas had shown that they were ready and able to expand production for the market – for example some 30,000 cotton growers were located in the lower Shire area at the end of the 1920s – but peasant production was unsupported and restricted by the colonial state and 'never allowed' to develop (28, pp.60, 65). The government tried to encourage a prosperous rich peasantry under the relatively favourable arrangements of Federation in the late 1950s; inputs, advice, and cash bonuses were available but, according to Vail, little was achieved in the long run. By the early 1960s, the peasant sector produced cotton, tobacco, maize, groundnuts, and rice, but its underdevelopment was such that it could market only as little as 11 per cent of its output (28, p.72). These induced weaknesses contrasted sharply with the export capacity of the estate sector. It was towards the latter that the greater continuity of the state policy, from colonialism to independence, was seen, and the so-called nationalist challenge to the plantations was, as Chanock notes, rather brief (2, p.403). The estates in Malawi exported tea and tobacco, but their numbers were much smaller than in Zambia, let alone in Zimbabwe.

The implantation of commercial agriculture in Zimbabwe was economically and institutionally deep and broad. The massive appropriations of land from the 1930s soon led to the introduction of tenure, a fundamental of sustained commercial agricultural development, over some 42 per cent of land, in white-owned and in Purchase Area lands among a rising rich peasantry. The quick growth of export production provided a 'nucleus' around which a whole range of agricultural development services grew up (3, p.121). The basis of the country's increasing capacity to produce successfully a range of commodities – notably maize, tobacco, cotton – simultaneously resulted, in the perspective of the 1980s, from 'fifty or more years' investment in research and development', much of this by and through the settler state (3, p.66).

Diversification and the rate of development quickened after the Second World War, Zimbabwe gained a 'substantial and responsive export orientated large-scale agricultural industry'. This was in turn 'supported by a high quality infrastructure of marketing organizations and other allied service and input industries, both parastatal and private (3, p.56). Development and diversification were extended through the growth of manufacturing industry where, as noted above, much of the impetus came from the settler state, and a large integration between commercial agriculture and manufacturing was made: the former not only providing a large percentage of the raw materials required by the latter, but also constituting a growing domestic market and demand for the products of the manufacturing sector. Nothing like this diversification and integration was obtained in Zambia or Malawi. The contribution of export agricultural capacity and a strong and activist state were at its heart.

Such agricultural development represented long-term unequal gains for all Zimbabweans and, for a specific indigenous class, viz. a rising rich peasantry, definite material advantages fairly quickly. This was the dimension of colonial state action which helped to ensure that the resources and advantages of commercial agriculture were directed to a limited extent to certain African farmers. Broadly similar policies were initiated in all three countries at different times, with differing degrees of strength and coherence. Much the earliest programme, however, was in Zimbabwe.

Special areas were designated for purchase by 'emergent' black farmers in Zimbabwe in 1930. No specific qualifications were required for purchasing farms until the mid-1940s, though Cheater suggests that the aspirant landholders were sometimes educated men, and those naturally with some money. Experience at government agricultural training centres was introduced only after the numbers of applicants for farms increased substantially in the early 1950s (4, p.7).[4] Extension services were for some time provided only after requests from the officials and farmers of a particular Purchase Land (4, p.7).[5] The settler government's concern for agricultural development in the Purchase areas, notes Cheater, was actually 'scant'. But she also says that 'in practice' the state assisted 'the capitalization and development' of Purchase area farms: between 1931 and 1950 direct state investment of Z$1.6 m was made in the infrastructure of the Purchase areas – roads, bridges, water, fencing, dipping, etc. – in addition to assistance in fields like education and health (4, pp.7–8, 13).

The colonial government also 'funded capital investment on individual farms in the Purchase Lands', through offering credit for fencing, dams, and boreholes from various agencies – the Land and Agricultural Bank, the African Loan Fund, and the Agricultural Finance Corporation. The new black farmers were able to buy their land 'at nominal prices' from the state, with interest-free payments spread over long periods. These rich peasants gained access to bank credit from government and private sources, the basis for which was the ownership of land which they had acquired (4, p.13). The rise of the Rhodesia Front party in the early 1960s threatened for a time the very idea of freehold tenure for blacks, although by 1963 there were 23 white extension officers and 155 black extension assistants employed full-time in the Purchase Areas. In the mid-1960s seasonal loans for inputs (seeds, fertilisers, etc.) were available from the African Loan and Development Trust (4, pp.8, 13–14). By 1977 there were 66 separate Purchase Lands covering in total 1.42 m hectares or some 3.8 per cent of the country. Some 8,500 farmers then owned land in these areas, of whom around 60 per cent were full titleholders while 40 per cent held lease agreements.[6] Despite a highly exploitative colonialism, a very small rich peasantry had gained control over significant agricultural resources with the aid, however spasmodically, of the settler state.[7] Their increasing capacities were indicated rather quickly; for example, in 1958 they were able to market about two-thirds of what they produced,[8] and in 1960 they were said to employ 56,000 labourers.[9]

The colonial government in Zambia began to support the formation of a rich peasantry only in the late 1940s. The African Farming Improvement Scheme provided its members with credit and extension services, the chance for a cash bonus, and the same price for their marketed maize as that accorded to white farmers, unlike small peasants who received a lower price (11, p.140; 19, pp.283–4)[10]. The programme operated only in the relatively developed provinces, Southern, Central, and Eastern, and it therefore encouraged both uneven development and social differentiation. The Peasant Farming Scheme was introduced in parallel with this, but here the rising farmer was provided with a new block, with superior soils and water facilities, as well as some loan capital for the purchase of equipment and farm stock. The Peasant Scheme was not introduced to Northern province, but it 'met with remarkable success' in Southern, Central, and Eastern provinces in just a few years (11, p.139). In 1959 there were 2,424 farmers under this scheme in Zambia, and most were in Eastern provinces (11, p.140). The

Farming Improvement Scheme also made a definite impact. In 1954 in Southern province, where peasant commercial agriculture existed before the 1920s, 'improved' farmers were producing five bags of maize per acre compared with three per acre for the 'unimproved' farmers (19, p.284). In 1962 there were 1,311 improved farmers in Southern province and 1,072 in Central (11, p.140).

African marketed maize production (through official channels) rose significantly through the mid-1950s: 1952, 179,000 bags; 1953, 576,000; 1954, 658,000; 1955, 433,000; 1956, 746,000; 1957, 883,000.[11] The government's relationship to agriculture, however, remained in general one of neglect, sometimes of direct opposition. As African farmers in Southern province increased their production of maize in the 1950s, the colonial state reacted by aiming to restrict their output. When in 1957 peasants in Mazabuka produced a total of 300,000 bags of maize, and those in Choma produced 140,000 – both centres of relatively advanced commercial agriculture – the government deemed this, says Hellen, as overproduction.[12] The introduction of tenure reform was slow and very limited. Only in 1962 was a law introduced which enabled farmers to register title to land through their Local Native Authority, whereas in Ghana, for example, a permanent, heritable and transferable land title had existed, notes Hellen, since 1897.[13]

State policy towards agriculture in Zambia has shown long continuities, at least until 1982–83, and some observers suggest that the same is true in Malawi.[14] What is distinctive about Zambia, however, is that here the continuities are outstandingly those of omission. As the ILO's Jaspa mission reported in 1977, 'for nearly 50 years now' Zambia has experienced 'the neglect of domestic agriculture, particularly small-scale production . . .' (16, p.83). While the government has favoured the rising rich peasantry over the poor peasantry, and large-scale and parastatal agriculture most of all, the strength of state support has declined over the independence period. Extension staff, at the beginning of the 1980s, said the World Bank, were 'less mobile, less trained, and . . . less effective' than in the early 1970s, and the government's extension services generally reached perhaps about five per cent of smallholders (30, pp.52, 68). Credit facilities, similarly, were distinguished by 'cumbersome' procedures, 'late deliveries of inputs, and delays in marketing and crop payments', which together represented serious constraints on small-scale farmers. By 1981 some 87 per cent of the recurrent expenditure of the Ministry of Agriculture consisted of grants and subsidies mainly to parastatals and cooperatives (30, pp.17, 52), institutions which were in fact notorious for their acute inefficiencies and mismanagement (30, pp.10, 9 passim).

An overall consequence has been the formation of middle and rich peasantries in Zambia which tend to be both relatively large in size, vis-à-vis Zimbabwe and Malawi, and weak as regards their control over and access to productive resources. Precise analysis of rural class formation is bedevilled by data that is only rough and approximate and by dissimilar classifications of the data. Sources do agree that there is a so-called subsistence sector, or poor peasantry, totalling 463,000 to 610,000 households in the years 1975–80, and characterised by the land holdings of less than two hectares, and by the notable fact that they market up to 50 per cent of what they produce.[15] Thereafter the World Bank identifies 'small-scale commercial' farmers, totalling 122,400 farm-units in 1980, holding up to 10 hectares of land, and 'medium-scale commercial', numbering 21,350 farms at that time, holding 10–40 hectares (30, Table 1)[16], and which might be understood for comparative purposes as respectively middle peasants and rich peasants. Finally the World Bank identifies a 'large-scale commercial' class, totalling in 1980 some 730 farms, which indiscriminately exceed 40 hectares in size;[17] these might be interpreted as a rural capitalist class.

TABLE 1
SOME NATIONAL DIFFERENCES

	Malawi	*Zambia*	*Zimbabwe*
Population (est.)1983	6.6m.	6.3m.	7.9m.
Area	118,000 sq.km.	753,000 sq.km.	391,000 sq.km.
GNP per cap. 1983	$210	$580	$740

Source: World Bank, *World Development Report 1985*

On this basis, a middle peasantry of 122,400 and a rich peasantry of 21,350 had arisen in Zambia by 1980. These together were rather large in size compared to the Zambian poor peasantry of some 500,000 to 600,000, and to the rich peasantry of the former purchase area of Zimbabwe numbering then only some 9,000.[18] But whereas this small Zimbabwean rich peasantry owned land averaging 123 hectares, and ranging up to 800 hectares in size, its Zambian counterpart held less than 40 hectares.[19] The Zambian rich peasantry is also large in size relative to the country's 'large-scale commercial' or rural capitalist class, totalling only 730, all of which are realistically 'heavily capitalised farms' (30, Table 1 and p.5). While this number is less than one-sixth the size of the large-scale farming class in Zimbabwe – about 4,700 around the same time – the Zambian rural capitalist category was also different in that 'about half' the number were indigenous Zambians (3, p.27; 30, p.5). Since included in the total of 730 are many corporate owners – Lyons

137

Brooke Bond, Lonrho, etc. – indigenous owners might form the majority among privately-owned large capitalist farmers. The relationship of this class to the Zambian state, and to a somewhat lesser extent that of the rich peasantry also, was vastly different from that of the poor peasantry. Within the parameters of the government's overall indifference towards agriculture, the two leading rural classes had done well in terms of state subsidies, credit, extension, pricing and marketing arrangements.[20] It was largely because of such supporters that the indigenous component among the highly capitalised farmers of Zambia was so large, much larger than the relative number in Zimbabwe, and possibly larger than that in Malawi too.

The independent state in Malawi quickly assumed an activist role in agriculture, much more so than its colonial predecessor and its contemporary Zambian neighbour. Yet there were broad and loose similarities with Lusaka, in that Zomba strongly supported the large-scale sector, and assisted the *achikumbe*, doing both, particularly the former, at the direct and heavy expense of the poor peasantry.

Unlike most African countries, including Zambia but excluding Zimbabwe, the Banda government emphasised agricultural production as the motor for economic development. Within agriculture, Ghai and Radwan have shown, 'government policy has concentrated on the estate sector and the *achikumbe* . . .' Assistance to the large-scale sector is broad and substantial: 'a growing proportion of [state] expenditure on economic infrastructure has been geared to [agriculture]'; encouragement is given to 'foreign private investment in plantations and agro-industry' through 'a favourable tax system and a liberal policy on imports and repatriation of profits and capital'. Additionally, a 'major incentive' to investment in plantations, by foreigners, by government agencies, and by Banda's own Press Holding Ltd., has been 'the existence of cheap labour', the provision of which has been 'the main objective' of the government's incomes policy. Largely due to the 'rigorous' operation of this policy, the country in general and the estate sector particularly enjoyed an expansion of wage-employment, through the later 1960s and mid-1970s, 'in the context of declining real wages'. The estates obtained the double boon of a 'massive' expansion of their work-force and a fall in the real wages of their workers. State policy operated actually 'to prevent' a rise in the value of wages (7, pp.93–4, 77, 84–5).[21]

The state has also aimed to promote cash crop and export production through assistance to a rich peasantry. The *achikumbe* are granted certain benefits which the mass of the peasantry do not receive – priority in marketing crops through ADMARC, permission to take certain crops such as tobacco direct to the auction floor rather than being required to sell to ADMARC from which they would obtain only one-quarter or one-third of the auction price, priority in the supply of farm inputs, and advice on farm planning.[22]

The establishment by the government, in association with international agencies such as the World Bank, of four major rural development projects since 1968, has provided indirect benefits to rising rich peasants. These have come to comprise about 20 per cent of the total rural population, and it is largely here and from among this sizable minority (not all of whom could profit quickly or directly from their opportunity) that certain valuable agricultural resources have been made available. Individual land tenure was introduced on the Lilongwe Land Development Project, where a total of 287,500 hectares was demarcated by 1977. Under these projects, the use of improved tools and modern inputs – fertiliser, better seeds – also became available, and assisted the formation of the middle-to-rich peasantry. At the same time, the concentration of available resources on these projects resulted in 'a neglect of the majority of farmers in the country' (7, pp.94, 81–2). Smaller agricultural projects in Zambia had similar consequences.[23]

The rise of the 'progressive' farmers in Malawi as cash-crop producers assisted by the state, accompanied policies which discriminated against the poor peasantry as potential small-scale commercial producers. Ghai and Radwan estimate that the total number of middle-to-rich peasants had grown in the later 1970s to about 100,000, representing some 10 per cent of the whole peasantry (7, p.81). Comparisons with Zimbabwe and Zambia are very approximate; this, however, would seem to represent larger rich peasantries than those in Zimbabwe, but smaller perhaps than Zambia.[24] With the help of the state, the *achikumbe* have not only acquired access to productive resources, but have also enjoyed on this basis a rise in their real incomes since 1969; this contrasts starkly with the decline in real incomes experienced by the bulk of rural people.[25] Vail states that the number of 'full-time smallholders actually decreased' during the 1970s (28, p.77), though the population was growing rapidly, as elements of the poor peasantry were forced to abandon their struggle on the land and to accept domestic wage labour.

ADMARC has served as leading agency of the state in the combined process of increasing agricultural production and rural class formation. The role of this parastatal is far more profound than its seeming equivalents in Zimbabwe and Zambia. Unlike Namboard in Zambia, for example, ADMARC operates chiefly in relation to the poor peasantry. Only they are required by the state to market their produce through this agency, in itself a 'significant discriminatory measure' in favour of the estates.[26] The Chavunduka Commission presented what might

139

amount to a 'best possible' interpretation of ADMARC's activities. Under the Banda government, marketing has been organized to enable a smallholder to sell his or her produce without travelling more than five kilometres, to sell small amounts of produce at any time for cash, and supposedly to obtain other services at the same place. ADMARC is engaged in rural transportation and distribution, operates extension services, and assists rural development broadly. Unlike the marketing boards of Zimbabwe, ADMARC is therefore engaged in what is of necessity a high-cost marketing system, and its producer prices are low in consequence (3, pp.102–4).

Closer examination reveals that ADMARC is engaged in the systematic and heavy exploitation of the poor peasantry, and its enforced monopolistic position and very low producer prices vis-à-vis only that rural class are the instruments chosen to achieve this end. ADMARC's resource-extraction from the mass of the peasantry in the 1970s, according to Kydd and Christiansen, amounted to some K20 m per annum, roughly equivalent to at least one-third of the average per capita income of the poorest 90 per cent of the population (17, pp.368, 374). The corporation's activities, according to Ghai and Radwan, resulted in 'a massive transfer of surplus from the smallholder sector to finance urban development and other government expenditure' (17, p.90). The state utilised ADMARC's growing assets – 1970–71, K13.6 m; 1977–78, K115.5 m – to further the growth of the estate sector (17, pp.95, 368). The mutuality of interest between ADMARC and the estates was established early, and in 1972 Press Holdings and ADMARC jointly owned 28 tobacco plantations (7, p.80).

The Malawian state's engagement in agriculture – significant, almost unique in itself – has as its cutting-edge and dominant feature the systematic exploitation of the poor peasantry. This is not done merely to further the consumption of an urban elite. It occurs in the interest of the growth of commercial agriculture generally and of the large-scale sector primarily; the rich peasantry are secondary beneficiaries. Such activities bear no comparison with the independent state in Zambia. There it is the disregard of farming which has predominated, the abandonment of the poor peasantry, and almost only a residual support offered inconsistently to large-scale farming. Within agriculture in Zambia, vital inputs are regularly unavailable, extension services are grossly undersupported, farmers wait months for payment for their crops, and so on.[27] The Rhodesian settler state with its farmer-politicians seems to offer the only realistic comparison with independent Malawi. Banda's direct, personal engagement in farming is important. Not only is he himself a leading estates' owner, but he also signs the *achikumbe* certificates which are

140

bestowed as tangible benefit on officially recognised 'progressive' farmers and,[28] at an age of about 86, he carries out an annual month-long crop inspection tour of the country which is both serious and symbolic.[29] Kaunda has no comparable involvement,[30] and Mugabe's appreciation of agriculture is of a different, more cerebral order.

RURAL CLASS FORMATION

Peasant class formation is everywhere the accompaniment of increasing production for the market, but certain interpretations serve to disguise this fact. The 'inward' view and 'moral economy' approaches to the understanding of peasantries are perhaps the most important of these and represent an orthodoxy within the field.[31] They tend to see peasant societies as unique, as subsistence-orientated, as unusually homogeneous and egalitarian, as detached from market, towns, and state, and as relatively static as a result. There is much stress upon the supposed autonomy of the peasant household and village, and on a 'subsistence ethic', a 'collective solidarity', and an 'economy of affection' which are said to characterise peasant societies.[32]

These very similar and over-lapping approaches therefore have inherent difficulties in coping with the reality of peasant production for the market in developing countries. The response when confronting such activities is frequently simply to ignore their existence or to minimise their importance.[33] When this proves difficult, the tendency is to define the new production activities as non-peasant, and to refer, not to middle and rich peasants, but to 'entrepreneurs', petty commodity producers, small businessmen, and so on, who are said to have both emerged from the peasantry and left them behind. It thus dichotomises rather sharply all supposedly small peasants engaged largely in subsistence production, on the one hand, from all commercial farmers, small and large, on the other. Even when small peasants are clearly seen to be increasing production for the market – as in Zimbabwe's 'communal lands' since independence – it tends to be implied that they do this while remaining egalitarian.[34] Peasant market production, peasant class formation, and the whole idea of process and change, are all obscured in this perspective.

The alternative 'outward' or so-called 'rational peasant' approach recognises inequalities in pre-capitalist societies and sees elements of the peasantry as readily disposed to increase production for the market when resources are available and personal gain is involved.[35] The household and village are segments of the wider political economy where the non-peasant sectors of market, towns, and state, nationally and internationally, are dominant. Class formation is a process of change in which under market conditions a minority of peasants gains greater control over productive resources while others lose it.

This view accords with the reality of early and spontaneous expansion of peasant production for sale and the gradual rise of rich peasantries in southern Zambia. Here Tonga farmers were located close to the railway and possessed fertile land. Perhaps equally importantly, as Carpenter expressed it, 'their traditional social structure facilitated the change . . . to individual ownership' (1, p.10).[36] By 1913 they were 'beginning to compete with Europeans for the local market' (20, p.56), and Southern province became the centre of advance in African agriculture (11, p.128). Maize production among the Tonga rose from an estimated annual average of 10,000–15,000 bags in 1918–1920, to 20,000 in 1926–27, and to 30,000 in 1928–30. By 1933 some 75 per cent of taxpayers on the Tonga Plateau paid their taxes through selling maize or cattle and not through wage-labour for whites.[37]

Expansion of marketed output was accompanied by increasing differentiation. At the end of the 1920s, wagons, scotch carts, ploughs, and planters were being purchased in increasing numbers by certain farmers in Mazabuka, one of the most advanced areas of the province. Bikes were being purchased, and 'one native' had acquired a car. A few years later another official report referred to 'the rich and progressive Batonga farmers of the railway strip', and observed that 'in most villages' there were 'two or more substantial men' who cultivated 'up to twenty five acres of maize and employ[ed] up to six people at an average wage of 8/– per month' (22, p.15). In 1937 a report on the province said that 'a class of peasant farmers' had come into existence, the individual member of which 'acquires and retains wealth'.[38]

By the mid-1940s there was a close inter-relationship between the comparatively high marketed output of the rising rich peasantry and their control over resources and income. In 1945 in Mazabuka, while 85.3 per cent of the surveyed peasant population marketed less than 10 bags of maize each year, 14.3 per cent marketed between 11 and 100 bags, and 0.4 per cent of peasants sold in excess of 100 bags. The great majority of small peasants had an annual average income of only about £5, but the very small class of rich peasants gained on average some £380 each year.[39] In 1953, when the state had recently begun to assist the rich peasantry, so-called Grade A farmers in Mazabuka were producing 9.78 bags of maize per acre, Grade B 8.83, and unassisted small peasants only 4.35 bags per acre. The same Grade A farmers possessed farms of some 22.8 acres with fixed capital of £416, representing a capital investment per acre which was considerably better than that of many white farmers.[40]

The rich peasantry in the Southern province had therefore made notable advances in some 40 years in terms of their acquisition of productive resources and in the effective commercial use of their land and capital as reflected by their output and investment figures. These were 'the most developed' rich peasantry in Zambia by 1964, but those in Central province probably ranked second, and those in Eastern third (19, p.283). Their achievements must be understood relative to white large-scale farmers, as well as the most obvious case of the poor peasantry, and they had been gained without benefit of support from the colonial state over most of the period. The many grievances against the government held by those in the advanced districts of Southern province in the 1950s were a measure of what the whole class had struggled against – the hardship of taxation, low producer prices, poor marketing facilities, inadequate services, and the general discrimination in favour of white large-scale farmers (19, p.286). But the capacities of at least sections of the peasantry for commercial agricultural development were clearly demonstrated, and were there to be encouraged and supported properly by an independent government.

In Malawi peasant production of cotton, aimed at the accumulation of wealth, arose before 1910 in some favourable locations. It was borne upon a ready and enthusiastic response among the peasantry to produce for the market, which was dissipated subsequently under colonialism as growers lost both opportunities and resources (28, pp.47–9). Interpretations of colonial Zimbabwe have referred to the rise and early decline of peasant market production, in ways similar to but slightly later than the trajectory of peasant production in South Africa (23, passim). Nevertheless, some 46,000 acres of land were in the hands of 19 African farmers in Zimbabwe in 1925, and 'a number' of blacks were operating farms of up to 5,000 acres, which they had bought or leased, 'as efficiently as white producers on similar acreages' (4, pp.2–4). The spontaneous rise of a rich peasantry in Zimbabwe had an impetus and determination quite comparable to that in Southern province in Zambia.

The drive towards 'rich peasantization'[41] was channelled and furthered, albeit inadequately, with the establishment of the Purchase Lands. Cheater identifies three phases in the development of these areas – 1930–45; 1946–62; and 1963–82 – with the 'consolidation' of the special status of the areas and the black freehold farmers thereon occurring only after the second phase.[42] Her book is important because it presents a detailed description of the rise of freehold farmers on one of the Purchase Lands, Msengezi, located west of Harare. It falls into land category 11 (B), which means that it is favourably placed for crop production and cattle (4, p.35). She assesses Msengezi to be 'an example of a successful, developing Purchase Land', which is at the same time typical of other such freehold areas, since it is 'nowhere near as productive as more recently settled areas' (4, pp.14, 178). The reasons for the typical success of Msengezi were found in the determination, activism, and ambitions of the rising landowners themselves. The freeholders, 'from the very beginning ... recognized the potential class differences' that existed between them and the mass of the peasantry in the Tribal/Communal lands (4, p.158). They also 'pushed the government' to 'provide the capital and services that they need[ed]' to operate as commercial farmers (4, p.14). Their organisation and action was the impetus to the commercial agricultural development of the area. The period 1962–1973 saw a 'general rise in prosperity' in Msengezi: 'the numbers of privately owned dams, boreholes, tractors, motor vehicles and mechanized equipment rose sharply; larger acreages were brought under crops; tobacco and later cotton were planted ... to an increasing extent; and facilities in the Purchase Land as a whole improved considerably' (4, pp.32–3).

By the 1970s a significant proportion of the farmers had gained access to and control over important productive resources. Average size of freehold farms was 180 acres, but farm sizes ranged from 80 up to 400 acres. Many landowners utilised family labour, but the majority hired casual farm labourers, and 33 per cent employed 'resident labourers on a supposedly "permanent" basis'. One-quarter of owners used oxen to till their land, while some 16 per cent of them possessed tractors (4, pp.39, 57). Cheater interprets the ownership of a functioning tractor and disc-plough as the minimum for recognising a farm as mechanised. Fifty-four farms representing 16 per cent of the total qualified for this category. However, 'most producers' possessed 'large numbers of ox-drawn implements'. Additionally three farmers owned two tractors each, 'some' had bought lorries or pick-ups, and 'a couple' had acquired more specialised farm equipment (4, pp.47, 82–3).

Commercial agricultural development has been gained through the formation of a sizeable and reasonably strong rich peasantry, some of whom were apparently moving further into a larger capitalised class or category. The fencing of their farms, the provision of water supplies, and mechanisation on the basis of access to bank credit, were important sequences in the developmental process. By 1973 some eight per cent of owners had moved into the capitalised category, and there were also 'a large number of semi-capitalized farms only one step away from full capitalization' (4, p.84). Substantial economic diversification was occurring within the small class of rural capitalists. Twelve of these capitalist farmers 'owned 30 separate businesses' or a variety of kinds, and more than half of them combined relatively large capitalist farming with other business activities in both rural and urban areas. The capitalised farmers derived additional income from contracting-out and hiring-out their equipment and vehicles, sometimes to neighbouring farmers, and from the salaries or pensions of elected office (4, p.96). Mechanisation, capitalisation and diversification appeared to be the hallmarks of the successful emergence of a small rural capitalist class from out of the ranks of the rich peasantry. But both had arisen and commercial agricultural development had been brought about largely through 'the demands made by the farmers themselves' upon the colonial state (4, p.136), and of course through bank credit which their ownership of land in turn opened up to them.

The rich peasantry in Zambia in the later 1970s were less well equipped: in general they relied upon hand or oxen power, some were able to hire tractors, but very few owned them; fertilizers were used, and limited bank credit was available to those who were favourably located.[43] They, and the rural capitalists even more so, were heavily concentrated in the most developed provinces – by 1980, some 99 per cent of the rich peasantry were found in Southern, Central, Eastern, Copperbelt and the new Lusaka provinces.[44] All the large-scale commercial farms, at that time, were concentrated in Southern, Central, Eastern, and Lusaka provinces.[45] Some 375 indigenous farmers had by then climbed into this rural capitalist class and were in possession of what the World Bank classified as heavily capitalised farms.[46] But this topmost indigenous farming class was possibly not composed of a majority of full-time, professional farmers. Of large-scale commercial farmers in Lusaka province in the early 1980s, for example, 'politicians, businessmen and civil servants in Lusaka' constituted 'a substantial share' (24, p.11). Usually a rather reticent group, one Emmanuel Kasonde might well be representative of their number: chairman of the Standard Chartered Bank in Zambia, he owned a mixed farm of no less than 2,500 hectares near Kasama in 1985.[47]

Zambia's rich peasantry has grown in numbers since independence, and in the areas of more advanced commercialisation it has come to include more women; thus in Eastern province in the late 1970s 'nearly 30 per cent of all emergent farming households', or the middle-to-rich peasantry, were female-headed (14, p.26). But they have not advanced significantly in resource ownership and control. This is directly attributable to the weakness of the independent state and to the low priority accorded to agriculture. Nevertheless peasant differentiation is ubiquitous in contemporary Zambia: at the level of the district, if not lower, there is no homogeneous peasantry.[48] As Klepper observed, 'even the poorest areas have peasant farmers who are relatively better off and those who are relatively poor'.[49] It is likely that Zimbabwe and Malawi would not deviate markedly from this pattern.

The rise of the rich peasantry in colonial Zimbabwe shows that a peasantry needs resources and organisation if it is to place demands on the state for increased support. While three farmers' organisations are found today in Zimbabwe, for large-scale commercial farmers, for 'small-scale', and for those in the Communal areas,[50] in Zambia only the Commercial Farmers Bureau exists, and small and middle peasants possess no independent organisation. The Mugabe government has increased state aid to the peasantry. Loans to 'smallholders' from the Agricultural Finance Corporation have risen from a total of 4,400 in 1980 to approximately 100,000 in the 1984–85 season. The numbers of extension workers have gone up from one per 1,000 'peasant farmers' in 1980 to one for every 850 in 1985, and marketing parastatals have opened new rural offices closer to the small peasantry. Largely as a result the number of peasants registered with government agencies rose from 130,000 in 1981 to 330,000 in 1985, while the share of 'peasant producers' in total marketed output went from 10 per cent in 1981 to 15 per cent in 1984.[51] The small and middle peasantries in Zambia make a relatively good contribution to domestic marketed food production despite the lack of state support in any way comparable with Zimbabwe.[52] It would seem virtually impossible for the bulk of the Zambian peasantry, ill-equipped, dispersed, and unorganised as they are, to make effective demands on the Kaunda government.

POVERTY AND PRODUCTIVITY

Poverty is widespread and inequalities are deep in both Zambia and Malawi today, and it is the great bulk of the rural populations, the poor peasants and rural labourers, who suffer most. In Zambia in 1980, according to the ILO, 'four out of five households in the rural areas [we]re poor or very poor and about one out of four in the urban areas.' This meant that the monthly *household* incomes of 80 per cent of rural people were below K80, and as such were insufficient to meet even their 'minimum private consumption needs'. Of the country's total 'subsistence' or small peasant population then of 610,000 households, 572,000 were in this condition (14, pp.xxiii, 47).[53]

Unskilled rural workers in 1980 supposedly received a minimum of K1.20 per day or K31.20 a month (of 26 working days). But it was known that women working in rice harvesting at this time received merely a small dish of salt for their day's labour. Its approximate cash equivalent was 2.4 ngwee but, since the women-workers could resell the salt by the spoonful to their neighbours in exchange for beans and the like, they 'considered this a good wage' (14, p.23). From 1965 to 1980 the rural urban terms of trade 'deteriorated by 65 per cent', so that rural people had to pay in 1980 three times more in agricultural produce for the urban goods they bought compared with 1965 (14, p.xxvi). Over the six years, 1974–80, Zambia's GDP per capita fell precipitously by 52 per cent. At the beginning of the 1980s the great majority of Zambia's rural people experienced therefore conditions amounting to 'multiple deprivation' and compounded poverty: dispersal and remoteness largely in the more backward areas of the country;[54] the physical weakness of labour-short families; lack of a marketable surplus; inadequate state services for health, education, roads, and water, as well as for agriculture itself; and shortages of goods and their high prices in the shops (14, pp.xxv, 26).

It follows that the relative distribution of income in Zambia badly disadvantages the mass of the peasantry. Income distribution is not only inequitable but extremely so. 'Few countries', stated the ILO in the early 1970s, 'display a comparable degree of income inequality', and it 'seems to have widened over time' (16, pp.292–3). At the end of the decade they gave the following estimates: while the poorest 40 per cent of the total population received only eight per cent of total income, the richest five per cent of the country's population commanded 35 per cent of income.[55]

In Malawi in the 1970s both estate workers and 'the great majority of smallholders' received 'extremely low incomes'. As a result, said Ghai and Radwan, poverty was 'widespread'. This was corroborated by such indicators as infant mortality of 142 per 1,000; average life expectancy of 46 years; and adult literacy rate of only 25 per cent (14, p.93). Income inequalities in 1977 were, they believed, of 'staggering dimensions' – those they termed urban skilled or high-level employees

TABLE 2
INCOME DISTRIBUTION

% *Share of Household Income*	*Malawi* 1976–8	*Zambia* 1978
lowest 20% of households	10.4%	3.4%
highest 20% of households	50.6%	61.1%
highest 10% of households	40.1%	46.3%

Source: World Development Report 1985.

TABLE 3
HEALTH

		Malawi	Zambia	Zimbabwe
Life Expectancy	1965	37 years	42 years	50 years
at birth: Males	1983	43 years	49 years	52 years
Infant Mortality	1965	201	137	106
(under 1,/'000)	1983	164	100	69
% of under-	1969–71	19%	35%	-
nourished people	1972–74	14%	34%	-

Sources: *World Development Report 1985*, and Ghai and Radwan, *Agrarian policies and Rural Poverty in Africa.*

TABLE 4
MALAWI – PRODUCTION OF MAIN CROPS

	1978	1979	1980	1981	1982
Maize ('000 tons)	120.3	83.7	91.8	138.6	246.1
Cotton ('000 tons)	24.2	22.4	23.1	21.7	14.8
Sugar ('000 tons)	92.6	108.5	147.4	166.4	171.8
Tea (m kg)	31.7	32.6	29.9	32.0	38.5
Tobacco (m kg) (amt. auctioned)	67.5	69.8	59.3	99.3	133.8

Source: *Economic Intelligence Unit.*

received 32 times the rural minimum wage (14, pp.90–1). However, it is not obvious that Malawi's income distribution is significantly worse than Zambia's. The data in Table 2 are not directly comparable on time. As regards health and life-expectancy, Malawi was worse than Zambia on two relevant indices and much better on a third, while Zimbabwe appeared to have been superior to both (see Table 3).

If the mass of the peasantry of both Zambia and Malawi have endured deep poverty and inequality, it is only the latter country which has enjoyed growth and increased productivity. After independence, Malawi gained 'remarkable' economic growth, said Ghai and Radwan, and GDP (at constant prices) rose by 6.8 per cent per annum from 1964 to 1972, and by 6.4 per cent per annum from 1973 to 1978 (7, p.73). Over the whole period, exports grew by 6.5 times, composed almost entirely of agricultural products. Three main crops, tobacco, tea, and sugar, provided an average of 83 per cent of exports from 1976 to 1981. The 'rapid growth' of agriculture, rising at 4.5 per cent per annum to 1978, gave impetus to 'the entire economy' (7, pp.74–8; 5, p.29).

148

Agricultural Development in Zambia, Zimbabwe, Malawi

The contribution of estates' production to total agricultural production almost doubled from 1964 to 1978 and, consistent with the strong support from the Banda government, the large-scale sector achieved a differential in output per person of the order of 3.5 over the smallholder sector (7, pp.78–9). In contrast even with Zimbabwe, the rate of agricultural expansion which Malawi achieved was 'well in excess' of its population growth. But the peasantry in general and the comparatively well-supported rich peasantry in particular also contributed to development through 'higher yields' and by 'bringing new land under cultivation', in addition to their export crops and their successful production of sufficient food for domestic consumption (7, p.96).

Table 5 below suggests both Malawi's comparative superiority over both its neighbours in terms of domestic food production per capita and Zambia's relative inferiority. Yet Zambia's total area is almost six times larger than Malawi's, and it is said to have a 'vast' potential of arable land. Of Malawi's land area, however, only some 37 per cent is arable, of which 86 per cent was already cultivated in 1977 (14, p.45; 7, p.73).[56]

TABLE 5
SOME INDICES OF FOOD PRODUCTION

		Malawi	Zambia	Zimbabwe
Cereals Imports	1974	17,000	93,000	56,000
(tonnes)	1983	21,000	247,000	124,000
Food Aid in Cereals	1974–75	–	1,000	–
(tonnes)	1982–83	3,000	83,000	6,000
Average Index of Food Production per capita (1974–76=100 to 1981–83)[57]		101	74	79

Source: World Development Report 1985.

Zambia's agricultural production is seriously inadequate as regards domestic consumption requirements and many commodities are regularly imported. Maize production attained a brief self-sufficiency in 1976, 1977, and 1981: in 1982–83 the importation of the national staple cost K11.3 m in scarce foreign exchange; K25.47 m the next year; and K27.6 m in 1984–85, when Malawi supplied Zambia with 20,000 tonnes of maize at a cost of K7.8 m, and Zimbabwe 50,000 tonnes priced at K19.8 m. Production of rice is about 40 per cent of domestic consumption needs, and production of wheat satisfies only some 10 per cent of total demand. The importation of wheat, often from South Africa, is particularly costly – in 1981–82 wheat imports reached K46 m. Tobacco

149

TABLE 6
ZAMBIA – PRODUCTION OF MARKETED CROPS

	1982	*1983*	*1984*
Maize (90kg bags)*	5.67 m	5.90 m	6.34 m
Soyabean (90kg bags)	0.057 m	0.076 m	0.105 m
Seed Cotton (kg)	12.8 m	20.72 m	40.91 m
Tobacco (kg)	1.9 m	2.10 m	2.35 m
Sugar (tonnes)	1.01 m	1.09 m	1.18 m

* National consumption requirements for the staple, over this period, were not less than 8 million bags per annum.
Source: Planning Division, Ministry of Agricultural and Water Development, *Agricultural Statistics Bulletin*, July–September 1985.

output fell disastrously from 13.2 m kg in 1964 to an average of about 2 m kg in the early 1980s. Cotton production, however, has gone up, although the quality of the lint is said to require improvement.[58] Total agricultural production declined steeply from 13.7 per cent of GDP in 1965 to only 9.4 per cent in 1974, and has yet to exceed the 1965 level. This is very small by African and regional standards, and mirrors the state's enduring over-reliance on copper.

Zimbabwe's broad agricultural productivities contrast totally with Zambia. In the early 1980s, agricultural exports in Zimbabwe represented on average 30–40 per cent of total exports each year. Over the preceding 30 years, crop yields rose markedly. Maize increased threefold, and cotton six times, largely as a result of successful research (3, pp.33, 177). Soyabean yields within the large-scale sector are, according to the Chavunduka Commission, 'comparable to those in the USA and in some years higher'. The large-scale maize sector similarly 'has long been among world leaders'. Average wheat yields are 'among the world's highest' at around 4.5 tonnes per hectare, and the country is one of the few in Africa which can satisfy its own requirements. Tobacco is the most important non-food crop and is usually the leading export commodity, and the 'highly sophisticated' industry is built upon 'one of the world's best' research programmes. A large proportion of cotton is exported, and 'consistently achieves above average world prices' (3, pp.39, 41, 44, 78).[59]

Zimbabwe's overall position as an agricultural producer within Africa was described as follows in 1984:

... a relatively efficient marketing system, reasonable prices, and Africa's best research and extension services. While Kenya imports all its fertilizer, Zimbabwe produces 15 domestic varieties. While grain spoilage averages nearly 15 per cent in the rest of sub-Saharan Africa, in Zimbabwe it is less than 1 per cent. (6, passim)

The diversification present within the country's agricultural production reflects the diversification and integration of the economy as a whole. The structure of the Zimbabwean economy differs markedly of course from its neighbours (except South Africa) as Table 7 suggests.

TABLE 7
ZIMBABWE – INDUSTRIAL ORIGIN OF GDP: LEADING SECTORS

	1977(%)	1982(%)
Agriculture and forestry	16.1	16.2
Manufacturing	22.2	26.4
Mining	7.2	5.9
Distribution	11.7	15.8
Public Administration & Defence	9.9	8.6
Transport	8.0	8.1
Construction	4.1	3.6

Source: Economic Intelligence Unit.

Serious uncertainties, however, now confront Zimbabwean agriculture. While agricultural productivity improved through the 1970s, it was neither as fast nor as broad-based as was needed to meet the demands of a rate of population growth greater than both Zambia and Malawi (3, p.72). Overall agricultural productivity was inadequate in a particular and additional sense. By independence the underdevelopment of the so-called Tribal/Communal areas was such as to produce a situation where 'approximately a third of the nation's land [was] rapidly becoming useless for anything, much less for productive agriculture . . .' (3, p.9). This cut the already low reserve of good land – only some 17 per cent of the total – and weakened the ability of the poor peasantry to contribute effectively to production. At the same time, but a comparatively lower level of significance, wage-labour employment in large-scale farming was beginning to decline as the result of the increasing productivity of this sector (3, pp.23, 89).[60]

Yet the independent state increased support to the small peasantry, as noted already, and the small-to-middle peasantries greatly expanded their food production for the market. Marketed maize production from the Communal areas rose some 500 per cent between 1980–81 and 1981–82, from about 54,000 to some 253,000 tonnes. The number of landowning rich peasants in the Purchase Areas increased from 8,500 in 1977 to 9,500 in 1982 (3, pp.31, 187).[61]

151

The poor peasantry appeared to favour engagement in the market albeit on much improved terms. Those in Makoni district during the liberation struggle in the 1970s seemed uninterested in collectivisation, while the poor peasantry nationally, according to Ranger, supported the war in order to see the establishment of a state which would both 'no longer interfere in peasant production' and would 'back black farming against white' through high producer prices, good marketing facilities, etc. (25, pp.177–8). Even the squatting phenomenon, which sprang into existence against the large-scale farms in 1981–82, expressed strong inegalitarian tendencies as well as the desperation of the landless and deprived. 'A high percentage of squatters', said the Chavunduka Commission, were 'either employed or already have land rights in the communal areas' (3, p.68) and other sources reported on the role and influence of so-called 'squatter kings' in certain areas (25, pp.311–13).[62] When the Mugabe government set its face against the squatters at the end of 1982 (25, p.313) it acted in accordance with its expressed support for productive commercial farming. The squatters' farming practices 'usually' presented a 'serious threat' to the lands they occupied (3, p.68) while as early as 20 May 1980, Mugabe had told a meeting of white farmers that they had a safe and guaranteed future, and that full and fair compensation would be paid for any land acquired for resettlement.[63]

It is the policy of resettlement which promised the most thorough change in the conditions of the small peasantry on the over-crowded and destitute Communal lands. It was planned to reallocate some 8 m hectares of land out of the 14.4 m hectares which were reserved for large-scale farming in the early 1980s. This proposal therefore went straight to the heart of the whole agricultural problematic in Zimbabwe; whether to provide land for the needy or to those able to farm it productively, the equity versus productivity issues. The programme could release the productive energies of the small peasantry in the future. On the other hand, it placed big uncertainties against the existing productivities and capacities of the large-scale sector immediately.[64] Land purchases on the terms envisaged and reallocations on a proper basis were soon seen as very costly.[65] As of mid-1982, only 1.35 m hectares had been acquired by the state, and most resettlement was planned to occur in the country's less fertile land, regions III, IV, and V (3, p.60; 8, p. 358). Such land was presumably then unused or underutilised by large-scale farming. The government's preference was for the productivity argument. The Minister of Lands stated in March 1981 that redistribution was 'not merely to give land to the landless', but to create a community which was 'commercial in orientation' and so able to 'meet the needs of the non-agricultural sectors of the population'. Land was intended, as was said in September 1982, for the farmer determined to make use of it.[66]

As the Chavunduka Commission recognised, Zimbabwe's agricultural productivities in the 1980s had grown out of more than 50 years' investment in research, development, and other aspects of a diversified farming sector. Successful food production and export production, the Commission pointed out, worked together in mutually supportive ways. Successful export agriculture had promoted efficiency in food production and encouraged the development of a range of good agricultural services (3, p.121). In an average year nearly 50 per cent of total agricultural production was exported (3, p.113). Such an agriculture offered little scope for an ill-equipped and inefficient small peasantry. Production of the country's main export commodities towards established levels of efficiency inherently promoted the formation of middle and rich peasantries with strong drives towards mechanisation and capitalisation. This had already occurred on a small scale, and if the developed agriculture was maintained while the state backed black farmers instead of whites, it could only broaden and grow quicker.

The Mugabe government also recognised that continued control over the large-scale sector by some 4,700 whites was neither desirable nor politically tenable.[67] Of equal importance for the long-term was, however, the identity of the groups and classes which would replace the white farmers. If these valuable farms were to be acquired by the new urban bureaucratic bourgeoisie, national productivities might well be endangered. The rising capitalised rich peasantry, on the other hand, would have a greater capacity for operating the large-scale farms efficiently. The outcome, in either case, will have a big effect on national export capacities, which are vital both to Zimbabwe and to its agriculturally weaker neighbours, Zambia, Mozambique, and Angola.

Many uncertainties confront agriculture in Zimbabwe today – very high population growth; the historic deprivation of the poor peasantry; the untenable position of white commercial farmers. Uncertainties also affect Malawi's agriculture – the smallness of the estates' sector; the role of the state following Banda's death; the very heavy exploitation of the small peasantry. Malawi's achievements in agriculture are superior to Zimbabwe's in terms of rising per capita production, but output is of course on a much smaller scale than in Zimbabwe and it is less diversified. The agricultural productivities of both countries nevertheless represent a great resource for future national development. Small Malawi's successes highlight the failures of Zambia where the bulk of the rural population has no prospect of future development as recompense for the long neglect which they have suffered. Here there is little or no agricultural surplus; no self-sufficiency; negligible investment resources; high indebtedness. A rich peasantry which was an early, active, even dynamic force for development under colonialism is now relatively ill-equipped and supported. In Zambia a weak state and backward agriculture stand in a long and close relationship.

NOTES

1. It is regrettable that this useful book contains no essay on the settler-colonial state, that some of the chapters are influenced by irrelevant notions of Zimbabwe as an underdeveloped country, and that the obviously oppressive nature of settler colonialism is stressed at the expense of consideration of its developmental contribution.
2. Despite this, Vail declares unconvincingly that 'the people saw cotton production primarily as a means to an end' – taxes – 'and not as an end in itself'. He also notes that by 1909 some peasants in the lower Shire area began growing cotton on individual plots with the aim of 'accumulating wealth'.
3. In agreements signed in 1936, Vail, 'Railway Development', p.389.
4. In early 1950 there were no less than 2,000 outstanding applicants for land, due not only to a strong drive for land-ownership among blacks, but also, states Ranger, to the government's slowness in surveying and preparing farms for sale (25, p.148).
5. From the late 1920s, African Agricultural Demonstrators had been sent into selected Reserves, where they had been of particular assistance to rising 'entrepreneurial peasants' (25, p.62).
6. See Chavunduka Report, pp.30–1 and Table 29, p.64. This table indicates that in 1980 the then re-named 'small-scale farming areas' covered a total of 1.48 m hectares.
7. Very small by comparison both with the poor peasantry in Zimbabwe, which numbered around 650,000 households, and with the rich peasantry in Zambia, at that time.
8. Despite rudimentary marketing facilities then (4, p.10).
9. Ranger quoting Barry Munslow (25, p.237). The rich peasantry's control over productive resources will be considered further below.
10. See Robert Klepper, 'The State and Peasantry in Zambia' in *The Evolving Structure of Zambian Society*, p.146.
11. Figures quoted by Robert Klepper, 'The State and Peasantry in Zambia', Table 3, p.150.
12. Op.cit., pp.130–1.
13. Ibid., p.134. Ghanaian cocoa farmers, as is well known, took firm advantage from such title.
14. For example (2) p.407 and (28) p.40.
15. The lower figure is that of the World Bank (30), Table 1, p.104; the higher that of the ILO (16), Table 2.3, p.16. The World Bank's figures are based on those of the Ministry of Agriculture, while the ILO's are compiled from a wider range of sources over a longer period. So-called subsistence farmers in Zambia are officially defined as those marketing up to but no more than 50% of their total production.
16. Land holding and farm size was of course not the only determinant of class here and in Zimbabwe and Malawi. It was rather the basis around which the possible acquisition of other resources, e.g., credit, subsequently hinged. It naturally covered a variety of forms, from simple usage or control, most typical of the small peasantry, to recorded claims and titles, and to leasehold and freehold ownership. The possession of legal ownership typified large sections of the rich peasantry and all rural capitalists.
17. The ILO unhelpfully identifies merely 'emergent' and 'commercial' farming classes. The former numbered only 90,000, and held anything between 2 and 40 hectares. The ILO stresses that its figures are 'very approximate' and represent only 'rough orders of magnitude' (14, Table 2.3).

18. As already noted, this figure for the Zimbabwean rich peasantry ignores those sections of the class located in the so-called communal areas and on new settlement schemes. The position of these two sectors or sub-categories is unrecognized in official statistics.
19. National comparisons of this kind are the more difficult and approximate because of the differing official 'class' classifications in Zimbabwe and Zambia: in the former 'small-scale farmers' owning an average of 123 hectares, and in the latter 'emergents' with less than 40 hectares each. Additionally, the official baseline of the Zambian 'commercial' class, ownership of more than 40 hectares, places it within the bounds of the Zimbabwean government's 'small-scale farmers'.
20. A recent consideration of the alignment of the state with large-scale farming is found in (8).
21. Press Holdings Ltd. is said to be 99% owned by President Banda, 'the largest company in Malawi', with 'extensive farming interests'. As the country's biggest producer of tobacco, with 60,000 acres of maize and over 6,000 acres of groundnuts, it is a leading member of the estates' sector. It also shares ownership of many major companies with the leading parastatals, the Malawi Development Corporation and the Agricultural Development and Marketing Corporation (ADMARC) (5, p.32). Banda is thus a large and direct beneficiary of his government's policies.
22. David Humphrey quoted in Ghai and Radwan (7, p.94).
23. This has been discussed in a number of places including (14, pp.xxxix, 51).
24. Combining a mid-peasantry of some 122,000 with a rich peasantry of 21,000 and comparing them to a poor peasantry of some 600,000.
25. The bulk of rural people had earlier been constrained to depend upon remittances from migrant labour in South Africa, and when these became sharply curtailed and controlled in the later 1970s, they suffered large losses of real incomes, which 'completely swamped' any modest gains from cash crops (7, p.92). This was a measure of their existing poverty, and a mechanism through which the Malawian government increased the domestic labour supply to the particular benefit of the rich rural classes.
26. Which 'must in part be held responsible for the relatively low growth of smallholder productivity' (7, pp.94–5). The estates are left free to deal directly with international buyers (17, p.368).
27. There is a good analysis of the weakness of the extension services in ILO, *Narrowing the Gaps* (16, pp.88–9), and the overall contemporary situation is discussed in (9). On the important issue of payments to farmers by government agencies, Zimbabwean practice highlights Zambian weaknesses. The Cotton Marketing Board in Zimbabwe makes payment 'usually within ten days of delivery', and the Grain Marketing Board is said to do the same 'within a short period' (3, pp.96–7).
28. This personally signed certificate, in Humphrey's view noted above, was the very first of the tangible benefits received by *achikumbe*. Quoted in (7, p.94).
29. *Economist*, 13 April 1985.
30. His government's detachment from agriculture has deep roots. What Palmer referred to as the land question 'never featured prominently', he said, 'in the nationalist demands of the 1950s and 1960s' (20, p.56). Momba also notes that 'UNIP as a party' was 'characterized by a strong "urban bias" from the very beginning' (19, p.292). The government's indifference to agriculture has been maintained while certain ministers and party chiefs became sizeable landowners, and was modified somewhat only recently (8).
31. They are examined respectively in (31, pp.80–5), and in (18, pp.34–7).
32. These are key terms in the work of James C. Scott on the peasantry in Southeast Asia and are also present in Goran Hyden's studies of Tanzania.
33. Usually by placing the stress upon the limitations and incompleteness of the new production activities – that it involves only a minority of peasants, that their output is small, that few resources are individually owned and sold on the market, and generally that no significant change has occurred at the time of observation.
34. The newly formed National Tobacco Company in Zambia stated in May 1986 that it had embarked on an 'ambitious programme' for developing tobacco production: in 1987, a total of 4,500 tonnes of tobacco would be produced of which commercial farmers would

contribute 80% and small-scale farmers 20%; in 1988, 7,000 tonnes would be produced of which small-scale farmers would contribute 50%; in 1989, small-scale farmers would produce 70% of the total of 10,000 tonnes; and by 1991, the output of small-scale farmers would be no less than 90% and that of commercial farmers just 10% of the total of 20,000 tonnes (*Zambia Daily Mail*, 16 May 1986). In other words, tobacco production will rise rapidly over some four years from 900 tonnes to 18,000 tonnes while being produced by farmers who remain uniformly small peasants. Producers will achieve a twenty-fold increase in output although resource acquisition and distribution among them remains static.

35. The terms used respectively by Worsley (31) and Lieberson (18). The notion of 'rational peasant' is closely considered by Samuel L. Popkin in his book of the same name sub-titled *The Political Economy of Rural Society in Vietnam*, Berkeley and Los Angeles, 1979.

36. Hellen noted not dissimilarly that the Tonga were 'cattle owners with a marked interest in and appreciation of European connotations of wealth, backed by traditions of bride wealth . . .' (1, p.76).

37. Palmer (22, pp.8–9) suggests that the Tonga's expansion of marketed production dates from 1912.

38. Also referred to as 'a class of Native Farmers', among whom the 'tendency towards individualism continues' (11, p.128).

39. Data of the 1945 Reconnaissance Survey, noted in Momba (19, p.283).

40. In the late 1950s farm sizes among the Tonga ranged up to 300 acres (11, pp.130–1). Momba also notes that the 1945 survey found that 'a few rich peasants' in Mazabuka produced in excess of 200 bags of maize each year, production which 'compared favourably with those of a number of white commercial farmers' (19, p.283).

41. To borrow from Ranger's expression 'self-peasantization' which he uses in conjunction with what he refers to as 'the choice of *the* peasant option' (my emphasis), when in reality there would appear to be at least as many 'peasant options' as embryonic classes and categories of peasants in particular places and times, e.g., a small peasant option, middle and rich peasant aims and drives, and perhaps a readiness to combine temporary wage-employment with small-scale farming (25, pp.25, 31 and passim). Ranger's usage is of course perfectly compatible with the notion of the homogeneous (small) peasantry, and the corollary that rich peasants are small businessmen or entrepreneurs.

42. As suggested above, the colonial state was 'essentially neutral' on development in the Purchase Lands prior to 1962 (4, pp.136, 156, 164).

43. These broad generalisations are those of ILO, who noted that in 1977–78 88% of all agricultural loans were issued to farmers in the line-of-rail provinces (not including Eastern province) (14, pp.15–16). As stated above, their farms ranged up to 40 hectares in size.

44. Of the national total of 21,350 rich peasant (or medium-scale commercial) farm units, only 90 were in Northern, 80 in North-Western, 50 in Luapula, and none at all in Western provinces (30, Table 1).

45. Of the national total of 730 large-scale farm units, 320 were in Southern and 300 in Central provinces (ibid.).

46. In the assessment of the ILO in the late 1970s, the large-scale farmers in Zambia utilised the 'most sophisticated machinery' and were 'among the best in the world' in their application of knowledge, capital, and skill (16, p.91).

47. Kasonde's farm was atypically located in Northern province, but this was suitable for the coffee and rain-fed wheat on which he was concentrating, and he was near the Tazara railway (*Times of Zambia*, 10 May 1985).

48. On the data presented by the World Bank, only Western province had no 'medium-scale commercial' farmers in 1980, but it did possess the comparatively high number of 5,450 'small-scale commercial' farmers or middle peasants, as well as 85,400 small peasants, which was the second largest class in the country (30, Table 1).

49. See Klepper, *op.cit.*, p.139.

50. Respectively the Commercial Farmers Union, the Zimbabwe National Farmers Union, and the National Farmers Association of Zimbabwe (3, p.31).

51. *The Economist*, 12 January 1985.
52. For example, 'small non-commercial farmers' in the later 1970s produced 'over 60 percent of marketed maize'. (These 'non-commercial' farmers in official terminology were actually small and middle peasants who sold less than K500 of maize – 14, pp.xxxiii, 61.)
53. On the exchange values current in 1986, K80 per month represented a household income of approximately $11.
54. The more developed and accessible areas had near this time a population of about 1.5 m with in addition 'generally larger and stronger families, lower outmigration, larger farms, higher per capita incomes, and more production'; while the commercially backward areas held about 2.1 m people with 'higher outmigration, smaller and weaker families many of them with only female adults, smaller farms, much lower per capita incomes', etc. (14, p.16).
55. See (14) Table 0.1, p.xxi. The year to which the estimates applied was 1976.
56. The Economic Intelligence Unit said in 1983 that while some 38% of Malawi's surface area was arable, 37% of this was already cultivated then (5, p.29).
57. As regards *agricultural* production per capita, and on a base-line of 1969–71=100, an alternative assessment of the three countries' performance by 1980 is as follows: Malawi 98; Zambia 82; Zimbabwe 87 (3, Table 34, p.72).
58. See Republic of Zambia, National Commission for Development Planning, *Economic Review and Annual Plan 1986*, Lusaka, the Government Printer, 1986, pp.62–3. *Zambia Daily Mail*, 13 Sept. 1985.
59. Zimbabwe's success as a cereals' producer has given it the position of a granary state among the 9 member countries of the Southern African Development Coordination Conference.
60. Good land refers specifically to zones or natural regions 1 and 11.
61. The increased total of established rich peasants was partly or largely due perhaps to the return of farmers forced to flee from the guerilla struggle.
62. Ranger (25, pp.311–13), with reference mainly to *Moto* and to officials.
63. Quoted in Good (8, p.357).
64. The intended programme threatened to reduce wage-employment within large-scale farming, at a time when as noted it was beginning to decline although the population was rising rapidly.
65. Thus the assessment of a cost of Z$600–$800 m 1982–1985 on existing plans (3, p.66).
66. The second speaker was also a Minister of Lands. Quoted in Good (8, p.258).
67. For example the statement to this effect by Minister of Lands, Moven Mahachi, in *Moto*, July 1982.

REFERENCES

1. Carpenter, Frances, 'The Introduction of Commercial Farming Into Zambia and its Effects to 1940' in Robin Palmer (ed.), *Zambian Land and Labour Studies*, Vol.1, Lusaka 1973
2. Chanock, Martin, 'Agricultural Change and Continuity in Malawi' in R. Palmer and Neil Parsons (eds.), *The Roots of Rural Poverty in Central and Southern Africa*, London, 1977
3. Chavunduka, G.L. (chairman), *Zimbabwe, Report of the Commission of Inquiry Into the Agricultural Industry*, Harare, 1982
4. Cheater, Angela P., *Idioms of Accumulation*, Gweru, 1984
5. Economic Intelligence Unit, *Quarterly Economic Review, Zimbabwe and Malawi*, Annual Supplement, 1983
6. Frankel, Glenn, 'An African Success Story', *Guardian Weekly*, 16 Dec. 1984
7. Ghai, Dharam and Radwan, Samir, 'Growth and Inequality: Rural Development in Malawi, 1964–1978' in D. Ghai and S. Radwan (eds.), *Agrarian Policies and Rural Poverty in Africa*, Geneva, 1983

8. Good, Kenneth, 'Zimbabwe' in Timothy M. Shaw and O. Aluko, *The Political Economy of African Foreign Policy*, Aldershot, 1984
9. —, 'Systemic Agricultural Mismanagement: the 1985 "Bumper" Harvest in Zambia', *Journal of Modern African Studies*, Vol.24, No.1, 1986
10. Hart, Keith, *The Political Economy of West African Agriculture*, Cambridge, 1982
11. Hellen, John A., *Rural Economic Development in Zambia, 1890–1964*, Munich, 1968
12. Hyden, Goran, *Beyond Ujamaa in Tanzania*, Berkeley and Los Angeles, 1980
13. Iliffe, John, *The Emergence of African Capitalism*, London and Basingstoke, 1983
14. International Labour Office, *Basic Needs in an Economy Under Pressure*, Addis Ababa, 1981
15. Jackson, Robert H., and Rosberg, Carl G., *Personal Rule in Black Africa*, Berkeley and Los Angeles, 1982
16. Jaspa Employment Advisory Mission, *Narrowing the Gaps*, Addis Ababa, 1977
17. Kydd, Jonathan and Christiansen, Robert, 'Structural Change in Malawi Since Independence: Consequences of a Development Strategy Based on Large-scale Agriculture', *World Development*, Vol.10, No.5, 1982
18. Lieberson, Jonathan, 'The Silent Majority', *New York Review of Books*, 22 Oct. 1981
19. Momba, Jotham C., 'Peasant Differentiation and Rural Party Politics in Colonial Zambia', *Journal of Southern African Studies*, Vol.11, No.2, 1985
20. Palmer, Robin, 'Land in Zambia' in R. Palmer (ed.), *Zambian Land and Labour Studies*, Vol.1, Lusaka, 1973
21. —, 'The Agricultural History of Rhodesia' in R. Palmer and N. Parsons (eds.), *The Roots of Rural Poverty in Central and Southern Africa*, London, 1977
22. —, 'The Zambian Peasantry Under Colonialism: 1900–1930' in *The Evolving Structure of Zambian Society*, Centre of African Studies, University of Edinburgh, Proceedings of a Seminar, 30–31 May 1980
23. Phimister, Ian, 'Peasant Production and Underdevelopment in Southern Rhodesia, 1890–1914, with Particular Reference to the Victoria District' in R. Palmer and N. Parsons (eds.), *The Roots of Rural Poverty in Central and Southern Africa*, London, 1977
24. Provincial Planning Unit, *Blueprint for Agricultural Development in Lusaka Province*, Lusaka, 1984
25. Ranger, Terence, *Peasant Consciousness and Guerilla War in Zimbabwe*, London, 1985
26. Stoneman, Colin, 'Agriculture' in C. Stoneman (ed.), *Zimbabwe's Inheritance*, London, 1981
27. Vail, Leroy, 'Railway Development and Colonial Underdevelopment: the Nyasaland Case' in R. Palmer and N. Parsons (eds.), *The Roots of Rural Poverty in Central and Southern Africa*, London, 1977
28. —, 'The State and the Creation of Colonial Malawi's Agricultural Economy' in Robert I. Rotberg (ed.), *Imperialism, Colonialism and Hunger: East and Central Africa*, Lexington, 1983
29. Wield, David, 'Manufacturing Industry', in C. Stoneman (ed.), *Zimbabwe's Inheritance*, London, 1981
30. World Bank, Regional Mission in Eastern Africa, *Zambia: Agricultural Research and Extension Review*, Report No. 4591 – ZA, 22 June 1983
31. Worsley, Peter, 'Village Economies' in Raphael Samuel (ed.), *People's History and Socialist Theory*, London, 1981
32. Young, Crawford, *Ideology and Development in Africa*, New Haven and London, 1982

5

The Modern Economic History of Botswana

ANDREW MURRAY AND NEIL PARSONS

INTRODUCTION

Botswana today is a paradox of political economy. It is a capitalist economy based on central planning. More capitalist than any of its neighbours (including South Africa) in lack of state ownership, control and management of industry or agriculture or even of infrastructure. But also more planned than even supposedly-socialist states in Southern Africa, in terms of state machinery identifying, projecting and inducing the growth of economic sectors over five-year periods.

The role of the state in recent economic development has been the product of necessity. For twenty years before 1971–72, state revenue from an impoverished economy – one of the world's ten poorest nations – was insufficient even to cover the recurrent government budget. For more like seventy years Botswana (then Bechuanaland Protectorate) had been reduced to the poorest of the poor by almost complete subordination to the interests of the South African economy.

The 'break-out' of the Botswana economy – thirtyfold growth in the past two decades – has been made possible by the exploitation of diamonds and beef under state patronage. State revenue has burgeoned, from 15 to 1195 million Pula between 1967–68 and 1986–87, making Botswana a classic test case of whether development can really 'trickle down' from the urban mineral top to the rural subsistence bottom. It is also a test of whether the state can tackle the two inheritances that loom largest for the Botswana economy – the vagaries of climate, and the proximity of South Africa.

HISTORICAL BACKGROUND BEFORE 1899

Between the imposition of colonial tax in 1899 and the renegotiation of the South African Customs Union in 1969, the pressures of colonial

159

state intervention in the Botswana economy almost entirely originated from South Africa. But there were pre-colonial Tswana states within Botswana which survived colonial rule as 'tribal reserves', and which continued to express elements of autonomy. It is necessary to look back to the formation and florescence of those states to grasp the nature of their political economies.

The earliest states in Southern Africa may have originated in Botswana about 1000 A.D. Recent archaeology around Toutswe Hill in the Central District has shown the existence of three hill towns dating from that period (34). Each town covered approximately 70,000 square metres on a flat hill-top, and was based around a very large cattle corral. Similar but smaller villages of 10,000 square metres were located on other hill-tops, while small hamlets were based on small corrals on the plains. This is the earliest evidence of centralised cattle-keeping and nucleated human settlement of hundreds of thousands of people in Southern Africa, and indicates the existence of a state or states with centralised wealth and authority.

The characteristic type of state formation in precolonial Southern Africa, from Toutswe (c.900–1200 A.D.) and Great Zimbabwe (c.1200–1400 A.D.) onwards, is normally known among historians as the *mafisa* system. *Mafisa* refers to cattle which were lent or loaned in trust from patron to client, in return for tribute, services, and allegiance. Hence the *mafisa* system is not improperly sometimes translated as 'cattle-feudalism'.[1]

The *mafisa* system was the organisational principle of the Tswana states which spread across the Kalahari from the south-east of modern Botswana in the later eighteenth and early nineteenth centuries. Though the acquisition of cattle played its part in the wars of conquest, particularly during the *Difaqane* invasions of Kololo and Ndebele armies traversing the sub-continent, the main incentive of Tswana political expansion appears to have been the capture of trade in hunting goods. Lines of conquest followed the supply routes of ivory, feathers and furs. Thirstland hunters were incorporated into Tswana societies in servile status – while the chiefs of conquered mixed farming groups continued subject to Tswana kings through the holding of *mafisa* cattle and tribute in grain as well as hunting produce (59).

The trade in ivory, furs and feathers, and the introduction of the horse, wagon and gun, account for the articulation of the 'feudal' states of Botswana into the expanding mercantile economy of the Cape during the nineteenth century, an articulation that was to take the eventual political form of a British Protectorate over Bechuanaland in 1885. It was a protectorate with political origins in alliance of Batswana and British against Boers and Amandebele.

The hunting trade was rapidly depleted by the extermination of wildlife in the 1870s–80s, but Botswana took on vital strategic significance as the 'Road to the North' for British interests from the Cape to the Zambezi. The defeat of the Amandebele in 'Rhodesia' during 1893–96 and of the Boers in 'South Africa' during 1899–1902 opened the way for fuller imposition of British hegemony on the Bechuanaland Protectorate. It was no longer such an important piece in the Southern African strategic jigsaw (64; 26, pp.119–28).

YEARS OF IMPOVERISHMENT 1899–1933

It was no accident that the beginnings of decline from a developing to an underdeveloped economy were marked by the beginnings of regular colonial administration around 1900. Internal boundaries between the Tswana 'tribal' states were fixed and a system of colonial 'Hut Tax' was introduced in 1899, at a time when people were still recovering from the rinderpest pandemic of 1896 which had killed off as many as nine out of every ten cattle (85). The Mafeking–Bulawayo railway, which had opened in 1897, was also in process of rapidly replacing the international waggon trade which had been the infrastructure for the growth of nineteenth-century Tswana states. Thus, even as the British began to turn 'protection' into colonial rule the local economy of the Protectorate was slipping into ever deepening depression.

Cattle herds could be, and were, quickly replenished in the early 1900s, but not so cattle markets. Few cattle or small stock could be marketed between 1902 and 1910 because of export embargoes imposed by neighbouring colonies due to East Coast fever, anthrax and rinderpest. But cash still had to be found to pay the Hut Tax of 20 shillings per adult man. With the decline of the waggon trade and a series of droughts in the 1900s all but eliminating the sale of crops as a source of income, more Batswana were obliged to migrate to the mines in South Africa – increasingly to the Witwatersrand as well as to Kimberley. What had been one of a number of options was becoming unavoidable, not just to pay Hut Tax, but also to maintain the patterns of consumption to which people had become accustomed in the 1880s and 1890s.

Restrictions on the export of cattle were partly lifted in 1910. For a few years dependence upon the income derived from migrant labour was mitigated by the sale of cattle to Southern Rhodesia and the Union of South Africa, albeit at low prices. Khama III of the BaNgwato, acutely aware of the social evils which accompanied the system of migrant labour, made vain efforts to re-establish his state's economic autonomy. He started a royal trading company in 1910 and used it to ensure that 'tribal' state revenues benefitted from the cattle trade. State capital combined with local labour, which would otherwise have been exported, was employed in projects such as the building of a great church and schools. But Khama's very success in diverting trading profits and labour into his country from abroad proved to be his downfall. Foreign business interests, backed by the South African press, succeeded in pressurising the colonial administration to dismantle and forbid royal participation in trade (65). The 1923 Credit Sales to Natives Proclamation then effectively put African retailers out of business by banning wholesale credit to them.

In 1917 cattle exports to the Union of South Africa were again stopped due to bovine pleuro-pneumonia. Though the market was opened up two years later for the southern half of the Protectorate, in 1924 the Union imposed weight restrictions on cattle imports to protect the large South African producers from cheaper imported cattle (35). The decline in the quality of Tswana cattle herds caused by disease, pasture erosion and drought in the previous decades ensured that few cattle would reach the required weight. The result was a traffic in smuggled cattle across the borders that brought some profit to white traders and speculators with border farms, but which gave little income to Batswana cattle owners in the 'tribal' reserves. The long-term economic results can be seen in the Bangwato Reserve by 1930. In that year the Ngwato state imported goods worth £25,611 more than it exported. Its people also had to find a further £30,000 to render unto the colonial state in taxes and levies (64, pp.134–5).

Once accumulated cash reserves were eaten up, the only alternative was increasing dependence on migrant labour – a dependency which had become vital to the survival of the economy of the Protectorate as a whole. By 1933 when the Pim Commission made the first serious critical inquiry into the economy, the Bechuanaland Protectorate had become little more than a labour pool and an impoverished market for the Union of South Africa.

The colonial administration, headed by the High Commissioner in Cape Town (or Pretoria) who deputised to a Resident Commissioner at Mafeking, acted as midwife to the birth of the labour reserve economy. Since 1899 the administration's goals had been to maintain law and order in the Protectorate, to extract revenues in the form of the Hut Tax, and to balance the budget books so that expenditure did not exceed revenue. It abandoned the collection of import and export statistics in 1909 in preparation for the revised Customs Union with South Africa of 1910. The fiscal autonomy of the Tswana states was further eroded in

1919 by the establishment of a Native Fund for educational and welfare development along South African lines, capitalised by a surcharge of three shillings on the Hut Tax. 'Native Tax' replaced and standardised the school taxes already collected by the Tswana states on top of the annual Hut Tax. The Tswana states or 'tribes' remained responsible for the collection of both the Hut Tax and Native Tax. In return for their loss of discretion over local development, chiefs and headmen were rewarded with a central representative institution in the form of a Native Advisory Council. The Tswana states thereafter sometimes resorted to their own developmental levies. But even where the political will survived, the economic muscle was wasting away. Their economies were being starved of markets, devastated by drought and disease, and drained of accumulated cash reserves.

Impoverishment was unequally distributed regionally and by social strata. In Ngamiland, for example, the period 1899–1933 seems to have been one of relative prosperity. Rinderpest had pushed back the tsetse-fly into the swamps by destroying its wildlife hosts, and thereby temporarily opened up the Okavango region to pastoralism. Such prosperity, however, benefitted stock-holders rather than crop farmers and fisherpeople (55). The trend towards unequal distribution of wealth between stock-holders and non-stockholders in the rest of the Protectorate became evident after the market value of livestock recovered in the 1940s.

Drought, opportunities of male migration, depressed livestock prices, and 'tribal' levies obliged or persuaded a growing percentage of Batswana, particularly among the politically subordinate subject peoples, to surrender their livestock and become dependent upon wages earned by men in the South African mines. Such redistribution of cattle, concomitant with increase of male labour migration, had begun with the collapse of the Kalahari hunting trade before 1899, and probably became most intensive in the three decades after 1933. Cattle were passed to those whose herds and water or pasture resources were large enough to withstand the demands of the environment and of the state. These larger cattle-owners, mostly chiefs and headmen, sometimes organised in syndicates, and white settlers with border ranchers, stood to benefit from market recovery or current smuggling (52; 67).

THE YEARS OF FRUSTRATION AND STAGNATION 1933–1954

The doctrine of the balanced budget was temporarily abandoned in 1933–34, when the British government began once again to contribute a grant-in-aid towards administrative expenditure in the Protectorate. Depression and drought, as well as foot-and-mouth disease, had resulted

163

in the falling off of payment of Hut Tax since 1928–29, and domestic revenues had failed to cover recurrent expenditure. The administration had attempted to stop the rot by instituting a new Native Tax of 25 shillings, collected as a poll tax on every male over eighteen years of age – but to no effect, as the previous Hut Tax had despite its name always been collected as a tax on adult males rather than as a tax on housing. A grant-in-aid of £177,000 from Britain had to be given to make up the deficit. Revenues from taxation only regained pre-1930 levels in 1939 and the British grant-in-aid continued to be provided until 1941 – having contributed one-third of recurrent expenditures during the years 1933–41 (41, pp.92–3).

Even before the Depression, the Dominions and Colonial Secretary in London, L.S. Amery, had determined to make a start on the development of Bechuanaland. He recruited an energetic administrator, C.F. Rey as Resident Commissioner, who took up his post in early 1930 (70). But the effects of the Depression, and political changes in London, delayed any action until a review, carried out by Alan Pim in 1933, of the financial and economic position of the territory (69). His report, backing the Amery-Rey line of expenditure on public services and the reform of Protectorate administration in order to provide infrastructure for development, was influential in securing the British grants-in-aids for the territory.

Rey's efforts to boost the economy of the Protectorate were largely frustrated and only partially successful. The Depression put paid to plans for copper mining by knocking the bottom off metal prices. But dams were built in collaboration with the 'tribes', a small abattoir was re-opened at Lobatse in 1934, and schemes to exploit the water resources of the Kalahari desert and swamps were mooted. However, as Rey discovered, the British government still lacked any serious commitment to the development of the Protectorate in the face of 'inevitable' transfer to the Union (70, Prologue and Epilogue). With the coming of the Second World War, the territory was expected to contribute an enormous quantity of labour to the war effort in the South African mines as well as on the North African military front – at the expense of its own economic development (46).

The pace of labour migration from the Protectorate quickened considerably during the 1930s. It has been estimated that during 1938–40 27.7 per cent of adult males (i.e. 23,500 men) were working outside the country (73, p.39). The same authority estimates that in the year 1930 little more than 4,000 Batswana men had been employed in South Africa (73, p.32). This extraordinary growth reflects not only the parlous state of the Protectorate economy, but also the greatly increased labour demand of the gold-mining boom in post-1933 South Africa. The Witwatersrand Native Labour Association became very active in the northern half of the Protectorate during the later 1930s, building a road from Francistown to Ngamiland (and later airfields) to transport labourers to the Rand. The colonial administration gave every assistance to the recruitment drive. Rey himself remarked: 'it will help the natives to get a little money which they badly need, and will enable the Administration to get in a certain amount of additional hut tax, which they need no less badly' (80).

While colonial state-sponsored development spluttered and then died during the 1930s, indigenous state development efforts recovered, particularly in the field of education. In 1933 there had been 98 African primary schools with 7,960 pupils. Five years later, in 1938, there were 131 African primary schools with over 15,000 pupils. Funds for education were supplied by tribal levies and after 1938 by capital allocated from the newly created Tribal Treasuries which were entitled to 35 per cent of the Native Tax collected. There were no colonial government schools for African children either primary or secondary, until the eve of Independence in 1965. Secondary education was provided outside the borders of the Protectorate, notably at Tiger Kloof in South Africa run by the London Missionary Society. Some primary schools attempted secondary classes in the later 1930s, but the first school designed to include secondary classes was opened by the Catholic Church in 1944. After the Second World War, four 'tribes' managed to finance and build their own secondary schools, the most famous of these being Moeng College, which opened with upper primary classes in 1948, and which was built with the aid of a tribal levy, mainly cattle, amounting to £100,000 (66).

Such was the contribution made by the Protectorate to the war effort in terms of men (10,000 adult males out of a total population of 400,000), money (a war levy realised £89,000), and food (labour and land was provided by each tribe to produce grain for sale), that many Batswana expected a 'new deal' from the British in 1945 as they had in 1902. They were to be disappointed again. Though the Colonial Development and Welfare Act of the British Parliament in 1944 had made provision for the expenditure of £120 million in the British colonies and protectorates, very little found its way to Bechuanaland in the immediate post-war period. The function of the Protectorate administration was still considered to be the minimal one of maintaining law and order subject to the doctrine of the balanced budget. The official briefing given to a new Resident Commissioner in 1947 was simply to do nothing to disrupt labour supplies to South Africa (76). Even in the first years of the 1950s when paltry revenues actually began to exceed expenditures (the

Studies in the Economic History of Southern Africa

1952–53 reserves stood at £419,000), practically nothing was done to promote development.

The logjam was not unstuck until 1954. The Symon Commission of that year, given a similar brief to the Pim Commission, came to similar conclusions. As Symon remarked,

the apparently satisfactory financial position was only achieved by the curtailment of practically every activity of Government. Social and administrative services were maintained at a dangerously low level and the construction and maintenance of public works drastically restricted (79, p.52).

TRANSITION TOWARDS DEVELOPMENT 1954–1972

A cynic might well conclude that the reason Britain began to pump money into the Protectorate in the 1950s was to provide the minimum infrastructure necessary to facilitate a legitimate transfer of power to some other Power. (The idea of political independence rather than incorporation into a neighbouring state or federation was not accepted until the early 1960s.)

The building of a new abattoir at Lobatse in 1954 (the previous one had closed in 1941) marks the birth of the modern livestock industry in Botswana. It was accomplished largely through funds and expertise provided by Britain's Colonial Development Corporation. In the same year, thanks to the Symon Commission, the British government decided to use up the Protectorate's financial reserves and then to resume grants-in-aid. So for the first time the colonial power now made some long-term commitment to the development of the economy of Bechuanaland. Development expenditure, in the form of grants and loans, was to increase from £123,500 in 1953–54 to £550,000 in 1956–57 and £1.8 million in 1964–65.

However, as commentators have noted, all this was 'rather little and rather late' (31, p.31). The bulk of British aid was to be spent on projects, notably the building of the new capital at Gaborone, which merely up-graded the machinery of government to an acceptable level for independence. As late as 1964 a UNESCO educational mission described Bechuanaland government machinery as 'barely sufficient for the maintenance of the daily administration of a country rapidly advancing towards self-government' (84, p.55). Money was also spent on encouraging the stronger peasant farmers – and on veterinary projects, in particular the control of foot-and-mouth disease, and water development. The government continued the policy, begun in the early 1950s, of converting state land around the borders into commercial ranching

166

areas for white settler owners. But the colonial administration, under the enlightened leadership of Peter Fawcus as Resident Commissioner (1959–65), became more sympathetic to black social and economic aspirations than ever before. However, the pace of political change was such that neither sufficient time nor funds were available to more than begin the transition towards significant economic development.

Britain conceded political independence to Botswana in 1966. But the new Republic, in the words of a later planning minister, 'inherited almost nothing by way of physical and social infrastructure so necessary to foster economic growth and development' (60, p.xv). Five years of drought had killed a third of the cattle and made one in five Batswana dependent upon famine relief. Botswana was one of the ten poorest countries in the world with a per capita income of less than U.S.$75 per year. According to the 1964 Census, only 73,000 of the total population of 580,000 were in formal employment, and most of these were employed outside Bechuanaland as migrant labourers. A third of the adult population could read, but there were less than 250 people with qualifications at junior secondary level or above (7). A report compiled by the British Ministry of Overseas Development in 1965 concluded that Botswana would not be able to balance its government budget without external aid for many years to come (8). There were no prospects for significant economic growth, it suggested. Development efforts would have to be focussed upon cattle production as the bulwark of the economy.

The pessimism of the old imperial government was not shared by the new independent government. Though its Transitional Development Plan of 1966 was concerned mainly with the re-organisation of central and local government, one of its major objectives was budgetary independence by 1971. Yet the Plan contained no indication as to how this was to be achieved. Reference was made to a project called the 'Shashe Complex' which would turn Francistown and its hinterland into a centre for mining-industrial development but even this was dependent upon the as yet undecided whims of multinational capital (10; 49).

The end of the great drought fortuitously coincided with the beginnings of political independence, thus facilitating the recovery of cattle production. Were it not for the good rains, and manna from Britain in the shape of substantial grants-in-aid, the GDP would have grown little if at all. As it was the GDP increased from P14.5 million (£7.25 million) in 1966 to P23.2 million (£13.8 million) in 1968–69. An encouraging trend, but still insufficient to prevent a widening deficit of government revenue on recurrent expenditure.

Yet by 1972 not only was Botswana no longer in need of foreign budgetary aid, but its recurrent revenue had almost doubled, the

167

GDP had tripled, and development expenditure had increased sixfold. Botswana's finances had undergone an extraordinary transformation. At last significant economic and social development was feasible, and it could be accomplished without over-dependence upon external aid. How had this 'miracle' come about?

The essential prerequisite for budgetary self-sufficiency was the securing of customs and excise revenue by re-negotiation of the Customs Union with South Africa (and Swaziland and Lesotho) in 1969. Under the previous system Botswana government revenue would have scarcely benefited from any rise in exports and imports resulting from development of the country. Botswana's share of the revenue pool of the whole Customs Union was fixed at 0.30971 per cent (and that had been raised from 0.27622 per cent in 1963 by the British at the expense of Lesotho's share with no loss to South Africa). Customs and excise raised only a meagre P1.4 million (£833,000) in Botswana government revenues during 1968–69. After much negotiation, with South Africa demanding 'protection' from its minuscule neighbours, a new customs agreement was reached on the basis of recorded annual trade instead of fixed percentages. Customs and excise then brought in P5.1 million to Botswana in 1969–70 and by 1972–73 had increased to P12.5 million – 45 per cent of total domestic revenues (48; 71).

Revenue from the re-negotiated Southern African Customs Union was boosted between 1969 and 1972 by the sharp rise in capital imports from outside the Customs Union, mainly as a consequence of developments in the mining sector. It was mining, and to a lesser extent the beef export industry, which by 1972 pushed Botswana into a period of sustained economic growth at a rate unmatched except by oil-exporting countries.

Diamonds had been discovered at Orapa in 1967 and production began, at what was then the world's second biggest diamond pipe, in 1971. Orapa fitted neatly into the infrastructure planned for the 'Shashe Complex', replacing the lapsed salt and soda ash project on the nearby Makgadikgadi Pans. But De Beers financed most of the project themselves, lending the government finance for its share and investing P21 million before the mine had opened. In 1972 the government of Botswana received P2.8 million in profits and revenue from De Beers – a figure which would leap to over P18 million in 1975 when its share of the equity was negotiated upward from 15 to 50 per cent (31, pp.149–56). The other, original half of the 'Shashe Complex' proved less successful – the copper and nickel mine at Selebi-Phikwe, run by R.S.T./Amax, for which government was investing much more heavily in roads, railways, power, water and township development. A multi-national donor package had been put together by government by 1973 after five years' effort. Copper and nickel production began in 1974 but was beset by low world copper prices and technical difficulties with the flash-smelting process of making copper-nickel matte. All this resulted in company restructurings that have since achieved efficient production but have never since surfaced from the accumulated debt.

The better annual rains continued through the late 1960s and early 1970s giving rise to improved crop harvests and growth in the national herd, from 1.2 million cattle in 1966 to 2.2 million in 1972. Negotiations with the European Economic Community, as part of Britain's entry to the EEC in 1971–73, resulted in privileged access for Botswana beef into Europe and a doubling of beef exports in 1971–73 at a time of rapid rise in world beef prices (44). Total payments to cattle producers rose from P12.1 million in 1971 to P31.8 million by 1976. Government planning machinery in negotiation with foreign powers and foreign capital had facilitated the growth of livestock and mining exports and customs revenues, in ways that the colonial regime would not or could not attempt. But there was as yet scarcely a dribble of development 'trickle down' from managers to masses, or outside the new mining villages and the administrative capital of Gaborone – growing so rapidly from such a small base.

YEARS OF RAPID DEVELOPMENT 1972–1987

Botswana's apparent success as a functioning multi-party democracy, albeit with only one large party at its heart, is often remarked upon. The dominance and success of the Botswana Democratic Party in four post-Independence elections was in large part attributable to its success as the government which delivered the goods. The B.D.P. government has not shrunk from claiming responsibility for the extraordinary growth of the economy since Independence. This has helped to close the electorate's eyes to the unequal distribution of new wealth (62).

The second National Development Plan of 1970–75 tried to come to terms, at least rhetorically, with social justice in development. But it said that redistribution of wealth to the people would be 'almost entirely dependent on the successful creation of a mining sector' (13, p.17). Government Paper No.1 of March 1972, *Rural Development in Botswana* spelt out the implications of such a 'dual economic strategy'. The income derived from mineral-led development was to be re-invested 'to promote labour intensive activities and improve services in rural areas' (14, p.2). Surplus government revenue was to be used to promote rural development. The first fruit of this strategy was the Accelerated Rural Development Programme, timed to coincide with the 1974 general election. It generated new schools, clinics, roads, and water-supply projects in the major rural centres.

In the long term, direct investment in rural development projects was comparatively small. During the 1973–81 period over half of domestic development expenditure was spent on the development of urban areas and main trunk roads. The much vaunted Tribal Grazing Lands Policy, the vanguard of the rural development programme, used up only 6.2 per cent of government development expenditure from the date of its inception in 1976 up to 1981. Only 4.4 per cent of domestic development expenditure went on rural development projects in 1979–85 (63, p.84). In part this was a consequence of the failure of the rural development programmes themselves, designed to benefit those graziers and farmers who were already 'strong'. In part this was a reflection of the reluctance of the government to intervene in the 'private sector' or to support cooperative production. There was much talk but no action about the 'liquidity problem' of commercial banks holding the surplus cash of rural cattle producers but refusing to loan funds to communal rural areas – because of purely 'commercial' lending criteria biassed towards highly profitable projects on freehold land (51). Government expenditure on rural areas was also constrained by the increasingly complex demands of the infrastructural projects of roads, schools and clinics to which it became politically committed in the early 1970s.

Concern with the educational system in the mid-1970s drew attention to the school-leaver problem of too many people chasing too few jobs. There was an ever-widening gap between the production of school leavers and the expansion of formal sector employment which such school leavers expected to find (86). This was highlighted by officially commissioned reports by Christopher Colclough in 1973 and by Michael Lipton in 1978 (30; 50). The fifth National Development Plan of 1979–85 reflected this concern by identifying the creation of employment opportunities as its new priority. The employment problem was further exacerbated by the breaching of the government's previous wage restraint, under pressures of world inflation, in the mid-1970s. The government had argued that higher pay meant fewer employment opportunities, against the counter-argument that higher formal sector wages were passed on to the rural economy through remittances. A serious strike by workers demanding more pay at the new Selebi-Phikwe mines was crushed by the police in 1984, but government proved less able to resist the demands of civil service personnel, and government salaries – which by convention set the levels of private sector salaries – doubled between 1974 and 1980.

Meanwhile the labour movement was brought under control with the assistance of the U.S. government-funded African-American Labour Institute, to institute discipline over workers by training trade union leadership – so that the somewhat draconian labour legislation already on the books (along the lines of other ex-British colonies such as Zambia), making official strike procedures incredibly protracted, could be successfully applied (32).

As the decade came to an end economic growth slowed, reflecting world market depression and regional insecurity. Diamond sales faltered. Foot-and-mouth disease, spilling over from the Rhodesian civil war, reduced cattle exports. Drought conditions returned, and at the time of writing (1987) have still not abated – though Botswana boasts a drought relief programme that has not yet led to one drought-related death. However diamond exports recovered by 1982, and foot-and-mouth disease was contained after Zimbabwe's independence in 1980. The growth of GDP revived after fits and starts in the early 1980s, but is predicted to level out by the end of the decade because of the lack of new large development projects.

The slogan for the twentieth anniversary of Independence celebrations in September 1986 was 'Twenty Years of Progress'. Not a particularly original slogan, yet one that rings less hollowly in Botswana than in many other countries. Development since 1966 has enriched the lives of most Batswana, particularly in the fields of education and health. The suffering they experienced during the drought of the 1960s has not been repeated during the drought of the 1980s – that is progress enough. Yet these achievements are fragile ones. Botswana is no longer a labour reserve economy, largely dependent upon capital supplied by migrant labour in South Africa. Nor yet is it a one crop economy or a one mineral economy. It is however dangerously dependent upon an industry, diamond mining, which is controlled by South African monopoly capital. It is also excessively dependent for its imports and export routes on South Africa – its politically hostile and militarily aggressive giant neighbour.

ECONOMIC PLANNING

For much of the colonial era, what passed for economic planning in the territory was rudimentary and short-term: the objective was to try and ensure a balanced budget for the forthcoming financial year which would include the least possible expenditure of a non-administrative nature. In 1946 multi-year fiscal planning techniques were introduced for the first time and, partly as a consequence, by the early 1950s government revenues began to exceed expenditure. However it was not until 1956

171

that government fiscal planning broadened its scope to include economic development.

The '1956–60 Development Plan', as it was later called, was a result of the radical shift in colonial policy towards the Protectorate which had begun in 1954 (4). Early in that year London had agreed to recommence grants-in-aid in order to improve the standards of administration which had fallen to a dangerously low level in the post-war period. In the same year the Symon Commission recommended a package of grants-in-aid, Colonial and Development Welfare Fund grants, and loans designed to serve development needs in the territory (79). So in December 1955 the primitive plan of development, based largely on the recommendations of the Symon report, was drawn up. The plan was essentially a shopping list of development schemes, each funded by separate Colonial Development and Welfare Fund grants. Symon had suggested that the livestock industry should be the focus of development, and to achieve this the *sine qua non* was the upgrading of water supplies in order to expand the cattle population. Out of a total CD&W budget of £1.3 million, £500,000 was to be spent on developing water supplies, in particular the drilling of boreholes in the Eastern Protectorate. The Geological Surveys Department was to concentrate on the discovery of underground aquifers. Remaining schemes included tsetse-fly control in Ngamiland, veterinary services, and the building of 'tribal' primary and junior secondary schools. There had been no central planning process however. As a later planner remarked, 'the choice of projects submitted for funding and the priorities attached to them tended to reflect the strength of the personalities of individual Department Heads' (41, p.107).

In 1960 an Economic Survey Mission under Prof. Chandler Morse visited the High Commission territories, reporting directly to the High Commissioner, who until 1963 retained responsibility for economic planning for all three territories. The Morse Mission was charged with making 'recommendations on the utilization of the financial resources that are or might be made available to the [each] territory' (55, p.3). Morse merely recommended that the stimulus offered the Bechuanaland economy in 1956–60 should be sustained and extended. The rationale was the familiar one of injecting capital into the territory in order to increase economic activity which would result in increased revenues.

The '1960–64 Development Plan' therefore differed little in content or style from its predecessor. Water supplies, veterinary services, education, communications – the building of roads and bridges – received the bulk of development expenditure though the development budget did show a marginal increase: from £4.7 million during 1956–60 to £5.2 million in 1960–64 (5).

The High Commissioner's office showed little interest in the economic development of the territory, which began to chafe on Peter Fawcus, the Resident Commissioner for Bechuanaland 1959–65. On his own initiative, Fawcus began to formulate a development plan in 1961, and was able to implement it in 1963 when the High Commissioner was removed from the 'chain of command' between Mafeking and London.[2] The '1963–68 Development Plan' was a radical departure from previous plans in that it was itself planned by intensive consultation (6). The plan was drawn up by a small coterie of 'experts' and members of the new Legislative Council 'to equip the territory for early self-government' (6, p.25). There were three main priority programmes – the building of a new capital at Gaborone inside Botswana, the expansion of secondary education to provide skilled manpower, and increased expenditure on water development and communications. There was also talk of a national development bank to stimulate the development of the private sector. These priorities – administrative development, urban infrastructure, education, and stimulation of the private sector – have remained the principles of development expenditure, if not always of the rhetoric, since Independence. The 1963–68 plan was still essentially a list of projects, but it was informed by a statement of cautious pragmatism. It recognised the role of government as central to the process of development, yet at the same time looked forward to the withering away of the state by private enterprise which it regarded as the proper engine of economic development.

A Transitional Plan for Social and Economic Development was published on 30 September 1966, the first day of independence for the new Republic of Botswana. An extension of the Fawcus plan in style and content, it echoed the colonial document in stating that 'a rationally planned and guided economy is the objective of Government policy. However a balance must be struck where private initiative has ample scope within the general confines laid down by Government' (10, p.6). Botswana was in desperate need of capital; the plan recognised that if the country was to attract foreign capital for mineral development it would have to provide a 'stable and friendly environment'. It went further to propose a novel scheme of infrastructure for mining development called the 'Shashe Complex' – roads, power and water supplies from the Shashe river near Francistown to support copper mining and salt/soda extraction in the northern Bamangwato Reserve (Central District).

The Transitional Plan was supposed to pave the way for a comprehensive five-year development plan to be published in 1967. However, the new possibilities opened up by the discovery of diamonds at Orapa made, in the words of the planner, 'long-term projections impossible'. The small Economic Planning Unit set up by Fawcus was also engaged in an epic struggle to make its voice heard against the high priests of the balanced budget in the Ministry of Finance (40). So the 1st National Development Plan (hereafter NDP-I), published in August 1968, proved to be yet another 'transitional plan'. Not until it was published was a new Ministry of Development Planning instituted to draw up a real five-year development plan.

NDP-I for 1968–71 contained few surprises. Infrastructure was to eat up 67.4 per cent of projected capital expenditure for the period and more than half of that was to be spent on the Shashe Complex, but all of it had to be raised from abroad. For the first time a wages policy was ventured: in future there would be a minimum living wage for government employees, which was 'intended as a guide to the private sector' (11, p.9). Government also gave notice of an unspecified intention to reform landholding, with a view to encouraging 'progressive' and 'modern' agriculture.

In September 1970 the long-awaited comprehensive five-year plan, the 2nd National Development Plan (NDP-II) was published. It broke new ground as an optimistic, confident document laying out government policy aims and objectives, and appealing to popular participation in development. In his foreword President Seretse Khama acknowledged that 'mining and the resources we expect to accrue from mining activity have transformed our economic prospects' (13, p.III). The overall architect of the plan was Vice-President Quett Masire, who was so bold as to predict that Botswana would now achieve budgetary self-sufficiency by 1975. The plan unabashedly proclaimed the four 'national principles' recently enunciated by the ruling party: democracy, development, self-reliance, and unity – and translated these into the development 'objectives' of social justice, equality of opportunity, and the use of persuasion over compulsion to bring about change. The foreword of the 1970–75 plan proclaimed that 'the greatest challenge' was rural development, and the development process would 'not favour the wealthy and deprive the poor'. Much effort was then put into popularising the plan by radio extension classes in the villages, and into drawing up local district development plans which were published as a massive appendix to NDP-II.

However the actual content of NDP-II was little changed in strategy from the previous plans – despite the new rhetoric adopted. Sixty per cent of capital expenditure was to go on physical infrastructure – mostly the Shashe Complex, and urban development the rest. After the explanatory chapters, the core of the plan was a 'shopping list' of projects which had little to do with rural development, and which were to be almost totally financed from abroad. Popular participation in planning was after the event, and village consultations and district development plans had propaganda value rather than actual input into the planning process.

The 3rd National Development Plan for 1973–78 (NDP-III) built on the rhetoric of the previous plan and went further down the road of confusing central government development with the development of the total economy. NDP-III was strongly influenced by a White Paper (Government Paper No.1 of 1972) titled *Rural Development in Botswana*, which pointed to 'the great inequality of wealth within the rural sector' disguised by the average *per person* income figure of R35 to R40 per year (14, p.i). The introduction to NDP-III asserted that 'Botswana now has the resources to undertake a major assault on the problems of the rural areas' (15, p.xi). A dualistic (i.e. 'trickle down') strategy was put forward: to earn income from the export of diamonds, copper and beef and to re-invest that income in 'education and training, promoting agriculture and labour intensive manufacturing, and improving services in the rural areas'. Once again analysis of actual projected expenditure makes it difficult to see how the rural areas were being favoured. The bulk of capital expenditure was allocated to infrastructural projects which, as in the case of main road construction, made only an indirect contribution to rural development.

Central government development planning became increasingly institutionalised with the reintegration of Finance and Development Planning into a single Ministry, which coordinated and controlled development planning by other ministries through a system of planning officers placed as its eyes and ears within each Ministry. Meanwhile the Division of Economic Affairs within MFDP acted as hand-maidens to an ever-changing Macro-Economic Model of Botswana (MEMBOT) upon which the succession of over-lapping ('rolling') National Development Plans was based (37).

The original theme of rural development, latched on to the original objectives of NDP-II, was further developed by NDP-III and by the Accelerated Rural Development Programme of 1974. The timing of ARDP was dictated by the need for visible development of infrastructure in rural district centres to be evident during the General Elections of that year. The thinking behind it can be traced back to the Chambers and Feldman consultancy of 1972, and the White Paper *National Policy for Rural Development* which followed from it in 1973. Chambers and Feldman had argued that the way forward was to create 'income earning opportunities' in rural areas, but no clear guide was given as to how this was to be achieved. The consultants also recommended that the commercialisation of agriculture would be greatly aided by land reform (27, p.x).

175

But when NDP-IV was published in May 1977 there was little in it to suggest that ARDP was more than a 'one-off' measure. The strategy for rural development had shifted in the direction of land reform suggested by Chambers and Feldman. The vague plans to commercialise livestock farming of NDP-I became the Tribal Grazing Lands Policy, formulated in 1975. As with ARDP, TGLP originated outside the mainstream of the planning process. Hence despite all the brouhaha, TGLP proved to be peripheral in terms of development finance compared with infrastructural projects. Furthermore, since monitoring of TGLP was relegated to a Line Ministry (Agriculture) rather than MFDP, its original objectives were progressively overturned by vested interests in district and central government – converting it from primarily a land conservation measure into a land grab (62).

NDP-IV was published for the period 1979–85 in November 1980, at a time when economic growth was slowing down while population boomed. NDP-IV introduced a new rhetorical 'theme' to rival that of rural development. A study of employment opportunities had been proposed by NDP-IV, and it had been undertaken by Prof. Michael Lipton in 1978 (50). Lipton reflected fashionable concerns with rural poverty and the importance of the 'informal sector' in towns. He advocated redistribution of cattle and land in order to provide more work and incomes for the rural poor, while commercial deregulation and *lower* minimum wages in towns would stimulate business and thereby provide more jobs. Not surprisingly, only the latter suggestions were taken seriously by Government. The war against unemployment was to be waged with a package of fiscal incentives for employers known as the Financial Assistance Policy adopted during the NDP-V Plan period (19).

The current development plan, NDP-VI for 1985–91, perhaps belatedly recognises that 'a "project" is not necessarily the appropriate solution to every problem' (21, p.54). It also comes full circle in the state's stance towards private enterprise, by contradicting the trend of bureaucratic centralisation of the economy with the promise of (eventual) reduction of the role of Government in Botswana's development. State provision of basic infrastructure for large-scale capital development will decline because opportunities for mining development have reached a plateau. As a result future economic growth is not expected to rise above 5 per cent a year. The onus is on the 'private and parastatal sectors to generate growth and employment opportunities' (21, p.56). The trend towards privatisation and lip-service to deregulation in NDP-IV was inspired by the Presidential Commission on Economic Opportunities of 1982, chaired by Vice-President Peter Mmusi. Its report assumed that deregulation would be to the advantage of indigenous entrepreneurs while clinging tenaciously to the principle of regulation of foreign enterprise (19).

Economic planning in Botswana since Independence has therefore elaborated on, but not veered too far away from, the priorities established by colonial plans. The highest priority has been given to large-scale mining development, followed by the cattle export industry. The ultimate aim has been to create an environment in which private indigenous capital can flourish. In order to create this environment, Government has had to intervene directly in almost every sector and aspect of the economy – a role which the would-be capitalists of the ruling party have adopted rather uneasily and which they now propose to shed. The proof of the pudding will be in the eating. Will the vested interests of centralised bureaucracy really be prepared to hand over direction of the economy to 'market forces'? And will the 'private sector' be coherent or competent enough to maintain national economic growth and integrity?

AGRICULTURE

There can be few countries where the risks associated with farming are as great as they are in Botswana. Only 5 per cent of its land surface is generally considered suitable for crop-growing. Family or peasant farms are relatively efficient by Third World standards because of almost universal use of the plough rather than the hoe, but subsistence let alone surplus harvests are extremely precarious because of the vagaries of climate and soils. The country is generally better suited to pastoralism. Yet the economies of herd management in countering drought and disease make even pastoralism an unreliable and insecure pastime for all but the larger stock-owners. Such owners have therefore been the major beneficiaries of government veterinary measures and the opening up of new watering points by drilling of artesian wells over the last 30 to 50 years. The national cattle herd grew from perhaps as low as 50,000 in 1896 in the aftermath of the rinderpest epidemic to a peak of over 3 million before drought set in at the end of the 1970s. According to the Rural Income Distribution Survey of 1974–75, 75 per cent of the national herd was owned by 15 per cent of the households and almost half of all rural households owned no cattle at all (16, p.113). Cattleholding is the main determinant as well as indicator of inequality in rural society.

Crop production is the Achilles heel of the Botswana economy. It is insufficiently productive to feed the population with staples or to provide cash-crops for families to buy essential imports. The income gap has been crossed by migrant labour remittances, cattle-sales, and more recently, by income derived from urban and industrial employment within Botswana.

One can argue that agriculture was underdeveloped by the Protectorate's colonial transformation into a labour reserve: labour migration withdrew the male (and some female) labour essential to the new plough cultivation. One can also argue that crop production has been the victim of successive droughts. An alternative argument is one of critical population density (1). Widespread adoption of the plough in the nineteenth century increased acreage under tillage, and thus food production within the limited rainy season, to levels that could support increased population. But by the mid-twentieth century the population had reached a critical level under that technology and existing land use practices. But the mixed cultivation of (indigenous) sorghum and (exotic) maize proved to be a safety net, drought-resistant sorghum providing something approaching bare subsistence even when the 'surplus' crop of maize failed.

The colonial administration seems to have been sporadically aware of such Malthusian problems but they made little effort to solve them. The conventional wisdom was that wages from migrant labour abroad both paid local taxes and helped stave off famine, so there was no pressing need to attempt to develop agriculture. The lion's share of government's agricultural attention was given to cattle production.

The Veterinary Department was established as early as 1905 to safeguard cattle exports from the plethora of stock diseases that had more or less accompanied the spread of colonialism in Southern Africa. By 1930 East Coast fever and bovine lung sickness had been banished from the territory. Foot-(hoof-) and-mouth disease was however endemic in the wild buffalo population of the Okavango Delta. It was not contained properly until the 1950s when a system of cordon fences was initiated. Stock disease control was the long-term success story of colonial development in the Protectorate (36).

After attempts to establish an abattoir, blocked by international meat monopolies in the 1930s, an abattoir was successfully established by the Colonial Development Corporation at Lobatse in the 1950s. This development gave the Protectorate the chance to cash in on the overseas boom in cheap (hamburger-type) meat consumption, and the first exports were made to the United Kingdom in 1958. The colonial government also funded the drilling of hundreds of new artesian wells to open up trek routes for cattle across desert areas.

A Department of Agriculture was founded in 1935, but the limits of its effectiveness are reflected in the fact that total acreage planted in 1966 was less than the acreage planted in the 1930s. From the 1930s onwards the territory had to import at least 10 per cent of its grain requirements each year. The colonial government had tried to introduce new farming techniques through wartime coercion, and then through 'cooperator' and 'pupil/master farmer' schemes aimed at the most progressive farmers in the most ecologically favoured zones (9). But in 1966 tried and trusted methods of risk-aversion still held sway in agriculture. The 'lands' (*masimo*) were in general kept separate and geographically distant from the 'cattle posts' (*meraka*). Fields were ploughed slowly and crops sown with mixed seeds by broadcasting, taking advantage of each rain storm for different rates of germination; and the resulting harvests of greatly mixed quality could only be selectively cropped. However, without fertilising by manure, or annual rotation of successive individual crops, fields were exhausted and shifted every few years, and the supply of arable land grew ever more restricted.

Cattle production continued to receive the lion's share of agricultural development funds after Independence, mainly in the form of funds for borehole drilling and the modernisation of the Lobatse abattoir to meet the demands of overseas markets. The Botswana Meat Commission was established as a parastatal corporation to take over the abattoir and the marketing of beef in 1965. It secured very favourable terms for beef exports first with the United Kingdom, and then through the U.K. in 1975 with the European Economic Community. The BMC thereby sold beef to Europe at four times the world market price. The value of BMC sales increased from P8.6 million in 1966 to P53.4 million in 1976. It was not until 1978 that the value of diamond exports surpassed that of beef. Such growth, however, was accomplished at the cost of overgrazing and the rapid deterioration of the range. In 1976 it was calculated that there was enough grazing land to support only 2 million cattle without infliciting permanent damage to the range, provided there was rain (31, p.119). In the late 1970s the range was having to support 3 million cattle.

In 1976 the Tribal Grazing Land Policy (TGLP) was initiated in an attempt to conserve the range and also to reduce inequality of income in the livestock sector. The strategy adopted was to divide the land into three zones: commercial farming areas, communal grazing areas, and reserved areas which were to be protected from development. The objective was to attract the large cattleholders out of the overgrazed communal areas into new commercial ranches in the thirstland, dependent on drilling for water, which would be held on 50-year leases. The small cattleholders would thus be given the chance to expand their herds in the communal grazing areas left vacant, though limits were to be set on the numbers of stock held there. In practice TGLP has proved very difficult to implement, though it has not yet been abandoned by Government. There were three major problems. First, there was simply much less unused range than the planners had hoped. Instead of wide empty spaces they found that there was little land that was not already occupied. Second, when new ranches were established, the ranch-owners, often politicians or civil servants with political clout, insisted on their right to also continue grazing their cattle in the communal grazing areas. Third, stock limitation which was essential if overgrazing was to be tackled seriously, proved very unpopular and Government has not been able to enforce it. The result has been that cattle have often destroyed the new ranches through over-stocking, only to be withdrawn to over-stock the old communal areas even more critically (42).

Crop production in Botswana since Independence has been even more problematic. In drought years the country has had to import almost all its maize and much of its sorghum, the two main food staples and subsistence crops. Even in years when the rains were good, crop production has failed to keep pace with population growth. National self-sufficiency has dropped from an average of 90 per cent in 1966 to no more than 50 per cent in the early 1980s (60, p.161).

In NDP-V the Government set itself the task of achieving 'sustained self-sufficiency in basic grains . . . in all but the poorest rainfall years' (18, p.150). An Arable Lands Development Policy (ALDEP) was therefore implemented in 1981. It was designed to bring about national self-sufficiency. In addition the policy was intended, like TGLP, to reduce inequality in rural incomes as well as create jobs in the rural areas and contain the drift to the towns.

According to a survey carried out in 1981, the last year of good rains, only 14 per cent of farmers in Botswana are solely dependent on crop cultivation (60, p.162). These tend to be among the poorest farmers, having no access to animal draught power. Most farmers in Botswana (75 per cent) raise both crops and cattle; and it is a fair generalisation that the more cattle you have the more crops you can raise. Cattle provide draught power, security for credit, and can be turned into cash to provide farm implements. ALDEP was supposed to assist those small farmers who had no or insufficient cattle to enable them to grow crops efficiently. All households ploughing less than 10 hectares and owning 40 cattle or less became eligible to apply for subsidised packages of implements, fencing, water catchment tanks, and donkey draught power.

Like TGLP, ALDEP has probably increased rural inequality. The period of implementation coincided with a drought in which no amount of subsidies would have helped to significantly increase crop production. Secondly, those farmers who have taken advantage of ALDEP packages have tended to be the 'middle peasantry', those farmers holding 11 to 40 cattle. (This had indeed been predicted by a pilot scheme carried out during 1979–80.) In order to qualify for an ALDEP package a down-payment has to be made ranging from 15 to 40 per cent of the value of the package. Few farmers holding less than 10 cattle can raise the capital (63, p.99).

INFRASTRUCTURE

The economic history of Botswana since Independence has been infrastructural development writ large. This has come about partly through necessity since the country's administration, social services, and communications were all in such a parlous state in 1966; yet Government has also chosen to allocate most of its resources to these sectors in preference to more directly productive sectors, particularly after the mid-1970s when certain basic gaps in infrastructure, such as the provision of an adequate central government administrative structure, had been filled and there was an alternative strategy open to it.

In the colonial era, infrastructural development was limited, for the most part, to the maintenance of an administrative presence capable of maintaining the peace and supervising the collection of taxes. Expenditure on the police force was the largest single item in the Protectorate's budget until the mid-1930s. Britain's legacy to independent Botswana in 1966 may have included parliamentary democracy but it did not include adequate roads, schools or hospitals, and it is in these areas, in the fields of communications and social services, as well as administration, that the bulk of development expenditure has gone since independence.

Botswana, as each development plan since 1960 has pointed out, is a country with a large area and a low population density, 'consequently capital expenditure on the development and maintenance of an adequate transport and communications network has to be greater than most other countries' (21, p.262). Critics of the Government's development programme have asked whether its expenditure on transport, and roads in particular, need have been *so* great. Bitumen road building alone amounted to a quarter of total capital expenditure between 1966–67 and 1976–77. It has been cynically argued that this ordering of priorities was made not for economic or even strategic reasons, but simply because it was the most convenient, and the least controversial, method of absorbing surplus funds during the boom years of the 1970s (29; 63). Roads were necessary, they were easy to build, and road-building projects attracted aid with less difficulty than almost any other project. An average of 100 km. of new bitumenised roads have been built per annum since 1966. The new roads link some of the major villages and the urban areas, yet comparatively little money has been spent on the rural feeder roads used daily by the vast majority of the population. It could be argued that even for the urban areas the new bitumen roads should not have been of vital

181

importance since the railway line already linked Lobatse, Gaborone and Francistown, and since 1966 spurs have been run off the main line to Morupule and Selibe-Phikwe. However, the railway has predominantly been a freight line with passenger service limited to long-haul overnight operations providing a daytime link only to Mafeking and Bulawayo outside the country.

The main line of rail in Botswana, 641 km. from the South African to the Zimbabwe borders, was constructed in 1897 by the British South Africa Company to connect Mafeking and Bulawayo. Its initial impact on the economic development of the Protectorate was negative. The railway undermined the existing infrastructure of the Tswana states, then based on the waggon trade, and contributed significantly to deforestation with its early wood-burning locomotives and by facilitating the transport of fuel wood to Kimberley (64, pp.128–9). It was a considerable drain on the early colonial budget – the railway subsidy was the second largest item of expenditure up to 1909. Revenue from the railway was negligible and/or irregular until 1950 when an annual wayleave of £140,000 replaced the haphazardly collected income tax. Few Batswana used the railways up to the 1950s – except to travel back and forth from the mines.

Since Independence the railway has made a more positive contribution to the country's economy, and to the economy of the region as a whole, since the line also serves Zimbabwe, Zambia and Zaïre. Botswana's copper-nickel and beef are exported via rail, while spur lines link Morupule and Selibe-Phikwe for the transport of coal. Total internal traffic has tripled in volume since 1966, while transit traffic has more than doubled. Yet the railway has still been regarded as something of an alien presence, mainly because it has always been controlled from outside the country. In 1974 President Seretse Khama announced his intention to nationalise the line. In January 1987 Botswana was supposed to take over the operation of the railway from the National Railways of Zimbabwe but this has been postponed indefinitely, partly because of Botswana's unpreparedness but also because of Bophutatswana's refusal to cooperate with the transition unless it obtains recognition as a sovereign state from the Government of Botswana.

Another recent move towards the lessening of transport dependence has been the opening of a new international airport outside Gaborone in December 1984. For the first time wide-bodied jet aircraft are able to make regular, scheduled flights to Botswana. Direct flights linking London and Gaborone began in April 1987.

Progress in the provision of social services in Botswana has been extraordinarily rapid since Independence. Once again, however, part of the explanation for this advance lies in the very low base from which development started in 1966. In 1916 a London Missionary Society missionary, W.C. Willoughby, charged the colonial Government with 'never having shown the smallest desire to care for the health of body or mind of the natives it professedly exists to serve' (66, p.33). It would not be unfair to say that this attitude changed little in later decades: both education and health were left largely to missionaries and the initiatives of local communities. There was only one central Government-owned secondary school in the territory in 1965. In 1960 there were only eleven doctors.

However, the colonial era cannot be written off entirely as a period of 'no-development' in the fields of education and health. Primary education in particular was a shining example of an area in which local 'tribal' development initiatives were successful, and would have been more successful still if given greater encouragement and aid by the central state. In the early decades of the century, Batswana fought and won battles for control over the schools run by the missionaries, the latter being unwilling to teach the practical curriculum desired by the diKgosi. By the 1920s these schools were being run jointly by missionaries and *merafe* (tribe), with the Government as arbitrator. Finance was provided, initially, by a self-imposed tax which the Government formalised and regularised in 1919 as the Native Fund. One product of this era was the BaKgatla National School, built in 1919 by Kgosi Isang Pilane without the help of either missionaries or Government (55). Such a degree of autonomy was regarded as dangerous by the colonial authorities, and by the Second World War the arbitrator had become controller of education in the Protectorate, though finance was still the responsibility of the *merafe*.

The most adventurous local initiative of all was a post-war development: the building of Moeng College, a secondary school costing the BaNgwato *merafe* £100,000 (82). Though it was a tribute to the thirst for education among the Batswana, this thirst was slaked only at the expense of the Bangwato, many of whom were forced to contribute labour, cattle and cash so that their 'masters' might go to school. Other *merafe* secondary schools were built in the 1950s by the BaKgatla, BaKwena and the BaNgwaketse. Prior to the building of these schools, Batswana had to travel to South Africa or Southern Rhodesia for secondary education, and it was only when South Africa closed its schools to Batswana from outside the Union in the 1950s that the Protectorate Government began to take a serious interest in educational development. Primary school enrolment leaped from 16,000 in 1950 to 36,000 in 1960 and 71,000 in 1966 as the Government belatedly pumped money into education. As Independence approached another priority became the provision of

183

manpower for bureaucratic localisation. The Fawcus administration in particular was fully aware of the desperate need for trained personnel to staff the new state's civil service, but all it could do was to set goals – goals which it was thought at the time the new state did not have the resources to achieve.

Since Independence, universal access to primary education has been a goal of every development plan, but only between 1973 and 1985 was primary education given the same or greater resources than secondary education. By 1985 85 per cent of the primary school age population was reported to be in school. Only a third of primary school leavers could expect to enter secondary school. So secondary school building accounted for the bulk of capital expenditure in education in the NDP-VI: 'it is hoped by the middle of the 1990s there will be universal access to 9 years of basic education for all Batswana children' (21, p.123).

Up to 1973, health care in Botswana had been defined in terms of 'hospital care' (57). In that year the policy, carried over from the colonial era, of allocating funds to the expansion of hospitals located in the large villages and towns was replaced by a decentralised 'basic' (now called 'primary') health care system. At the most basic level this meant health posts, usually an ordinary house without special facilities, visited regularly by nurses. The next level of health care was a clinic, located in all villages of 1000 and over, permanently staffed by nurses, with a dispensary and up to 10 beds. Finally, in the major villages and towns were the hospitals – the most important being the national referral hospital in Gaborone. Eighty per cent of the population now live within 15 kms of a health facility. One of the most impressive results of this revolution in health care has been a decrease in the infant mortality rate: from 97 per 1000 in 1971 to 68 per 1000 in 1981.

The administrative headquarters of the Bechuanaland Protectorate was for nearly all of its 81-year history based outside the territory, in Vryburg and then Mafeking over the border in South Africa. This anomaly was only solved just before Independence when a new capital was built at Gaborone. Central Government employed just over 2000 people, nearly all based in Gaborone at Independence. In 1985 this figure had risen to over 21,000, a reflection of the vast expansion in the responsibilities and activities of the state and also of its increased wealth and patronage. However, while dependence on expatriates in key administrative positions has passed, Government has not yet managed to lessen its dependence on expatriates. The latest available statistics on the progress of localisation, those for 1983, show that 51 per cent of the professional grades and 22 per cent of superscale grades were expatriates. Of the administrative cadre as a whole, 28 per cent were expatriates, a figure not far short of the 31 per cent for 1964.

MINING DEVELOPMENT

'It is not impossible', suggested Lord Hailey in 1953, 'that mining developments may have a considerable influence on the economic future of the Protectorate' (38, p.154). He had hardly been the first to make such a prediction. Ever since the discovery and subsequent mining of gold in the Tati district during 1869–71, the first mining 'rush' in Southern African history, great things had been expected of mining in Botswana – not only gold, but copper, coal, manganese, asbestos, coal and even diamonds. Yet this promise seemed likely never to be fulfilled.

There was very little successful mining development during the colonial era. The small Tati gold mines closed during the Depression, Monarch mine re-opened and in 1938 was producing almost 20,000 ounces a year, but closed again in 1964. Asbestos and manganese were mined on a very small scale by open-cast methods in the Bamalete and Bangwaketse Reserves between the 1930s and 1960s. By Independence mining contributed nothing to the GDP and experts discounted it as a possible source of revenue in the foreseeable future.

All this may be seen as a symptom of the general indifference shown to all economic development by the Protectorate Administration. Another significant factor was the reluctance shown by some diKgosi, in particular the Regent of the Bangwato, Tshekedi Khama, to cooperate in the search for and exploitation of minerals. Tshekedi had no wish to see a new Johannesburg, with loss of land to white settlers and all its attendant social evils, arise in Gamangwato. It was not until Tshekedi's death in 1959 that the Bangwato, after negotiations which spanned decades, signed a prospecting agreement, hedged about with safeguards and guaranteeing local participation, with a mining company, from Northern Rhodesia rather than South Africa, Rhodesian Selection Trust (33).

Good fortune shone upon Botswana along with Independence. In 1967 diamonds were discovered at Orapa and the existence of major copper-nickel deposits were established at Selebi-Phikwe. Both these sites were in the Bangwato District, and the *morafe* not the central state held the mineral rights, but the Bangwato were persuaded to relinquish their rights to the state in the national interest in 1967. It is arguable whether this reflected the strength of national sentiment and the relative weakness of 'tribalism' in Botswana, or the respect and loyalty owed President Seretse Khama and the expectation that Botswana would really be Gamangwato writ large.

Botswana could not finance exploitation of these finds itself; in 1967 the country's budget was still heavily subsidised by the British Government. De Beers had to provide not only finance for the Orapa mine, but also loans to Government for the building of the roads, housing, power and water supplies for the remote mining township. Following the precedent laid down by Tshekedi's deal with RST in 1959, the company agreed to give the Botswana Government a 15 per cent interest in the mine in exchange for the concession. The financing of the infrastructure for the Selebi-Phikwe project, a much larger project in financial and employment terms seen as the pole of growth at the core of the ambitious Shashe Project, was raised in the form of loans by the World Bank, Canada and the USA. Costs were raised by the insistence of Canadian donors on the generation of electricity from local coal rather than importing it from South Africa. Most humiliatingly of all, the financial package could not be completed without raising further capital, and resort had to be made to South Africa's Industrial Development Corporation whose offers had previously been rejected. Bamangwato Concessions Limited, a local company owned and backed by American Metal Climax (Amax), was to run the mine itself, again in return for a cession of 15 per cent of the equity (3; 31, pp.139–58).

The two mines enjoyed contrasting fortunes. The Orapa mine began producing diamonds in July 1971 at a rate of 2.4 million carats per annum. Mining was open-cast and processing costs were negligible. Output increased steadily during the 1970s and new mines were opened at Letlhakane in 1977 and Jwaneng in 1982. In 1984 nearly 13 million carats were produced with an estimated value of almost 900 million Pula. The Government was at first reluctant to sanction the opening of the second mine, because of the limited capacity to spend the increased revenues, but was eventually persuaded in negotiations with Commonwealth Secretariat help (over the objections of the U.K.) by De Beers' offer to increase its share of the equity from 15 to 50 per cent (77, pp.112–16).

The 'partnership' between De Beers and the Botswana Government thereby created is an unequal one: all the diamonds have to be marketed through the Central Selling Organisation, controlled by De Beers. However having a significant share in such a hitherto profitable world monopoly is not to be sneezed at. Unofficial estimates have put the Government's share of De Beers Botswana as high as 70 per cent of total earnings. Diamond mining's 30 per cent or more contribution to the revenue has been larger than any other sector of the economy and diamonds account for the lion's share of the country's exports (70.4 per cent by value in 1984) (2).

The dream of copper (rather than diamonds) fuelling economic development was transformed into a nightmare by plummeting world metal prices and by technical problems in mining and smelting processes. Production did not get under way until 1974 and the mine only began to run efficiently in the early 1980s. A number of company restructurings resulted in Anglo-American Corporation of South Africa replacing Amax as the major shareholder in Bamangwato Concessions Limited, but by 1984 the accumulated deficit was P750 million. The justification for keeping the mine operational has been its efficient low-cost productivity, despite its massive accumulated debt. But the covert reason generally supposed in business circles is a trade-off by Anglo-American Corporation with the Botswana Government. In return for unimpeded development of diamond mining by De Beers within the AAC group, the Government does not have to face the abandonment of a town of 35,000 people and all its associated Shashe Complex infrastructure (58; 83).

The Morupule coal mine at Palapye was established to supply coal for electricity generation at Selebi-Phikwe. It has since increased its output to fire a new 90 MW power station commissioned in 1987 to provide power for a national grid independent of South Africa but interdependent with Zimbabwe. The Morupule mine produces less than half a million tonnes a year from coalfields conservatively estimated to contain 17 billion tonnes. The vision of exploiting these coalfields, which would eventually necessitate a new trans-Kalahari railway to Namibian ports, briefly flickered in the early 1980s (17) – but died because of future world over-supply of better quality coal from South America as well as existing South African competition. A similar story may be told for hopes of salt and soda ash exploitation from the 30,000 sq.km. Makgadikgadi Pans, though the flicker has not wholly died. Current hopes are centred on relatively small platinum deposits and on remoter hydrocarbon (more likely gas than oil) possibilities in the Kalahari, while further diamond pipes are being assayed.

WATER DEVELOPMENT

The people of Botswana are acutely aware of the crucial importance of the availability of water for economic development – living as they do in a semi-arid climate, with unreliable and scanty rainfall, and general lack of surface water (except in the northwest). Drought has scarred the country almost every other decade since the Protectorate was established in 1885. Only the wealth supplied by diamond mining has prevented the most recent drought of the early 1980s from adding to those scars – it has been a proud claim of the Government that thus far there have been no drought-related deaths.

The history of water development since 1885 has been largely the history of borehole development. Though surface water is scarce, subterranean groundwater is relatively plentiful. Prior to the late 1920s, the exploitation of this resource was limited to the digging of shallow pits, usually in dry river beds or where the water table was within a few metres of the surface. With the general introduction of petrol or diesel-engined drilling rigs, boreholes could be drilled to depths of a hundred metres or more. The new technology made possible the settlement and use for grazing of lands previously unoccupied because of their lack of surface water and wells – in effect this meant most of the country.

The potential of borehole development was first realised by Batswana rather than the colonial government. Isang Pilane, Kgosi of the BaKgatla, organised a Tribal Boring Scheme in the late 1920s, imposing a levy of an ox on each tax-payer to finance the drilling of sixteen boreholes at a total cost of £4000 (55). The colonial government was brought to realise how boreholes could help advance the livestock industry. In the 1930s, Resident Commissioner Colonel Rey managed to secure grants from London to finance borehole development for trek-routes across the Kalahari, but this ended with the onset of the Second World War. After the war, the Colonial Development and Welfare Fund financed the drilling of 220 successful boreholes during the years 1946–56. Government still lagged behind private initiative however: during the same period 395 private boreholes were drilled. At Independence it was estimated that there were around 5000 boreholes in Botswana (31, pp.235–8). In 1985 this figure had doubled, and an estimated 80 per cent of the people have come to depend upon boreholes for their water.

While the boreholes certainly helped to extend the land available for grazing, and thereby increased the national herd, only a minority of Batswana cattleowners benefitted directly. From the beginning in the 1920s and 1930s syndicates of cattleowners were formed to take charge of the new water-sources. Usually these men were already wealthier and more powerful. Control of the boreholes gave the syndicate-members control of the grazing land around the boreholes, in effect 'privatising' communal land (67). The proliferation of boreholes, particularly since Independence, has also contributed significantly to overgrazing.

Edwin S. Munger writing in the early 1960s noted that 'the two natural problems of Bechuanaland are too little water and too much' (56. p.63). The 'too much' he referred to is the Okavango Delta, a large expanse of surface water extending over 3000 square miles in the remote northwest of Botswana. Ever since the delta was 'discovered', schemes have been advanced to exploit this resource to benefit the territory and the region as a whole. Perhaps the most ambitious of these schemes was that of E.H.L.

188

Schwarz in 1920 who suggested that the climate of the sub-continent could be improved by channelling the Okavango into a series of lakes. The increase in evaporation, he theorised, would greatly increase the rainfall of Southern Africa (56, p.65).

The idea of re-channelling the waters of the Okavango has persisted – either for irrigated agriculture around the Delta or for piping to the water-starved East. Apart from limited marsh clearance to facilitate water flow to the Boteti River and thence to the Mopipi Dam serving Orapa, these schemes have come to nothing. Research, including computer models of flow and blockage through the myriad of papyrus-choked channels, has continued (22). In 1986 Government announced a comprehensive technical and economic feasibility study of water transfer from the Okavango-Chobe region. But such studies must be limited until the political problems associated with the international status of the Okavango and Chobe rivers in Angola and Namibia can be faced.

MANUFACTURING

During the colonial period, and for much of the post-Independence era as well, manufacturing industry has been of negligible importance to the economy of Botswana. Lack of capital and labour, high utility and transport costs, the relatively small domestic market, and the openness of that market to South African goods through the Customs Union, have been almost insuperable barriers to industrial development. In 1966 manufacturing accounted for 8 per cent of the total GDP. The only factory of any size was the meat cannery owned by Botswana Meat Commission in Lobatse. Also in Lobatse was a maize mill, and in Francistown a small tannery which processed game skins.

Fifteen years later, in 1981-2, manufacturing's share of GDP had hardly changed at 9 per cent, though the value of production had risen from P2.9 million to P71.2 million. By 1984 there were only 32 licensed manufacturing companies employing more than 10 people; the total labour force in the formal manufacturing sector was just over 10,000 – 11.6 per cent of the formal sector total. Employment in manufacturing advanced at the rate of 14.2 per cent during the period 1979-85, but was no solution to the problem of 20,000 school leavers coming on to the market each year (2, p.26).

The state-owned Botswana Development Corporation (BDC) was created in 1970 to promote industrial development and was given access to large amounts of state capital for investment. After a rather conservative beginning, in which the BDC pumped most of its money into property, a more adventurous attitude was adopted in the late 1970s. By 1984 it had P50 million to invest and had 45 subsidiary companies. However its major investment was in beer-brewing, and most of its companies were in the service sector – in hotels and air transport for example – with a reluctant investment in irrigated agriculture. Following the pattern of other Southern African states, a parastatal organisation called the Batswana Enterprises Development Unit (BEDU) was established in 1974 to promote indigenous-owned small industries – textiles, furniture manufacture, construction and light engineering. BEDU was not particularly successful and was reorganised in the early 1980s to provide a 'leadership' role in business development. The real success story in Government-funded incentive schemes has been the Financial Assistance Policy (FAP), launched in 1982. It is a system of state subsidisation of manufacturing (rather than retail or services) for indigenous entrepreneurs, based on a points system giving extra credit to remote areas and women etc., though in practice most of its funds have gone to established entrepreneurs. The growth in manufacturing – 155 new companies during the period 1981–84 compared with 104 for the years 1966–81 – has been attributed to FAP (19; 2, p.33).

POPULATION

Botswana is characterised by one of the lowest overall population densities in the world. The population is mainly clustered on extensions of the Zimbabwean and Witwatersrand Plateaux in the eastern half of the country. Population within the Kalahari Basin is largely limited to the river systems of the Okavango/Boteti and Chobe/Zambezi.

The first population census of 1904 was part of a British Empire census, delayed since 1901 by war in South Africa. Enumeration through the existing local government machinery of the Tswana states was based on a counting system devised by Rev.W.C. Willoughby. He had calculated the population of the Bamangwato Reserve (now Central District) by using a multiplier of 4.5 on the Hut Tax collection figures of 1899–1900. Tax had been collected from every male member of an adult age-regiment in each Tswana state, whom Willoughby guesstimated had an average of three and a half adult female and child dependents.[3]

The Willoughby methodology survived with modifications until the first systematic national census in 1964 before Independence. It had obvious deficiencies – notably the undernumeration of aged and infant females, and of males without full citizenship of a Tswana state. But it does provide a series of suggestive statistics with some internal consistency between the key censuses of 1904, 1946 and 1964. These show the total population little more than doubling from 120,000 to almost 300,000 in the first four decades; and then rising to over 500,000 in the next two decades. Since then the population has doubled again to exceed one million today – having been enumerated at 940,000 in 1981.

The censuses of 1911, 1921 and 1956 are generally discounted as inaccurate in estimating total population. There is also scepticism about the 1971 figures, and demographers prefer to work on the basis of the 3.4 per cent annual growth rate of population between the 1964 and 1981 censuses – rather than the ridiculously high 4.6 per cent between 1971 and 1981 (72; 81). But demographers should not rush to similar conclusions regarding the 1936 census, which was rather more energetically conducted. It may seem too high (266,000) compared with the 1946 census (296,000) – an intercensual growth of only 1.1 per cent. But this reflects the unusual data of almost zero population growth for Lesotho between the same two censual dates, and enormous urban-industrial growth in South Africa based on the 1930s boom in gold mining and the 1940s boom in manufacturing (61, pp.20–6). In other words this was a period of considerable and permanent out-migration to South Africa.

Crude social statistics were also collected in the colonial period. Most remarkable of all, but supported by other evidence, is the dramatic drop in literacy/education figures from 1921 to 1936, with some recovery from 1946 (though one-third of literates had never been to school). These figures also consistently show the peculiar pattern for Africa of more literate/educated females than males – reflecting the economic value of male child labour in cattle-grazing far distant from the traditional conurbations (44; 66).

CLASS, GENDER AND ETHNICITY

Popular consciousness in Botswana of the role of class, gender and ethnicity is no doubt in reverse order to the academic ranking of their significance in social and economic development. Even ethnicity has been the subject of relatively little finger-pointing in Botswana by universal standards, because of the relative success of the extension of Setswana identity to the whole of the Botswana population over the last century and a half.

Academic consciousness of class differentiation in Botswana dates from the 1967–8 Agricultural Census, substantiated by the Rural Incomes Distribution Survey of 1974 (12; 16). The Agricultural Census showed that little more than half of rural families owned cattle, and more than half the cattle were owned by the richest eighth – while the poorest eighth had no crops or cattle at all. Further investigation showed that most of the poorest families were single-parent, female-headed households –

dependent on cash remittances from a migrant adult male and/or informal sector activities such as beer brewing. The 1967–8 and 1974 surveys thereby 'completely undermined' both governmental assumptions of a largely self-sufficient rural population, earning cash by cattle sales, and academic assumptions of a relatively classless society.

Academic research on the economic history of Botswana therefore directed itself towards the origins of such inequality in cattle ownership. It was shown how royal and traditional state mechanisms of cattle ownership had been converted into personal property by the colonial cash-nexus, and how inequalities of cattle holding had been promoted by epidemics of stock disease and prolonged market depression – until the 1940s, when migrant labour was also fully established as an alternative means of rural income. Drawing on the wider Southern African literature, it was also accepted that the rural population was locked in an intermediate position between peasantisation and proletarianisation (61, pp.1–31; 62). However the precise nature and periodicity of such transformation was not debated.

These points were taken up by political scientists, particularly by Jack Parson in a 1979 thesis that led to the publication of his *Botswana: Liberal Democracy and the Labour Reserve in Southern Africa* (1984). Jack Parson coined the term 'peasantariat' to identify the colonial peasant-proletariat that still continued to exist after Independence while a new 'petty-bourgeoisie' had taken political power in alliance with foreign capital. Such a 'peasantariat–petty-bourgeois' model assumes that the present equilibrium between class forces will collapse when the milch-cow of mining growth begins to dry up – giving rise to class conflict in competition for now limited rather than limitless resources, as new fractions of the bourgeoisie and a stable urban-industrial proletariat emerge.

The Jack Parson paradigm has great persuasive value because of its coherence and simplicity, but like all heuristic devices has inherent dangers if accepted as a total explanation of all phenomena. The 'peasantariat' essentially equates the position of Botswana as a classic labour reserve of South Africa in the 1940s–50s with the structure of Botswana's political economy today. It not only confuses the external migration patterns between mine and reserve of yesterday with the internal migration patterns of today between town and country, but it obscures the dynamics of rural differentiation between larger and smaller cattle-owners and strata of crop producers – as promoted by Tribal Grazing Land Policy and Arable Lands Development Project. As for the petty-bourgeoisie, some may object that a social formation cannot be dominated by a 'residual category': the obvious answer to that is that the *grande bourgeoisie* is absentee mining capital – but that involves one in contortions of denying any measure of autonomy to the rulers of Botswana. There is surely some degree to which there is 'national capital', represented largely by cattle, which helps to explain Botswana's present political stability in balance against the interloping power of foreign mining and manufacturing capital. One can reproduce to some extent for Botswana the debate between social scientists over 'national bourgeoisie' and 'comprador bourgeoisie' in Kenya (78). One can also take a leaf from the Tanzanian concept of a 'bureaucratic bourgeoisie' – a class in transformation from acquisition of education to acquisition of capital through control of state machinery (75). That in turn helps to link back 'bourgeois' class formation to both the traditional aristocracies and the more productive peasantries of the Tswana states.

Gender as an issue of historical research has received remarkably little attention in Botswana. This is remarkable because the status of women in Botswana has been relatively advantageous within an essentially patriarchal society. Until recently Botswana was unique in that basic education and literacy were overwhelmingly female – though male enrolments overtook female in the higher echelons (44). This can be explained by the widespread adoption of the plough and of more extensive cattle herding over the past century, which reduced the female role in (previous hoe-based) agriculture and removed males from central settlements. This was accompanied by extension of basic legal-political rights to women within 'traditional' law and custom from royals around 1900 to commoners by the 1950s–60s – recognition of rights to property and a voice in Kgotla (74).

Academic attention has focused on 'female-headed households', resulting in a lively debate that has shown the term is insufficient to cover the range of family relationships of women in Botswana, and is too easily equated with the 'matriarchies' of Afro-American society (45; 68). The origins of 'female-headed households' are not difficult to identify in the culture of labour migration that emerged in the 1930s–40s – as Schapera's *Family Life in an African Tribe* (1940) eloquently shows. The anthropologist Adam Kuper has attempted to explain why single female parenthood should have emerged stronger in Botswana than in culturally-similar Lesotho, which had an even higher rate of male labour out-migration. Basotho male migrants financed their wives to improve cultivation back home, while Batswana ignored their women to finance their male relatives to buy cattle on their behalf (47).

Though ethnicity is not an unduly political issue in Botswana, there are roots of ethnic identity and competition that date back to pre-colonial and colonial political economies, and still have parts to play in the political arena. Their gradual conversion from 'feudal' to 'capitalist' society has for a start benefited many Tswana royals and aristocrats, through privatization of former communal property and through access to Western education for up to three or four generations. The only ethnic group from within the old Tswana states to significantly challenge the modern 'petty-bourgeoise' has been drawn from the Kalanga – a linguistic group constituting possibly one eighth of the total population. The Kalanga of the north-east (together with the more ethnically diverse 'Barolong' of the extreme south-east) constituted the most productive peasantry in Botswana. Some caught the educational fever of their Shona relatives in Zimbabwe from the 1930s to 1940s onwards, which paid dividends in being able to take advantage of access to the rapidly expanding higher educated elite of the 1960s–70s. Two less coherent ethnic groups of exogeneous origin fill out the 'bourgeoisie' in significant numbers: whites (or 'Europeans') and 'Asians' (Muslims) among whom there are differences based on citizenship, etc. The perceived growth of Kalanga and Asian wealth since Independence assumed to be promoted by the ethnic conspiracy, has resulted in recent rumours of a Tswana brotherhood pressing 'pure' Tswana interests in commerce and the urban property market.[4]

EXTERNAL ECONOMIC RELATIONS

The spectre of South Africa has loomed large in these pages. For almost sixty years the Bechuanaland Protectorate and Republic of Botswana was incorporated in a customs union in which it was entirely dependent on the fiscal and economic policy of South Africa.

Bechuanaland had joined the Cape Colony/Orange Free State customs union in 1891, which was extended as far as Southern Rhodesia and Swaziland in 1903–4. This was renegotiated in 1910 as the South African Customs Union, in which the Pretoria government held such a degree of unilateral control that Southern Rhodesia eventually withdrew in 1935. Not only did South Africa collect and operate all customs and excise, but the Bechuanaland Protectorate ceased to record its import and export statistics. The Protectorate's customs revenue was averaged out from the three previous depressed years, and fixed as 0.27622 per cent of the whole customs union's revenue from 1910 up to 1966. One of the last British acts before independence in 1966 was to take away some of Lesotho's share and give it to Botswana, so that Botswana's percentage rose to 0.30971 from 1967 to 1969 (42, pp.99–100).

South African 'free trade' with Britain, instituted in 1855, ceased in 1903, and was replaced by Imperial/Commonwealth preference for

South African goods entering Britain. The South African government passed its Customs Tariff Act in 1914, which was the legal basis for erecting ever higher tariff walls around the South African Customs Union from 1922 onwards. Between 1924 and 1941 South Africa imposed unilateral restrictions on cattle imports from its neighbours within the customs union. This contravention of the 1910 agreement led to Southern Rhodesia's break from the union in 1935, but was swallowed by the High Commissioner's office which regarded British relations with South Africa as paramount over the interests of the High Commission Territories.

The renegotiation of the Customs Union in 1969 was initiated by Botswana, which recognised it as the necessary precondition for government revenue to have any benefit from national economic growth. There was then no question of alternative arrangements with illegally ruled (Southern) Rhodesia to gain alternative access to the world market – at a time when South African goods were at higher than world prices (48).

Since 1980 Zimbabwe has become independent and Botswana has been able to exploit Zimbabwe's inherited status as a most favoured trading partner with SACU, allowing duty free exchange of specific goods by mutual agreement. The road to Zambia, across the Zambezi at Kazungula, has also been bitumenised – though a bridge rather than a ferry has yet to be built. But Botswana has proved remarkably cautious in its relations with SACU: preferring to build alternative bilateral economic relations elsewhere rather than to contemplate precipitate withdrawal from SACU.

Botswana was the main initiator, and is now the secretariat headquarters, of the Southern African Development Coordination Conference (SADCC) – designed to build up bilateral economic relations between the states of Southern Africa (including Tanzania, excluding South Africa) as an alternative to economic dominance by South Africa (39).

However South Africa remains the most convenient source of supply for Botswana of most manufactured goods, currently often at lower than world prices. Lines of communication and supply through Zimbabwe and Zambia are long and expensive and subject to (South African-backed) military attack. Ironically it is South Africa itself which is its own worst enemy in keeping open its lucrative and growing trade with the buoyant Botswana economy and through Botswana to the north. In response to international sanctions, South Africa has begun its own sanctions on its neighbours. And this despite the fact that Botswana publicly acknowledges it is in no position to impose sanctions on South Africa.

CONCLUSION

This paper has been written at a critical juncture in the economic history of Botswana. On the one hand there is a remarkable achievement of economic growth, generating a surplus that has yet to be productively invested to generate further growth. The steep climb of mineral-led growth is beginning to level out on to gentler slopes. On the other hand the great imponderable is the immediate future of its wounded giant neighbour, South Africa. Economic rationality seems to prevail on less than alternate days in the portals of Pretoria.

NOTES

1. The continuing importance of *mafisa* was underlined by research in the Rural Sociology Unit, Ministry of Agriculture, in the later 1970s. See for example, T. Hertel, 'The System of Mafisa and the Highly Dependent Agricultural Sector', Rural Sociology Unit Report No.11, Ministry of Agriculture, Gaborone, 1977.
2. Interview with Sir Peter Fawcus, Gaborone, 9–10 Oct. 1986.
3. Willoughby originally estimated 4 people per taxpayer on the basis of 1900 Bangwato figures. This was raised to 4.5 in 1903 and subsequently to 6 by 1910 – W.C. Willoughby Papers, Selly Oak Colleges Library, Birmingham, England, File 778.
4. For such stories on the so-called Leno Brotherhood see *Mmegi Wa Dikgang/The Reporter*, Gaborone, since January 1986.

REFERENCES

1. Allan, William, *The African Husbandman* (Edinburgh, 1965)
2. Barclays Bank of Botswana, *Botswana: An Economic Survey and Businessman's Guide* (Gaborone, 1985 edn.)
3. Barrett, John ed., *Accelerated Development in Southern Africa* (London, 1974)
4. Bechuanaland Protectorate, *Development Plan 1956–64* (Copy in Botswana National Archives)
5. Bechunaland Protectorate, *Development Plan 1960–64* (Copy in Botswana National Archives)
6. Bechuanaland Protectorate, *Development Plan 1963–68* (Mafeking, 1963)
7. Bechuanaland Protectorate, *Report on the Census of the Bechuanaland Protectorate, 1964* (Copy in Botswana National Archives)
8. Bechuanaland Protectorate, *The Development of the Bechuanaland Economy: Report of the Ministry of Overseas Development Economic Survey Mission* (London and Gaborone, 1965)
9. Bhila, Hoyini H.K., 'The Impact of the Second World War on the Development of Peasant Agriculture in Botswana, 1939–56', *Botswana Notes and Records* Vol.16 (1984), 63–72
10. Botswana, Government of, *Transitional Plan for Social and Economic Development* (Gaborone, 1966)
11. Botswana, Government of, *National Development Plan 1968–73* (Gaborone, 1968)
12. Botswana, Government of, Ministry of Agriculture, *The 1967–68 Agricultural Survey* (Gaborone, 1968)
13. Botswana, Government of, *National Development Plan 1970–75* (Gaborone, 1970)

14. Botswana, Government of, *Rural Income in Botswana* (Gaborone, Government Paper No.1 of 1972)
15. Botswana, Government of, Ministry of Finance and Development Planning, *National Development Plan 1973–78* (Gaborone, 1973)
16. Botswana, Government of, *The Rural Income Distribution Survey in Botswana 1974–75* (Gaborone, 1976)
17. Botswana, Government of, Ministry of Finance and Development Planning, *National Development Plan 1976–81* (Gaborone, 1977)
18. Botswana, Government of, Ministry of Finance and Development Planning, *National Development Plan 1979–85* (Gaborone, 1980)
19. Botswana, Government of, *Financial Assistance Policy* (Gaborone, Government Paper No.1 of 1982)
20. Botswana, Government of, *Report of the Presidential Commission on Economic Opportunities* (Gaborone, 1982)
21. Botswana, Government of, Ministry of Finance and Development Planning, *National Development Plan 1985–91* (Gaborone, 1976)
22. Botswana Society, *Proceedings of the Symposium on the Okavango Delta and its Future Development* (Gaborone, 1976)
23. Botswana Society, *Proceedings of the Symposium on Settlement in Botswana: The Historical Development of a Human Landscape*, R. Renee Hitchcock & Mary R. Smith eds. (Gaborone, 1980)
24. Botswana Society, *Proceedings of the Symposium on Education for Development*, Michael Crowder ed. (Gaborone, 1983)
25. Botswana Society, *Research in Botswana: Revised Proceedings of a Symposium on Research and Development*, Robert K. Hitchcock, Neil Parsons & John Taylor eds. (Gaborone, forthcoming)
26. Campbell, Alec & Thomas Tlou, *History of Botswana* (Gaborone, 1984)
27. Chambers, Robert, & D. Feldman, *Report on Rural Development* (Gaborone, Government of Botswana, 1973)
28. Cliffe, Lionel, & Richard Moorsom, 'Rural Class Formation and Ecological Collapse in Botswana,' *Review of African Political Economy*, Vol.16 (1980), 35–52
29. Cliffe, Lionel, 'A critique of Botswana's Development Path' in Botswana Society, *Proceedings of the Symposium on Education for Development*, Michael Crowder ed. (Gaborone, 1982)
30. Colclough, Christopher, Ministry of Finance and Development Planning, *Manpower and Employment in Botswana* (Gaborone, 1973)
31. Colclough, Christopher, & Stephen McCarthy, *The Political Economy of Botswana: A Study of Growth and Distribution* (London, 1980)
32. Cooper, David M., 'The State, Mineworkers and Multinationals: the Selebi-Phikwe Strike, 1975' in Cohen, Robin, Jean Copans & P.C.W. Gutkind eds., *African Labor History* (Beverley Hills, California, 1978), pp.244–77
33. Crowder, Michael, 'Resistance and Accommodation to the Penetration of the Capitalist Economy in South Africa: Tshekedi Khama and Mining in Botswana' (Unpublished seminar paper, Institute of Commonwealth Studies, University of London, copy in Botswana National Archives)
34 Denbow, James, 'A New Look at the Later Prehistory of the Kalahari', *Journal of African History*, Vol.27, No.1 (1986), 35–52
35. Ettinger, Steven, 'South Africa's Weight Restrictions on Cattle Exports from Bechuanaland, 1924–41', *Botswana Notes and Records*, Vol.4 (1972), 21–9
36. Falconer, J., 'A History of the Bechuanaland Protectorate Veterinary Services', *Botswana Notes and Records*, Vol.3 (1977), 74–8
37. Granberg, Per, *A Description of the Macro-Economic Model for Botswana (Membot): A User's Manual* (Bergen, 1983)
38. Hailey, Lord, *Native Administration in the British African Territories, Part V: The High Commission Territories* (London, 1953)
39. Hanlon, Joseph, *Beggar Your Neighbours: Apartheid Power in Southern Africa* (London, 1986)

40. Henderson, Willie, Neil Parsons, Thomas Tlou, *Seretse Khama: A Life* (Cambridge, forthcoming)
41. Hermans, Quill, 'A Review of Botswana's Financial History, 1900–1973', *Botswana Notes and Records*, Vol.6 (1974), 89–115
42. Hitchcock, Robert K., 'Water, Land and Livestock: The Evolution of Tenure and Administrative Patterns in the Grazing Areas of Botswana' in Louis A. Picard ed., *The Evolution of Modern Botswana* (London, 1985)
43. Hubbard, Michael, 'Botswana and the International Beef Trade, 1900–1981' (D. Phil thesis, University of Sussex, 1983)
44. Kann, Ulla, 'Problems of Equity in the Education System: the Provision of Basic Education in Botswana' in Botswana Society, *Proceedings of the Symposium on Education for Development*, Michael Crowder ed. (Gaborone, 1982)
45. Kerven, Carol, 'Academics, Practitioners and all kinds of Women in Development: A Reply to Peters', *Journal of Southern African Studies*, Vol.10, No.2 (1984), 259–68
46. Kiyaga-Mulindwa, David, 'The Bechuanaland Protectorate and the Second World War', *Journal of Imperial and Commonwealth History*, Vol.12, No.3 (1984), 33–53
47. Kuper, Adam, *Wives for Cattle: Bridewealth and Marriage in Southern Africa* (London, 1982)
48. Landell-Mills, Peter M., 'The 1969 Southern African Customs Union Agreement', *Journal of Modern African Studies*, Vol.9, No.2 (1971), pp.263–81
49. Lewis, Stephen R.,'The Impact of the Shashe Project on Botswana's Economy' in Charles Harvey, ed., *Papers on the Economy of Botswana* (London, 1981)
50. Lipton, Michael, *Employment and Labour Use in Botswana, Final Report, Vol.I and Vol.II* (Gaborone, Government of Botswana, 1970)
51. Makgetlar, Neva Seidman, 'Finance and Development: the Case of Botswana', *Journal of Modern African Studies*, Vol.20, No.1 (1982), 69–86
52. Massey, David R., 'Labour Migration and Rural Development in Botswana' (Ph.D. thesis, Boston University, 1981)
53. Morrell, Robert, 'Farmers, Randlords and the South African State: Confrontation in the Witwatersrand Beef Markets, c.1920–1923', *Journal of African History*, Vol.27, No.3 (1986), 513–32
54. Morse, Chandler, *Basutoland, Bechuanaland Protectorate and Swaziland: Report of an Economic Survey Mission* (London, 1960)
55. Morton, Fred & Jeff Ramsay, eds., *Birth of Botswana: The History of the Bechuanaland Protectorate, 1910–1966* (Gaborone, forthcoming)
56. Munger, Edwin S., *Bechuanaland: Pan-African Outpost or Bantu Homeland?* (London, 1965)
57. Mushingeh, A.C.S., 'A History of Disease and Medicine in Botswana, 1820–1945' (Ph.D. thesis, University of Cambridge, 1984)
58. Nganunu, J., 'Botswana's Minerals and Mining Policy' in OOmmen, M.A. et al eds., *Botswana's Economy Since Independence* (New Delhi, 1983)
59. Okihiro, Gary Y., 'Hunters, Herders, Cultivators and Traders, Interactions and Change in the Kgalagadi' (Ph.D. thesis, University of California, 1976)
60. Opschoor, Johannes B., 'Crops, Class and Climate: Environment and Economic Constraints and Potentials of Production in Botswana' in OOmmen, M.A., et al eds., *Botswana's Economy Since Independence* (New Delhi, 1983)
61. Palmer, Robin, & Neil Parsons, eds., *The Roots of Rural Poverty in Central and Southern Africa* (London, 1977)
62. Parson, Jack, 'Cattle, Class and the State in Rural Botswana', *Journal of Southern African Studies*, Vol.7, No.2 (1981), 236–55
63. Parson, Jack, *Botswana: Liberal Democracy and the Labor Reserve in Southern Africa* (Boulder, Colorado, 1984)
64. Parsons, Neil, 'The Economic History of Khama's Country in Botswana, 1844–1930' in Robin Palmer & Neil Parsons, eds., *The Roots of Rural Poverty in Central and Southern Africa* (London, 1977)
65. Parsons, Neil, '"Khama & Co." and the Jousse Trouble, 1910–1916', *Journal of African History*, Vol.6, No.3 (1975), pp.383–408

198

66. Parsons, Neil, 'Education and Development in Pre-Colonial and Colonial Botswana to 1965' in Botswana Society, *Proceedings of the Symposium on Education for Development*, Michael Crowder, ed. (Gaborone, 1983)
67. Peters, Pauline, 'Cattlemen, Borehold Syndicates and Privatization in the Kgatleng District of Botswana' (Ph.D. thesis, Boston University, 1983)
68. Peters, Pauline, 'Gender, Development Cycles and Historical Process: A Critique of Recent Research on Women in Botswana', *Journal of Southern African Studies*, Vol.10, No.1 (1983), 100–22
69. Pim, Alan W., *Financial and Economic Position of the Bechuanaland Protectorate: Report of the Commission Appointed by the Secretary of State for Dominion Affairs* (London, 1933)
70. Rey, Charles F., *Monarch of All I Survey: Bechuanaland Diaries 1929–37*, Michael Crowder & Neil Parsons eds. (London and Gaborone, 1987)
71. Robson, Peter, 'Economic Integration in Southern Africa', *Journal of Modern African Studies*, Vol.5 No.4 (1967), 469–90
72. Salkin, Jay S., 'Research on Employment and Unemployment in Botswana' in Botswana Society, *Research on Botswana: Revised Proceedings of a Symposium on Research for Development*, Hitchcock, Robert K., Neil Parsons & John Taylor eds. (Gaborone, forthcoming)
73. Schapera, Isaac, *Migrant Labour and Tribal Life: A study of Conditions in the Bechuanaland Protectorate* (London, 1947)
74. Schapera, Isaac, *Tribal Innovators: Tswana Chiefs and Social Change 1795–1940* (London, 1970)
75. Shivji, Issa, *Class struggles in Tanzania* (London and Dar es Salaam, 1976)
76. Sillery, Anthony, 'Working Backwards: Draft Autobiography, 1903–51' (Rhodes House Library, Oxford, Mss. Afr.r.207)
77. Smith, Arnold, *Stitches in Time: The Commonwealth in World Politics* (London and Ontario, 1981), pp.112–16
78. Swainson, Nicola, 'The Rise of a National Bourgeoisie in Kenya', *Review of African and Political Economy*, No.8 (1977), 39–55
79. Symon, A.C.B., *Economic and Financial Report on the High Commission Territories* (London, 1954)
80. Taylor, John, 'Mine Labour Recruitment in the Bechuanaland Protectorate', *Botswana Notes and Records*, Vol.10 (1978), pp.99–112
81. Taylor, John & N. Tumkaya, 'Demography and Migration' in Botswana Society, *Research on Botswana: Proceedings of a Symposium on Research for Development*, Hitchock, Robert K., Neil Parsons & John Taylor eds. (Gaborone, forthcoming)
82. Thema, B.C., 'Moeng College: A Product of Self-help', *Botswana Notes and Records*, Vol.2 (1969),71–4
83. Tibone, M.C., 'The Shashe Nickel-Copper Project' in M.A. Oommen et al, eds., *Botswana's Economy Since Independence* (New Delhi, 1983)
84. UNESCO, *Bechuanaland: Educational Planning Mission* (Paris, 1964)
85. Van Onselen, Charles, 'Reaction to Rinderpest in Southern Africa 1896–97' *Journal of African History*, Vol.13, No.3. pp.473–488
86. Van Rensberg, Patrick, *Report from Swaneng Hill: Education and Employment in an African Country* (Uppsala, Sweden, 1974)

6

Land and Labour in the Namibian Economy

PHILIP LONGMIRE

INTRODUCTION

The economic history of Namibia has been marked by land alienation, resource extraction and labour exploitation. For over a century from the time of colonisation in 1884 to the present impasse in independence negotiations the attention of the colonial rulers has been directed toward the mercantile value of the human and natural resources in the Territory. The territory was visited by Portuguese, Dutch, British and German interests in turn. Commercial operations based in Europe, the Americas and South Africa searched the seas off Namibia for whales, seals and guano deposits before exploring the interior. British and other maritime interests used offshore islands and the rare coastal harbour as whaling stations where their ships could wait out storms or make repairs while explorers from the Cape Colony to the south searched out the Territory to determine its potential mineral wealth. Traders and missionaries followed explorers and prospectors to Namibia. German interests pursued a policy of immigration and settler ranching that required ever increasing amounts of land. The scramble for mining and trade concessions from the traditional leadership in return for ephemeral 'protection' resulted in the loss of economic and political control over internal affairs (27, pp.158–73). The Union of South Africa, which captured the Territory in 1915, distributed land to transnational corporations involved in resource extraction and to South African settlers. The indigenous population was shuffled onto unproductive reserves in the periphery of the Territory that still form pools of labour serving colonial interests. Africans were stripped of their means of production (access to land and resources), reduced to dependency upon a wage economy sustained by foreign capital and forced into a class of migrant labourers employed by international interests.

200

Namibians have not been silent in the face of the loss of their land. Members of the South West Africa Peoples' Organisation (SWAPO) have had some success inside the Territory in organising worker resistance. Using strikes, boycotts and public meetings they have faced the full range of political, military and economic power of the South African regime based in the capital, Windhoek. Operating from bases outside the Territory members of the military arm of SWAPO, the People's Liberation Army of Namibia (PLAN) have made repeated attacks on the South African Defence Forces (SADF) located in the north of Namibia. The cumulative effect of this resistance has been a strengthening of SWAPO support but also a strengthening of South African resistance to change. Namibia has become a police state with restrictive legislation and unfettered police and army action against civilians, throwing normal social and cultural life into disarray. The struggle continues on a daily basis but despite twenty years of armed resistance the political and economic independence is still a dream, albeit one which may be realised at the beginning of the 1990s.

HISTORICAL BACKGROUND

Exploration and Settlement

The original inhabitants of Namibia appear to have been the San (Bushmen) who roamed southern Africa as hunters and gatherers in small kinship groups. Herero and Nama peoples entered the area sometime near the beginning of the seventeenth century. They were herdsmen. Their herds of cattle, goats and sheep provided them with sustenance, wealth and status. In the north of the Territory lived the pastoralists – the Ovambo and related groups. They were and continue to be the largest ethnic group in Namibia.

As Boer settlers trekked north out of Cape Colony in the mid-nineteenth century they pushed before them African and Christianised mixed race populations who crossed the Orange River to settle in Namibia. In this wave of migration came the Orlams and the Basters who competed with the Hereros for grazing land. By the time European settlers arrived in the Territory they found a variety of indigenous and introduced peoples each with separate social, cultural and economic systems. Later colonial administrations used the rivalry among these competing groups to 'divide and rule' and thereby acquired concessions over land and mineral rights in the Territory.

201

German South West Africa[1]

In the last quarter of the nineteenth century a newly unified German nation was competing with the long established British and French empires for power and influence in Europe. Although initially wary of a colonial empire German Chancellor Otto von Bismarck was persuaded by German commercial interests that overseas territories could provide raw materials for German industry and markets for German products. In order to save the Imperial Treasury the expense of colonisation, however, Bismarck encouraged German business interests to take responsibility for the exploration and administration of colonial territories, as, he reasoned, it was the German commercial classes who would benefit most from colonisation (5, p.88).

By the late nineteenth century there were few accessible regions left which were not already claimed or occupied by European powers. The southwest coast of Africa was one such area. Britain had laid claim to Walvis Bay and several offshore islands in 1878 but the coast north and south of Walvis Bay had not been occupied.

Adolf Luderitz, a German merchant adventurer, following his agent to South West Africa in 1883, negotiated agreements with local chiefs for land, trading and mining privileges in return for guns and gold. These agreements gave Luderitz access to a narrow strip of coastal Territory from the Orange to the Cunene Rivers (5, pp.66–87). Luderitz then persuaded the German Imperial Government to extend to him its protection and lay claim to the Territory, which it did in August 1884.

The Deutsche Kolonial Gesellschaft für Südwest Afrika (DKG) was created to carry out further exploration and treaty negotiation on behalf of the German Government and to develop and administer the Territory. Luderitz sold his claims in Namibia to the DKG in the following year (5, pp.88–97). These German moves undermined attempts by the Cape Colony to get Britain to annex the same area and went unchallenged by the British Government.

Chancellor Bismarck sent several expeditions to South West Africa to negotiate 'protection' treaties over the hinterland while German companies were formed to engage in prospecting and mineral development. The indigenous population, in the face of this determined intruder, sought to secure the best deal they could for continued access to the land for their herds of cattle. They held the upper hand for much of the remainder of the century, but with the increasing presence of German military and commercial interests confrontation was bound to erupt.

Graf von Caprivi, who replaced Bismarck as Imperial Chancellor in

1890, sent Major Theodor Leutwein to German South West Africa, where he was to become Governor (1894–1905), with these instructions:

> ... Our power over the natives must be maintained under all circumstances and must be more and more consolidated. You must inquire whether the troops are strong enough to accomplish this task. (21, p.28)

Leutwein's recommendations were for increased troop deployment and greater German immigration. The acquisition and control of land and cattle became the overriding concern of the German administration. It was also the overriding concern of the Africans. The Herero, numbering some 80,000 under their chief Maherero, occupied some of the choicest grazing land on the 'hardveld' of the central plateau. Their herds were estimated at upwards of 100,000 head. Before general European encroachment they had already been competing for land and cattle with the Nama of Hendrik Witbooi who occupied the south central highlands. As German colonization increased, the settlers coveted the choice 'hardveld'. It was their opinion that the object of colonisation was to take control of the land for white settlement and thereby reduce the indigenous population to a servant class or confine them to reserves established for them (27, p.194).

Maherero had tried to play the Germans off against the Capelanders, who also wanted concessions in the form of access to land and minerals. He had refused the 'protection' offered by the German administration and revoked the agreement he had made with them in 1885. This was an impediment to further German settler expansion and presented a threat to Germans already settled in the Territory, who feared being drawn into conflicts between the Herero and the Nama.

Major Leutwein, using the enmity between the Herero and the Nama, promised them German 'protection' in exchange for their land, which was subsequently divided up and sold or leased to German settlers. The Germans, however, were in no position numerically or militarily to deliver the 'protection' which the agreements promised. Conflict between the Herero and Nama for grazing land continued and erupted in raids and warfare. Leutwein himself acknowledged that German 'protection' was 'merely on paper' (21, p.29). Samuel Maherero, son of the former chief, wavered between cooperation with the German administration and resistance. He eventually called for a united front against German land encroachment. Although supported by the Namas his efforts were betrayed by the Rehobothers. One of the last indigenous wars against colonial expansion in Africa began in 1904.

General Lothan von Trotha was sent to German South West Africa to subdue the Herero. He issued his infamous extermination order on a weakened and defenceless people declaring,

> The Herero people must now leave the country, if they do not I will compel them with the big tube. Within the German frontier every Herero, with or without a rifle, will be shot. I will not take any women or children, but I will drive them back to their people or have them fired on. (27, p.208)

True to his word von Trotha drove the Herero into the Kalahari desert, the great 'thirstland', slaughtering all stragglers. Of an estimated population of 80,000 less than 20,000 survived. An armistice with the Herero was signed in December 1905. Samuel Maherero was exiled to Bechuanaland. The Nama, having joined the struggle somewhat later, continued guerrilla campaigns until 1907, but they too were eventually defeated and confined to prison labour camps. Ordinances passed by the German administration in 1906 and 1907 prohibited the Herero and Nama from acquiring titles or rights over land and debarred them from owning riding animals or cattle. They were forced to carry passes and faced punishment for vagrancy if found unemployed. The Government confiscated the 10 million hectares of Hereroland and the land of the Nama who had taken part in the struggle. Most of their stock animals had been destroyed or died of starvation. What were left were also confiscated. As a result of these policies, Governor Leutwein declared that the German administration had completely destroyed the economic assets of farming and two thirds of native labour leaving only the mining sector unscathed (27, p.213). In the decade that remained of German occupation developments in the Territory were impeded by a labour shortage.

German policy in South West Africa had been to eliminate the native population and their competition so that German settlers could freely settle the land and engage in commercial animal husbandry and mineral exploration. The discovery of diamonds in 1908 forced the German administration to change its policies from one of exterminating the African population to one of exploiting its labour. Following the Herero war labour intensive industries in mining and railway construction were short of workers. Legislation was introduced to force what remained of the African population to seek work with German employers. Taxes were introduced to force Africans into the labour market. The aim was to 'make every native dependent for a living upon employment by Europeans. If any native tried to do otherwise he was treated practically as a vagabond' (22, p.42). Despite the legislation South West Africa had to look elsewhere for labourers to make up the loss suffered through warfare and starvation.

Plans were drawn up to import labour from German East Africa, the Cameroons and India. Most foreign workers, however, came from the Cape Colony.

Inside the Territory the Ovambos of northern Namibia became the main source of labourers. Ovamboland along the northern border with Angola, which has about 45 per cent of the entire Namibian population, was never fully under German control. They still occupied their traditional lands and pursued their traditional way of life – agriculture and animal husbandry.

The period of German occupation was one in which the acquisition of land for ranching and settlement were priorities. The discovery of minerals and the mining of diamonds and copper along with the introduction of Karakul sheep and the growth of beef cattle herds was to form the basis for the future development of the Namibian economy.

For the Africans, German occupation meant the loss of land and livelihood. Shunted onto reserves, legislation and the horrors of a genocidal war deprived them of their land and cattle and, thus, their freedom to pursue their traditional way of life. By the outbreak of the First World War in 1914 white settlement had risen to 14,830, of which 1,587 people occupied 1,331 farms covering one sixth of the Territory or about 83,712 km^2. In addition five mining companies[2] had been granted concessions over another 150,000 km^2 of land.

The South African occupation of German South West Africa in 1915 held out the expectation that the Africans would regain possession of the land and cattle if not their trust in the colonisers. This was not to be, however. Africans waited in vain for the fulfilment of promises made by the South African occupation forces.

SOUTH WEST AFRICA UNDER THE MANDATE

The treaty of Versailles which brought the War to an end established a League of Nations to oversee the peace. The high ideals which were the background to the League's creation, however, were quickly buried in the self-interest of the powerful nations which formed it. Germany as well as other of the Central Powers were stripped of their colonial possessions. These were then given as Mandated Territories to the victors to administer as 'a sacred trust of civilisation'. German South West Africa was to be administered by South Africa on behalf of Great Britain 'under the laws of the Mandatory as integral portions of its Territory . . . in the interest of the indigenous population' (3, pp.209–10, Article 22). South Africa was to submit annual reports on its administration to the Council of the League for examination and advice.

South Africa had the authority and the responsibility to rectify any unfair labour or land policies of the previous German administration in Namibia. South Africa had implied that this was in fact what it would do and Africans in the Territory expected to see their lands returned to them. Contrary to its promises, however, South Africa began, as soon as its control of Namibia was secured, to strengthen the direction of German economic policies. South Africa confirmed legislation in pursuit of land alienation, resource extraction and labour exploitation which the Germans had introduced. It proceeded to govern the Territory, not in the interests of the indigenous inhabitants but in the interests of white settlers and foreign investment. German civilians were encouraged to remain in the Territory. They were allowed to keep possession of their land and businesses. The holdings of German companies however were confiscated and sold to South African interests.

When pressed to address the grievances of the African population over the loss of their land and stock in the Herero war Gysbert Hofmeyr, Administrator of SWA, declared that he was of the opinion that the 'native question was synonymous with the labour question' and that he did not 'have the time to study the conditions of native labour' (27, pp.275–6). Instead he set up a commission to report on the availability, for the colonial interests, of indigenous labour, its distribution and the administration of reserves. Instead of returning land to the Hereros and others or making more land for settlement and agriculture available to them the Administrator declared that it was too late to acquire land due to 'the vested rights having to be considered' (27, p.277).

One presumes that by 'vested rights' the Administrator was referring to the possessions of German residents who only a few years before had wrested the land from the indigenous population. South Africa had the authority to expel all German citizens and confiscate their holdings as part of its war reparations claims. Instead South Africa allowed German residents to continue to work their holdings and made separate reparations claims against Germany.

The Native Labour Commission appointed by Hofmeyr reported in 1922. It recommended a policy of 'segregation' and the elimination of 'black islands' of indigenous populations situated in Territory designated for whites only. The German administration had proposed the creation of reserves for Africans but had not fully implemented the policy before being caught up in the First World War. On the basis of the Commission report South Africa began to implement just such a policy. The reserves which the South African Government set aside, however, were in the arid sandveld in the east of the country along the borders of the Kalahari Desert – the very area to which von Trotha had pursued the Herero to their deaths in 1904–5 (27, p.279). Their grazing lands were then allocated to immigrant settlers from the Union of South Africa. The creation of reserves served two purposes. First, South Africa reasoned, it would ensure a settled and contented African population that could be controlled through native administrations. Second, it would create a pool of potential labourers who could be recruited to work on future developments in the Territory.[3]

One is led to the conclusion that South Africa had never intended to administer South West Africa 'in the interest of the indigenous population' but rather in the interests of the white settler population. In the first three years of South African administration an additional 4,844,626 hectares of land was allocated for white settlement. By 1935 a total of 25,467,628 hectares was reserved for the white population which had increased to 31,800 (7, p.248).

South Africa also made its intentions clear regarding labour. During the twenty years between 1920 and the Second World War legislation was proclaimed which continued German policies to force indigenous workers into dependency on the wage economy. A work force of poorly paid and ill treated Africans was created which did not have access or input into the laws governing them. The German administration had deprived the Hereros and the Namas of their means of production by confiscating their land and depriving them of their stock animals. This had not, however, ensured their participation in the wage economy. The South African administration proceeded to introduce taxes and legislation which would force them to participate in the wage economy. An example is the dog tax which was introduced on the hunting dogs owned by the Bondleswarts.[4] In order to earn money to pay it they were forced to seek work on white-owned farms.

After having thus assured themselves that Africans would not be able to provide for themselves the South African administration introduced vagrancy laws. 'Vagrancy' was defined as having an insufficient means of support and was punishable by arrest and subsequent allocation to white employers. Pass laws were strengthened and curfews applying to Africans only were imposed in urban settlements. All this was meted out to a people whose greatest restrictions before colonisation had been those of climate and terrain.

South Africa found the mandate system overseen by the League an impediment to its total economic and political incorporation of German South Africa. South Africa's intention had always been to annex the Territory. South Africa had agreed to invade and occupy German South West Africa during the First World War with the expectation that if the Allied Powers won the war South West Africa would become a part of the Union of South Africa. This had been opposed by President Wilson of the United States in 1919. The wording of the mandate agreement however allowed South Africa to administer Namibia as 'integral portions' of its Territory without further delay. South Africa's attitude was that the mandate was as good as annexation. In veiled understandings arrived at with other world leaders South Africa was assured its administration would not suffer interference from them. Prime Minister Jan Christiaan Smuts explained to the South African parliament that it was not necessary to annex the Territory as the Mandate gave the Union complete administrative and legislative sovereignty over SWA (7, p.210).

Accordingly South Africa's approach to the administration of the Territory was to encourage white settlement, develop infrastructural linkages with the Union and to continue trade and investment following the German strategy of development using the land and labour of the indigenous population.

Throughout this period (1920–39), as the white population more than doubled to over 30,000, the indigenous population stood at 253,305 including 41,305 so called 'coloureds' or people of mixed race. Of a total area of 82,290,860 hectares white-owned farms occupied 25,614,210 ha., while white-controlled crown land took up another 21,000,000 ha. The African population was confined to reserves established on some of the least productive land amounting to only 17,499,557 ha. (27, p.312), less than 22 per cent of the total land area. The Great Depression (1929–1933) and Second World War interrupted this trend, but it resumed with a new determination following the collapse of the League and the establishment of the United Nations in 1945.

THE UNITED NATIONS AND SOUTH WEST AFRICA

The United Nations took over the supervision of Mandated Territories from the League in 1945. It requested South Africa to continue to make annual reports on its administration of SWA and submit them to the UN Trusteeship Council. South Africa, however, saw the demise of the League as an opportunity to formalise full incorporation of the Territory into the Union of South Africa. It rejected the UN's supervisory interest in SWA, declaring that with the death of the League the Mandate system was also at an end and therefore South African sovereignty over Namibia was unrestricted.

Following the victory of the National Party in South Africa's general elections of 1948, economic and political ties between SWA and the Union were strengthened. Whites in the Territory were given six seats in the South African Parliament in 1949 and a new constitution for SWA was drawn up without reference to its Mandate status. After 1947 South Africa refused to submit any further reports on its administration of the Territory to the Trusteeship Council.

The United Nations instituted legal proceedings in the International Court of Justice to determine SWA's status. The Court ruled in 1950 that although the Territory's mandated status continued South Africa was not obliged to place the Territory under UN Trusteeship.

Ethiopia and Liberia, two of the original members of the League, and also of the UN, asked the ICJ to require South Africa to carry out its obligations as laid down under the League Mandate system. They argued that the introduction of 'apartheid' was not in the best interests of the inhabitants of the Territory. The Court was divided on the issue and six years later ruled that Ethiopia and Liberia had not established a legal right to bring the matter to the Court. This was a signal to SWAPO forces that they could not expect an easy or swift resolution of their long standing struggle for freedom, justice and an end to South African rule. In August of 1966 they launched an armed resistance against South African forces in the Territory.

The United Nations General Assembly then passed Resolution 2145 (XXI) to strip South Africa of its Mandate over South West Africa. It established the Council for Namibia (1967) to act as the *de jure* administration for the Territory and changed the name from South West Africa to Namibia (1968). South Africa refused to recognise or comply with either ICJ or UN decisions on the Territory. The UN Security Council condemned South African occupation of Namibia and set October 1969 as a deadline for its withdrawal. The ICJ, in yet another ruling on the Namibia question, declared South Africa's presence in the Territory illegal (1971). South Africa considered these measures an interference in its internal affairs and proceeded to strengthen rather than dismantle its administration of the Territory.

The coup that overthrew the Caetano regime in Portugal in 1974 led to the independence of Portugal's African colonies. Mozambique and Angola on the east and west flanks of South Africa became independent in 1975 under Marxist-inspired governments. In Rhodesia the rebel regime of Ian Smith was fighting a futile battle against liberation forces which eventually claimed victory in the polls in 1980. Within a short five-year period the balance of political power had suddenly changed direction in the subcontinent. In an effort to gain time and get control of the direction in the change South Africa agreed to sit down and talk over the Namibia Question.

Five of the Western powers sitting on the Security Council in 1977 (France, West Germany, the United Kingdom, the United States and

Canada) joined together as a Contact Group to lead the negotiations between South Africa, SWAPO, the Front Line States (FLS), Nigeria and others. Over the next eight years deadlines for independence came and went. While the Contact Group through the UN Security Council drew up plans for a negotiated settlement (SC Res. 435, 1978) South Africa pursued a two-track strategy of its own. On the one hand it increased its security forces and made repeated incursions into southern Angola in pursuit of PLAN forces eventually occupying the southern portion of Angola. Meanwhile, inside Namibia, the South African administration searched for a means to include Namibians in a transfer of power that would effectively exclude SWAPO supporters. South Africa began to treat Namibia as a laboratory to explore constitutional arrangements which could perhaps be applied at some later date to the Republic itself. It staged elections for an Advisory Council based on ethnic groupings within the Territory. After several attempts at a divestment of power, none of which ultimately worked or were acceptable to South Africa, it formed a Transitional Government of National Union (TGNU).

With the election of President Reagan in the United States in 1980 South Africa also saw an opportunity to divert the international negotiations by emphasising the spectre of a communist-backed government in Angola to an American President who saw the hand of an 'evil empire' behind every socialist struggle. South Africa obtained US support in negotiations then under way. The American administration called for a 'constructive dialogue' with South Africa over the Namibia issue. Progress toward independence was delayed by the introduction of 'linkage' that called for a withdrawal of Cuban forces stationed in Angola in exchange for a withdrawal of South African forces from Namibia. This issue split the Contact Group and was rejected by Angola, the FLS and the UN, at least until 1988. While these political moves were failing to bear fruit Namibia's economy was facing stagnation and decline.

NAMIBIA'S ECONOMIC BASE

At two thirds the size of South Africa, Namibia is larger than France and the two Germanys combined and over three times the size of the United Kingdom. It stretches approximately 1,280 kilometres from the Orange River border with South Africa in the south to the border with Angola in the north. It varies in width from 960 to 352 kilometres excluding the extension of the Caprivi Strip, which was designed to give the former German administration access to the Zambezi River. The total area of the Territory is 823,168 km² excluding the 1,124 km² enclave of Walvis Bay, which was administered from Cape Colony until 1910 and is claimed directly by South Africa, and is now administered separately from the remainder of the Territory.

Except for the northeast quadrant the land is composed mostly of arid hardveld on the upland plateau and sandveld in desert areas. Two deserts dominate: the Namib which spreads along the Atlantic coast and the Kalahari which extends into Botswana on the east. Rainfall is unreliable averaging from 86mm in the South and West to 575mm in the northeast. There are no permanent rivers within the Territory except for the Okavango which crosses the narrow extension of the Caprivi Strip. Periodic droughts occur in approximately fifteen-year cycles. The drought in 1980–81 was the worst in fifty years (10, passim and 27, passim).

Estimates put the population at near 1.25 million, which includes 100,000 whites (excluding the defence forces), 115,000 coloureds or persons of mixed racial origins, and 1,035,000 Africans. The African population is further classified by the South African authorities into eight ethnic groups. They are the Ovambo, Okavango, Kaokovelders, Damara, Herero, East Caprivians, Tswana and San or Bushmen. The Ovambo, comprising about 47 per cent of the total, is the largest population group. The Tswana, with a population of 5,000, is the smallest (23, p.3).

Until 1955, statistical information on SWA's economy had been listed separately in annual reports, but since this date South Africa has incorporated statistical information on Namibia within the statistics of South Africa itself. This makes it difficult to find current and reliable data on such factors as external trade, balance of payments, etc. This move from reporting separate information on Namibia followed instructions issued by the South African Government to administrative and economic agencies not to publish information on Namibia after the Territory was incorporated into the Republic of South Africa.

Namibia is characterised by a dual economic structure with a heavy reliance on export oriented industry in the primary resource sectors of mining, farming and fishing. It depends heavily on the investments of multinational corporations (MNCs) based in South Africa and the West and imports technology, expertise and training from there. It is tied heavily to South Africa not only politically and militarily but economically. Transport and communications are directed south and imports come through South Africa and the MNCs have exploited the resources of land, labour and minerals. The service sector is primarily oriented to support the export/import sector. The primary sector contributes over half of the Gross Domestic Product (GDP). In 1979 it was R850m and of that mining alone contributed R655m. The total GDP was R1425m. The secondary sector was R150m and the tertiary sector another R425m made up of transport, trade, housing, financial and government services (9, p.274).

Agriculture, including forestry, and fishing which together provided 15.5 per cent of the Gross Domestic Product (GDP) in 1970 fell to 9.6 per cent by 1980 (17, p.53).

Agriculture

Due to the arid climate and infertile soil vegetation is sparse. The traditional and modern rural economic base has been animal husbandry. The Herero, who were the second largest ethnic group at the time of German occupation, were estimated to have had between 100,000 and 150,000 head of cattle in the 1890s. Half of the 500,000 African labour force is still engaged in the subsistence sector, at least part-time, as many African workers in the white and/or foreign-owned sector are forced to leave their families behind to subsidise their earnings through subsistence agricultural production on the reserves (14, p.31).

Rainfall determines the pattern of agricultural land use. Below 250mm a year pasture is too sparse for cattle and the land is given over to small stock – sheep and goats. About 30 per cent of the entire land is used in this way, mostly in the southern third of the country. In areas receiving above 350mm of rainfall larger stock such as cattle can be raised. In the northeast corner where rainfall exceeds 500mm a year mixed farming (ranching as well as growing maize, millet, fruit and vegetables) is possible. This represents only 6.5 per cent of the land surface, however.

Early explorers, traders and colonisers found a population that was divided along similar lines. In the south lived the small stock herders – the Nama and Damara; further north the Herero cattle herders predominated and in the north dwelt the Ovambo and related peoples with their mixed crops. All groups supplemented their food production by hunting and gathering. The scarcity of vegetation and the uncertainty of rainfall created a widely dispersed population, nomadic in nature and living in family groups under a decentralised authority.

Trade linked these peoples, however, as copper and iron, mined in the north and worked by Ovambo smiths, were exchanged for cattle and reached to the far south of the country and east into Botswana.

Migrations from South Africa during the nineteenth century put pressure on the Namibian people. As the population increased competition for cattle and grazing land resulted in armed conflicts. The movement of people and animals spread diseases like the rinderpest epidemic of 1897. The traditional social and economic order began to break down.

Both the German and later South African colonisers took advantage of this situation to gain control of the land and resources. Their aim was to settle whites in the Territory. Through 'protection' treaties and wars of genocide the Germans acquired the most commercially viable lands on

212

the central hardveld plateau. South Africa maintained this division of territory after it took the colony in 1915. Although white settlement was banned north of the 'Red Line',[5] which represented the northern limit of German police authority, very little expropriated land in the southern 'Police Zone' was ever returned to Namibians. Today less than one fifth of viable farmland is under peasant, that is African, cultivation.

The colonial administration had three main objectives: to secure a stable pool of labourers, to lower labour costs and to regulate competition for labour between employers. This was done by the creation of reserves that enforced a communal land tenure system in which the unemployed and elderly could be confined to their own resources. The colonial administration limited the size of stocks which Africans could have and their access to markets and imposed 'influx control' laws which limited the time Africans could be absent from the reserves.

Africans, denied access to markets and productive land, were left with their labour as their only means of production. They were thus forced to seek employment in the white 'reserves' outside their 'Homelands' and away from their families. There is virtually no manufacturing industry in Namibia (contributing only 4.2 per cent to the GDP in 1980) so the African was limited to jobs in the primary sector – agriculture, fishing and mining. Other Africans found work in the tertiary sector in health, education, administration and domestic service.

A contract labour system was created to recruit Africans from the reserves. Namibian labourers in the Police Zone were sent to work on the white farms. Beyond the 'Red Line' the northern Ovambo were designated to work in the mines. All commercial activity which might offer the hope of an independent livelihood was restricted. The northern area was fenced off and any southward movement of cattle was banned. An increase in the population and the number of cattle has put a severe strain on the available land. This has resulted in declining per capita returns and a dependence on outside relief in times of drought.

White farm settlement rose from 458 farm units in 1904 to 5,216 farm units in 1960 at which time they occupied 39 million hectares (48.5 per cent) of land. (At about the same time Reserves comprised approximately 32 million hectares or about 39.6 per cent of the land area. The remaining 12 per cent of the land area was set aside as game parks and forestry land.) The average cattle ranch was 6,615 hectares with 580 head per farm. The average karakul sheep ranch covered 8,780 hectares and the average rancher grazed 1,520 sheep (16, pp.30, 38).

Production is designed for export to South Africa and the West. The two principal agricultural exports are cattle exported as beef, live animals or hides and karakul sheep pelts (Persian Lamb). One hundred per cent of pelts are exported, about 80 per cent of which go to Germany and Italy for high fashion and about 95 per cent of the cattle products are exported. These two items taken together comprise about 90–95 per cent of total agricultural sales.

The six-year drought of the late 1970s and early 1980s resulted in an agricultural decline. The number of cattle rose steadily from 546,126 head in 1927 to a high of 2,850,000 in 1976. As a result of the drought the national herd had declined to 1,882,200 by 1984. A similar rise and decline was experienced in the Karakul pelt industry over the same period, rising from 123,745 to 5,000,000 and then falling off by nearly half to 2,600,000 beasts. The market for Karakul pelts has also declined as fashion turned away from Persian Lamb. Exports of pelts rose from 1,718,697 in 1942 to 2,860,000 in 1955 before separate statistical information was no longer noted (19, p.29). A decline in demand meant that in 1976 still only 2,885,881 pelts were exported valued at 51.4 million rand (9, p.287). By 1982 sales were 60 per cent less than they had been two years before. A similar decline in the production of maize and wheat was felt due to the drought. The Food and Agricultural Organisation (FAO) estimates that Namibia produces less than half of its cereal consumption needs, creating a shortfall of 310,000 tonnes (16, p.101).

Combined with declining returns, drought and an uncertain political future, the extension of PLAN guerrilla operations to the triangle around Otavi, Grootfontein and Tsumeb in north-central Namibia in the later half of the 1970s caused many farmers to pull out of Namibia. They began by selling off their breeding stock and then put their farms up for sale as emigration increased.

Fishery

The whaling industry brought the first foreign commercial interests to the area of southwest Africa as long ago as the eighteenth century. The cold Benguela Current which carries plankton to the coastal waters off Namibia provides food for commercial fish species making this area a potentially rich fishing ground. With the decline of whaling in the early nineteenth century foreign interests turned to gathering guano (bird dung) deposits to be used as fertiliser. In the twentieth century fishing for pilchard and rock lobster was an important industry until recently. Fish processing factories were established at Walvis Bay to can pilchards caught off the coast. Unfortunately the resource was poorly managed throughout the 1960s and 70s. High quotas, small net sizes and licensed factory ships from South Africa as well as an abundance of foreign fishing boats from the Soviet Union and Europe resulted in overfishing and the depletion of stocks. In 1968, the best year in terms of fish landed, 558,000 tonnes were taken by two factory ships alone while another 829,000 tonnes were taken by shore-based factories. In 1978 172 foreign trawlers from 16 nations were scooping up hake and horse mackerel from offshore. The South African administration in Windhoek declared a 200-mile Exclusive Economic Zone (EEZ) in 1981. It has been ignored by foreign fishing companies since the South African administration of Namibia is deemed to be illegal. South Africa acquiesced in this belief since it made no effort to enforce the EEZ limit. As pilchard declined the fishery turned to anchovy and rock lobster, which met a similar fate. At its height the fishing industry was the second largest employer after mining, employing some 7,500 people in 1977 (9, p.264), but by 1980 it had hit rock bottom. Fish factories were closed, dismantled and moved to Chile and elsewhere along with some of the factory ships. Smaller operators went out of business and employment was cut by half (8, p.111). The catch declined from a high of 858,000 tons in 1969 to 241,000 in 1980 (17, p.61).

Mining

By far the greatest money earner, however, is mining. Mineral exports provided 85 per cent of export earnings in 1979 and were expected to increase to 91 per cent by 1986 (8, p.99) contributing 47.7 per cent to the GDP (17, p.53). This has fluctuated between 44 per cent in 1924 down to a mere 11 per cent during the Second World War and rose to 33 per cent by 1954 (2, p.15).

The value of production, and therefore of profits, at any one time depends on several factors, not least of which are market demand and price of the metal in question. Demand has periodically dropped, most recently during the early 1980s due to a world-wide recession. The value of production must also include the metal content of ore and the extent of the ore body itself. The costs of production include wages paid to workmen, the cost of machinery and installations to extract the ore and the cost of transport to processing factories and to the market place. In the last few decades mining operations in Namibia have gone to technically advanced operations using mainly imported material. Mining sites are widely dispersed requiring the construction of transport links, principally railways. Where costs have been minimised, these have been in workers' wages. The mines employ some 18,000 Namibian workers who have been consistently underpaid. For the most part they have been confined to single-sex dormitories in compounds with a bare minimum of facilities. Living conditions and access to health facilities are poor. They are required to leave their families at home on the reserves for up to 18 months – the period of their contracts.

215

The main revenue earners in the mining industry are diamonds, copper and uranium. In addition to these minerals, Namibia produces lead, zinc, vanadium, manganese, tungsten, cadmium, gold and silver (23, p.17). Exploration for oil and gas off the Namibian coast has continued with some promising finds off the mouth of the Orange River.

Copper deposits in the Otavi region were being worked long before European exploration began. European mining operations did not begin seriously until the beginning of the twentieth century. The Tsumeb Corporation, which took over copper mining, was operated by German concerns. It was confiscated as enemy property during the Second World War and sold to a complex of American mining companies (AMAX and Newmont). Copper production was valued at over 69 million rand in 1980, up from 32 million a decade earlier.

Diamonds, which were discovered in 1908, could easily be mined by shovelling up the Namib sands along the coast and on underwater terraces. It appears that diamondiferous rock was washed down the Orange River and carried northward along the coast by the upwelling Benguela Current. Diamond mining quickly outdistanced that of all other minerals in value of production, contributing an estimated 59 per cent of state revenue in 1978/79 (2, p.137). Mining was controlled by the Consolidated Diamond Mines of SWA (CDM).

Production suffered a series of interruptions – during the First World War, the Depression of the early 1930s and the Second World War. From 1908 to the beginning of the First World War diamond production amounted to £8,500,000. Following the War, in 1919, output was 462,180 carats selling for £2,081,863 (p.920). By the late 1920s diamond production reached 600,000 carats but fell to a low of 150,000 during the Second World War. Mineral exploration and development which had lain somewhat dormant between the Wars surged forward in the 1950s. Production rose again in the 1960s to 1,500,000 carats (2, p.20).

The discovery of uranium at Rossing indicated the wide range of strategic minerals that existed in Namibia. Prospecting for uranium began in the 1960s and culminated in the discovery of extensive deposits near Swakopmund. Production began in 1976 at the Rossing mine. Although no figures are published on uranium production Wolfgang H. Thomas estimates that the 1980 production was about 350 million rand (17, p.62). Diamonds became the number one export in value, reaching R398,932,000 in 1980 (17, p.63).

The growth of markets which followed the War, combined with favourable South African incentives to invest in Namibia and the availability of cheap labour from the reserves, with the consequent promise of substantial company profits, attracted multinational corporations from

West Germany, the United Kingdom, the United States, France and Canada as well as South Africa to Namibia. Between 1946 and 1962 CDM made R369 million profits, two thirds of which went to pay shareholders' dividends and tax. The Tsumeb Corporation over a similar period made R140 million, 90 per cent of which went for tax and dividends. It is estimated that only 5 per cent of revenue generated from mining in 1977 went directly to black workers (2, p.22). The rest was spent mainly outside Namibia for imports of machinery, tax to the South African Government, as dividends or wages to whites who also exported much of their savings. Mining in Namibia generated very little investment in other industry or long-term development in Namibia.

Although legislation and the set-up of the mining operations has been designed to limit contact between workers it has led to the development of communication between ethnic groups and the formation of social and political organisations. It was in the workers' compounds that the Ovamboland People's Organisation, which was to become SWAPO, developed with the objective of improving conditions for workers. Strikes and protest meetings had been organised as long ago as 1893. Their efforts culminated in a major strike in 1971–72 involving over 4,000 workers protesting against the living conditions on the mines, wage levels and the operations of the labour recruitment on the Reserves. Two of the largest mining operations had initially formed the Northern Labour Organisation in 1926 to recruit Ovambo workers to the mining operations. This was later taken over by the administration as the South West Africa Native Labour Association (SWANLA). The strike of 1971, although initially suppressed and greeted with forced repatriation to the reserves, did lead to an improvement in wages. Wages rose by 60 per cent between 1971 and 1973 and by another 56 per cent in 1976 but by 1982 the minimum wage was only R110 to R150 per month compared with the officially recognised subsistence level required for a family of five in Windhoek of R261 per month (2, p.24). Workers at CDM and Rossing uranium mines fared better, earning on average R398 per month in 1982. On the smaller mines living conditions and wages had not improved.

Trade and Investment

The development of mining sites requires an inflow of capital and technology which, as yet, is available only from outside Namibia. As well as requiring large amounts of investment the mining industry is also labour intensive and requires a sizeable and reliable source of workers.

Multinational corporations were encouraged to invest in Namibia. They were assured of a ready supply of cheap labour and a favourable economic climate. African labour unions were banned while labour bureaus were

217

established for the recruitment of Africans from the reserves. The South African administration introduced a policy of low company taxation. In addition it allowed investors to export the major portion of their profits for reinvestment outside the Territory (13, p.77).

The profits to be made from investment in Namibia under these favourable conditions attracted transnational corporations from South Africa's major trade partners – the UK, the USA and the Federal Republic of Germany. By the early 1980s at the height of foreign interest in Namibia, the UN Council for Namibia noted that there were over 240 MNCs operating in the Territory. Of those 190 were based in the five members of the Western Contact Group (USA – 75, UK – 68, FRG – 25, France – 12 and Canada – 10) that was then negotiating an end to South African control of Namibia. Another 19 were based in RSA (25 and 26, passim). Many of the MNCs were engaged in the mining sector. Others were involved in the transportation sector, construction, finance and high technology industries.

The diamond industry in Namibia is run by CDM, formerly Consolidated Diamond Mines, a de Beers company which itself is a subsidiary of the Anglo-American Corporation. De Beers is responsible for mining, processing and marketing diamonds from Namibia. In 1980 CDM operations in Namibia provided 17 per cent of the profits of de Beers from only 10½ per cent of the carats mined. In 1982 the company employed 5,000 workers. The minimum wage was set at R398 per month. Although CDM has indicated that mining will continue to at least the end of the century production has been falling. In 1965–67 100 tonnes of ore produced 16.9 carats of diamonds. By 1982 this had fallen to almost half, at 9.8 carats.

Uranium mining, which began after the 1971 ICJ ruling declaring such operations illegal, was controlled by a conglomeration of companies based in the West including Rio-Tinto Zinc (RTZ) of the United Kingdom, Rio Algom of Canada, Total of France and Gencor of South Africa as well as West German interests. The uranium yellowcake was sold to British Nuclear Fuels (later the Central Electricity Generating Board) and other Western European buyers. Agreements were also signed to sell uranium to Japan. It seems likely that uranium also found its way to Canada for processing and resale. Rossing is one of the world's largest open-pit mining operations with its attendant pollution and health uncertainties, and the fourth largest producer of uranium in the Western world. It employs about 3,200 and paid a minimum wage of R296 in 1983.

The copper operations of the Tsumeb Corporation are also owned by companies based in South Africa and the West. Their profits have fluctuated wildly, showing a deficit in 1981. In 1982–83 it employed 6,400 with a minimum wage of R125 per month. Other mines have been developed by other Western-based corporations including Falconbridge of Canada and Bethlehem Steel of the USA.

Like the mining industry, the fishing industry is owned by outside interests. A cartel of South African-owned companies controls a sizeable proportion of the fishing fleet, the fish processing and canning factories. A British manufacturer, Metal Box, supplies the cans from its factory in South Africa and another British company, Reed International, supplies the packaging. US companies – Star Kist and Del Monte – continue to supply the technology. Marketing is also heavily influenced by companies in the West, with Unilever having a monopoly over Namibian fish oil.

The result of these policies has been evident in a consistent gap between the Gross Domestic Product (GDP) of what is produced in Namibia and the Gross National Product (GNP) of what is consumed of about 30 per cent, indicating that this amount has left the Territory (11, pp.33–4). GDP ranged from R61 million in 1950 to 1,425 million in 1979 while over the same period the GNP was between 24 and 30 per cent less at R46.4 to 950 million (10, p.275).

It is clear from statistics up to 1950 that South Africa was becoming both a major source of imports and destination for exports from Namibia. In 1926, shortly after it formally took possession of the Territory under League of Nations mandate, Namibia imported from South Africa £620,000 out of a total of £2,507,625 worth of goods and services. By 1949 South Africa's share of Namibia's imports had risen to £9,703,213 out of a total of £11,790,774. Since the mid-1950s trade statistics on Namibia's economy have been unavailable.

As international pressure through the United Nations and the media directed public attention toward South Africa's control of Namibia and SWAPO stepped up its campaign to drive South Africa out of the Territory, a frantic effort was made to strip Namibia of its economic wealth before independence could jeopardise the profits obtained by multinational corporations. This prompted the UN Council for Namibia to issue its Decree No. 1 in 1974 forbidding foreign exploitation of Namibia's resource base without its consent (14, passim).

In 1966 SWAPO began a guerrilla campaign to wrest power from the South African authorities. SWAPO received a tactical boost in 1975 when Angola became independent. South Africa increased its involvement in the area when it invaded southern Angola and met Soviet-backed Cuban-supported resistance. The rising insecurity deterred some international capital and caused other interests to suppress their activities in corporate intrigue.

Namibia has become more and more of an economic liability to South Africa. World demand for raw materials has slackened with the result that commodity prices have fallen drastically. Karakul pelts are no longer in demand as they once were. Fish stocks have been depleted by overfishing and canning operations have been forced to close down and move out. Periods of recurring drought have reduced cattle and beef production. The guerrilla war has been costing South Africa over a million rand a day. With its small, underpaid population, market potential in Namibia is limited (4 and 20, passim).

CONCLUSION

The theme which dominates the recent economic history of Namibia is colonial dependency. It has a resource-based economy exploited by foreign capital for the benefit of outside interests. Initial German colonial policy was to establish a settler state through the acquisition of land and the elimination of indigenous competition by the introduction of policies of extermination and marginalisation. With the discovery of mineral deposits the need for labour became acute. Having massacred the nearby population, the German authorities began to bring in labourers from the Cape Colony and from Ovamboland and other areas in the north of the Territory.

The South African authorities, which took over the administration of the Territory in 1915, continued German policies. Immigration from the Union was encouraged while the indigenous population was restricted to reserves which served as the source of a cheap labour-force for the white-owned farms and mining interests. To finance development foreign capital from South Africa and the West was encouraged especially following the Second World War. Africans were further restricted by legislation limiting their access to the means of production, their share in the methods of production and their participation in the political process.

The National Party in South Africa and Namibia, although losing supporters to ultra-conservative elements, is still firmly in control. With the rise to power of President Botha, formerly Defence Minister, and the ruling clique of the National Security Council, military elements are now influential in running both the Republic and Namibia. Consequently, Namibia has not been allowed to develop political let alone economic polices of its own. Meanwhile, the economy is in decline, unemployment is on the rise, foreign interests are closing down their operations and whites are beginning to leave the Territory. Prospects do not look good for either its economic or political future.

Economic ties between Namibia and South Africa have been well established, however. Transportation and communication links are to the south. South Africa's claim to Walvis Bay with its port facilities and military bases also serves its interests in dominating the Territory. Hope for Namibian's economic survival lies in establishing linkages with its northern and eastern neighbours to offset its heavy reliance on South Africa. At independence priority will have to go to establishing trade and infrastructural links to other states in the region as well as to land redistribution and social programmes in health and education. Namibia will need an infusion of aid from sources other than South Africa. However none of this is likely until independence is achieved. And independence is unlikely in the present circumstances. South Africa seems determined to hold on to the Territory as long as is necessary to eliminate the threat of a SWAPO government, and until it is clear that a compliant regime can be established that will not provide a base from which anti-South African elements, such as the African National Congress, can operate.

International pressures, rather than freeing Namibia from colonial domination, have brought greater South African repression. Repression, in turn, has forced the indigenous opponents of South African rule to seek redress through guerrilla action led by SWAPO. South Africa's response has been to further militarise the Territory through the establishment of South-West African Defence Forces and the declaration of a state of emergency in the northern zone bordering Angola and Zambia from where the guerrilla forces operate. South Africa has expanded its state of conflict to its surrounding African neighbours since the fall of Portuguese rule in Mozambique and Angola and of Ian Smith's regime in Rhodesia, now Zimbabwe. Its aims have been to carry out economic sabotage and political destabilisation, since none of the neighbouring states poses a military threat to South Africa. International negotiations have so far failed to resolve the conflict. The rising cost of fighting a guerrilla war in Namibia and the declining revenue from mining and other interests there, however, combined with an increasing level of frustration and revolt within the Republic itself, may ultimately force a settlement of the Namibian question.[6]

NOTES

1. For a history of German colonisation see J.H. Esterhuyse, *South West Africa 1880–1894: the Establishment of German Authority in South West Africa* (Cape Town: C. Struik Ltd., 1968). The following provide general histories of SWA/Namibia: J.P. van S. Bruwer, *South West Africa: the Disputed Land* (Cape Town: Nasionale Boekhandel Beperk, 1966); Ruth First, *South West Africa* (Harmondsworth: Penguin, 1963); I. Goldblatt, *History of South West Africa from the beginning of the Nineteenth Century* (Cape Town: Juta, 1971). The period of the mandate is covered by G-M. Cockram, *South West African Mandate* (Cape Town: Juta, 1976) and J.H. Wellington, *South West Africa and its Human Issues* (London: OUP,

1967). The economic history of SWA/Namibia is well documented by Reginald Herbold Green in *Namibia: a Political Economic Survey*, Discussion Paper No.144 (Brighton: Institute of Development Studies, 1979); and by Green, Kimmo Kiljunen and Marja-Liisa Kiljunen, *Namibia: the Last Colony* (Harrow: Longman, 1982) among other publications. See also Allan D. Cooper, *U.S. Economic Power and Political Influence in Namibia, 1700–1982* (Boulder: Westview, 1982); Robert I. Rotberg, ed., *Namibia: Political and Economic Prospects* (London: D.C. Heath, 1983). Among other publications are the following: Catholic Institute for International Relations, *Namibia in the 1980's* (London: CIIR, 1981) and International Defence and Aid Fund, *Namibia: the Facts* (London: IDAFSA, 1980).

2. Five companies held concession areas in the Territory. The Deutsche Kolonialgesellschaft für Südwestafrika (DKG) was formed in 1885 to take over the land acquisitions of Adolf Lüderitz. The British Karaskoma Syndicate purchased the land of the Bondelswarts in 1889 and, although its holdings were later reduced in size, it eventually selected the best land and watering places to be made into farms for settlers. This became an issue in the Bondelswarts uprising in the twentieth century. The South West Africa Company (SWA Co.) based in Cape Town was formed in 1892 to develop the mineral resources of the Otavi district and bought the Kaokoveld holdings of the DKG. The German Settlement Company was granted land around Windhoek. Land belonging to the Khauas Hottentots was granted to the Hanseatic Land Company.

3. This continued to be the policy of the South African administration in Namibia as stated in Official Year Books from the time of South African control in 1921 up to the 1950s, when official statistics on Namibia were no longer listed separately or made available to an increasingly concerned public.

4. The Bondelswarts were a tribe of mixed Nama and Herero origin, living in the Warmbad district, which in 1903 rose against the German authorities and again after the First World War against the South African administration.

5. The Red Line demarcated the Police Zone in the south and centre of the Territory which the former German administration had penetrated with some authority. The northern areas beyond the Red Line were uncontrolled. The South Africans have fenced off this northern sector. Anyone travelling in or out of the area requires a police permit. Inside the northern area there is a dusk to dawn curfew. SADF is stationed there in force in bases from which it launches incursions into Angola. Residents are liable to search and seizure. Reports out of the region speak of arrest, detention, torture and execution without benefit of redress.

6. International negotiations over the future of Namibia resumed in earnest in 1988 in a replay of developments from eight years earlier. Negotiators from South Africa, Angola and the United States met in secret talks to resolve the long standing dispute over Namibia. One is struck by the parallels to the situation surrounding similar negotiations held in 1980–81: South Africa is once again facing mounting pressures both at home and abroad to end its apartheid system. Its supporters in the West – most notably administrations in the United States and the United Kingdom – are also facing demands from their legislatures and international bodies like Commonwealth to impose greater economic sanctions against the Republic of South Africa. The United States is facing a presidential election that will usher in a new administration and the prospect of a change of governing party. All of this has once again prompted South Africa to sit down at the bargaining table to foster an appearance of compromise and movement towards a solution. It is another attempt by the South African administration to divert attention from its own internal conflicts and delay the stringent calls for its total economic and political isolation. This time 'linkage' – of the presence of Cuban troops in Angola to South African forces in Namibia – forms a key element in the negotiations. This has been a pivotal issue in the dispute for the Reagan administration since its introduction in the talks in 1980. The Reagan administration, too, would like to end its eight years in office with a diplomatic coup and thus justify its adherence to the policy of 'constructive engagement' with South Africa. But for the Republic of South Africa its objectives remain the same: continued economic and political domination of Namibia to ensure a buffer state which will deny bases to the African National Congress and other anti-apartheid elements. Although the continued occupation of Namibia and southern Angola has become a costly drain on its economy South Africa is not yet ready to accept

Land and Labour in the Namibian Economy

the economic and political consequences that would result from the establishment of a truly free and independent Namibian state on its northwest frontier.

REFERENCES

1. Catholic Institute for International Relations. *Namibia in the 1980's*. London: CIIR, 1981
2. Catholic Institute for International Relations. *Mines and Independence*. London: CIIR, 1983
3. Cooper, Allan D. *U.S. Economic Power and Political Influence in Namibia, 1700–1982*. Boulder, Colorado: Westview Press, 1982
4. Dillingham, Robert L.Jr. 'Namibia and its Neighbours'. *Africa Today*, 26 (2), 31 Aug. 1979, pp.29–37
5. Esterhuyse, J.H. *South West Africa 1880–1894: The Establishment of German Authority in South West Africa*. Cape Town: C. Struik Ltd., 1968
6. First, Ruth, *South West Africa*. Harmondsworth: Penguin, 1963
7. Goldblatt, I. *History of South West Africa from the Beginning of the Nineteenth Century*. Cape Town: Juta & Co. Ltd., 1971
8. Green, Reginald Herbold. *Namibia: a Political Economic Survey*. Discussion Paper No.144. Brighton: Institute of Development Studies, 1979
9. Green, Reginald Herbold, Kimmo Kiljunen and Marja-Liisa Kiljunen. *Namibia: the Last Colony*. Burnt Mill: Longman, 1982
10. Hutcheson, A. MacGregor. 'Namibia (SWA): Physical and Social Geography'. *Africa South of the Sahara 1982–83* 12th edition. London: Europa Publications, 1982
11. International Labour Organisation. *Labour and Discrimination in Namibia*. Geneva: International Labour Office, 1977.
12. Krogh, D.C. 'Economic Aspects of the Karakul Industry in South West Africa'. *The South African Journal of Economics*. 23 (2), June 1955, pp.99–113
13. Lazar, Leonard. *Namibia*. London: The Mandate Trust, 1972
14. McDougall, Gay J. 'The Council for Namibia's Decree No.1: Enforcement Possibilities'. *Africa Today*, 30 (1,2), 15 Oct. 1983, pp.7–16
15. Moorsom, Richard. *Exploiting the Sea*. London: CIIR, 1984
16. Moorsom, Richard. *Transforming a Wasted Land*. London: CIIR, 1982.
17. Rotberg, Robert I., ed. *Namibia: Political and Economic Prospects*. London: D.C. Heath, 1983
18. South Africa. *Report of the Commission of Enquiry into South West African Affairs 1962–1963*. Pretoria: Government Printers, 1964
19. Steward, Alexander. *South West Africa: The Sacred Trust*. Johannesburg: Da Gama Publications, 1963.
20. Thomas, Wolfgang H. 'The Economy in Transition to Independence' in *Namibia: Political and Economic Prospects* edited by Robert I. Rotberg. Lexington/London: D.C. Heath, 1983
21. United Kingdom. *Report on the Natives of South-West Africa and their Treatment by Germany*. London: HM Stationery Office, 1918.
22. United Kingdom. *South West Africa*. London: HM Stationery Office, 1920
23. United Nations. Department of Public Information. *Plunder of Namibian Uranium: Major Findings of the Hearings on Namibian Uranium Held by the United Nations Council for Namibia in July 1980*. New York: UN, 1982
24. —*A Principle in Torment: III. The United Nations and Namibia*. New York: UN, 1971
25. —.UN Centre on Transnational Corporations. *Policies and Practices of Transnational Corporations regarding their Activities in South Africa and Namibia*. New York: UN, 1984
26. —.UN Council for Namibia. *List of Transnational Corporations and other Foreign Economic Interests Operating in Namibia*. New York: UN, 1983
27. Wellington, J.H. *South West Africa and its Human Issues*. London: Oxford University Press, 1967

Index

ADMARC, 138–40
see also Kamuzu Banda; Malawi
agriculture, 9, 33, 35, 45, 57, 58, 71, 81,
  85, 87, 90, 91, 97, 104, 108, 110, 111,
  115, 127–54, 174, 177–80, 205, 206,
  211, 212–14
see also cattle; farmers; food
aid, 149, 164, 165, 166, 167, 172, 221
alcohol, 42, 49, 62, 94, 100, 190
Amin, Samir, 15, 17
Anglo-American Corporation, 86, 90,
  92, 94, 98, 103, 117, 186–7, 216
Angola, 4, 8, 11, 13, 18, 19, 23, 30–71,
  76, 189, 209, 210, 219, 221
archeology, 1, 2, 4, 6, 7, 8, 9, 10, 11, 13
Asians, 62, 87, 91, 106, 109, 194
authoritarianism, 110, 128, 129, 130

balance of payments, 49–57, 69–70,
  105, 110, 211
Banda, Kamazu, 106–11, 127, 138, 139,
  140, 149, 153
see also Malawi
banking, 37, 43–4, 46, 49–52, 56, 59,
  68, 71, 107, 109, 117, 135, 170
see also capital; credit
Bantu, 3, 4, 6, 7, 9, 10, 13, 17, 21, 23,
  68
  Eastern and Western streams, 6, 9
Belgium, 46, 58, 59, 60, 76
Benguela, 42, 58
Berlin Conference, 23, 36, 76
Botswana, 2, 4, 5, 8, 10, 12, 13, 18, 21,
  23, 159–86, 212
  Makgadikgadi, 5, 168, 187
  Okavango, 5, 178, 188, 189, 190
bourgeoisie, 34, 36, 37, 38, 39, 43, 48,
  49, 62, 75, 76, 79, 80, 87, 91, 100,
  103, 112, 153, 192, 194
  factions, 34, 36, 48, 76, 91, 92, 100,
  101
see also class; peasants
Brazil, 32, 34
British, 22, 23, 24, 34, 36, 37, 50, 58,
  61, 68, 79, 80, 82, 83, 86, 88, 114,
  131, 161, 163, 166, 168, 179, 186,
  194, 200, 218
see also Europeans
British South Africa Company

(BSACo), 23, 40, 77–83, 89, 99, 182
see also Rhodes; Zimbabwe

Cabinda, 60, 67
  oil, 60, 67
see also Angola
Cameroun, 3, 204
Canada, 186, 209, 216, 218, 219
Cape, 5, 6, 8, 13, 23, 161, 200, 202,
  204, 210, 220
capital, 30–71, 76, 80, 81, 88, 89, 90,
  91, 92, 93, 95, 96, 97, 99, 103, 105,
  111, 112, 120, 121, 162, 167, 168,
  169, 171, 173, 176, 189, 193, 200,
  217, 220
  foreign, 38–63, 67, 76, 81, 86, 88, 89,
  90, 92, 96, 99, 169, 176
capitalism, 31, 33, 37, 43, 77, 87, 89, 96,
  102, 106, 109, 121, 130, 159, 177
cattle, 5, 6, 10, 11, 14, 160–3, 167, 169,
  171, 172, 177, 178, 179, 188, 191,
  192, 201, 202, 204, 205, 212, 213,
  214, 220
Chavanduka Report, 131–2, 139, 150,
  152, 153
class, 20, 21, 24, 34, 38, 53, 66, 76, 80,
  81, 91, 100, 101, 103, 105, 109, 120,
  121, 127, 128, 129, 134, 137, 139–46,
  191–4, 200
  class formation, 127–9, 134, 139–46
see also capital; labour; peasants
coal, 61, 82, 83, 90, 111, 115–17, 182,
  185, 186, 187
see also energy
coffee, 36, 45, 46, 57, 58, 65, 66, 109
colonialism, 30–71, 75, 129, 133, 135,
  154, 163–5, 178, 181, 183, 184, 200,
  201–5, 207, 212, 213, 226
see also British, German, Portuguese
companies, 39, 40–71, 77–9, 83, 96,
  137, 168, 216, 218, 219
see also multinational corporations
Contact Group, *see* United Nations
copper, 8, 9, 10, 33, 45, 80, 83, 86, 87,
  102, 113, 118, 132, 150, 168, 173,
  175, 187, 205, 215–16, 218–19
corporatism, 42–56, 71
cotton, 12, 36, 40, 43, 45, 46, 59, 69, 82,
  84, 89, 91, 106, 131, 133, 134, 150

224

Index

225

For Product Safety Concerns and Information please contact our
EU representative GPSR@taylorandfrancis.com Taylor & Francis
Verlag GmbH, Kaufingerstraße 24, 80331 München, Germany